PROMISES TO KEEP

Books by Robert Shogan

A QUESTION OF JUDGMENT: THE FORTAS CASE AND
THE STRUGGLE FOR THE SUPREME COURT

THE DETROIT RACE RIOT: A STUDY IN VIOLENCE
(with Tom Craig)

Robert Shogan

★

PROMISES TO KEEP

Carter's First Hundred Days

THOMAS Y. CROWELL COMPANY

Established 1834 / New York

(

Published simultaneously in Canada by Fitzhenry & Whiteside Limited, Toronto.

Designed by Lydia Link

Manufactured in the United States of America

Library of Congress Cataloging in Publication Data

Shogan, Robert.
  Promises to keep.
  1. United States—Politics and government—1977–
2. Presidents—United States—Election—1976.
3. Carter, Jimmy, 1924– I. Title.
E872.S53 1977   973.926'092'4   77–22818
ISBN 0–690–01497–X

---

1 2 3 4 5 6 7 8 9 10

For my mother and father

Contents

──── ★ ────

Photographic section follows page 140.

Author's Note

———————— ⊠ ————————

Jimmy Carter's arrival at the White House followed a period of upheaval that had shaken public confidence in political institutions in general, and the Presidency in particular. He had a fresh face, an intriguing personality, a vigorous and confident style. But his rise from obscurity had been so swift that his goals and character were only hazily defined in the public mind. He was a stranger and, to many, an enigma. Americans viewed his assumption of power, at a critical point in their nation's life, with a mixture of hope and anxiety.

I have tried to measure the expectations created by Carter's candidacy against the performance of his first hundred days in office and, in the process, to illuminate the man. Because the period is brief, my emphasis has been on the new administration's tone and direction, rather than on the substance of its policies and programs. I have reported events and reactions to them, including my own, as they took place. My hope is that this contemporaneous record will aid in understanding the Carter Presidency during its formative hundred days, and in the future.

This book owes an initial debt to the editors of the *Los Angeles Times* who assigned me to cover national politics four years ago, an experience which provided a framework for viewing Jimmy Carter. I am particularly grateful to Dennis Britton, the national editor, and to Jack Nelson, Washington Bureau chief, for their encouragement and assistance.

Arnold Dolin, senior editor of Thomas Y. Crowell, conceived of this project more than a year ago, and his advice and enthusiasm helped carry it through to completion. My agent, Philip Spitzer, was a patient and persistent ally. My friend, Tom Allen, took time from his own book to review this manuscript, thereby invariably contributing to its improvement. My wife, Ellen, served as first reader and chief researcher. Without her support there would be no book.

—Chevy Chase, Maryland, June 1, 1977

1

The Long Night

————————— ★ —————————

Atlanta, November 3, 1976—In the darkness at Hartsfield Airport
the two Carter campaign planes, *Peanut One* and *Peanut Two*,
wait on the runway, engines running, ready for takeoff. It is getting on toward five o'clock in the morning, the morning after
election day. Soon it will be dawn, the start of a new day and,
maybe, if the man of the hour is to be taken at his word, of a new
direction for our politics and for the Presidency.

At any rate, this night marks the end of an interminable
campaign and an incredible quadrennial. These were the four
more years Richard Nixon had promised us. Nixon has for some
time been removed from the scene. But he left his mark on the
period and, in a sense, paved the way to the White House for
Jimmy Carter.

The two planes warming up here have, during the past eight
weeks, carried Carter and his entourage nearly 50,000 miles, into
thirty-seven states. All told, since he first declared his candidacy

1

for the Democratic nomination twenty-two months ago, Carter has covered about 500,000 miles and been almost everywhere that mattered politically. On the evening of election day he made the final leg of his journey as Democratic nominee, flying here to Atlanta from his home in Plains, 140 miles away in south Georgia, to await the decision of the voters. Little more than an hour ago, in the unofficial but imposing judgment of the networks and wire services, he was proclaimed the winner. Now he is eager to return home, no longer merely a candidate, but the President-elect of the United States.

For the time being, though, the President-elect is grounded. All through the campaign his well-drilled organization had shifted the candidate and his retinue from one place to another with admirable efficiency. Now, in his moment of victory, in the capital of his own state, Carter's vaunted logistical machinery has gone haywire. It has lost the press corps.

Most of the reporters stayed behind when Carter left his hotel headquarters, granted twenty minutes' grace to file their victory stories. They departed on schedule for the airport, shepherded by Carter aides; but the Atlanta police escorting the buses inexplicably turned onto the wrong freeway. While the President-elect waited at Hartsfield Airport, the press corps was heading at 50 miles an hour in another direction.

Carter suffers neither fools nor delays gladly. In May 1975, at a time when his movements attracted far less attention, I had witnessed his quiet but stern dressing down of a young volunteer who had lost his way driving from one New Hampshire town to another. The long campaign had, if anything, only increased his irritation at any disruption in his schedule. And his election-night vigil, compressing the tension of the campaign into a few hours, was enough to wear down anyone's nerves.

Carter has been through a lot, this night and the past two years. He had started somewhere close to zero, as a little-known lame-duck governor, with no visible means of political support outside his own state. But he had a keen sense of the country's mood and total faith in his own capacities, fierce determination, a quick mind, and boundless ambition and energy. And these strengths propelled him, against enormous odds, to the Democratic Presidential nomination—an achievement so remarkable it was often described as not just a campaign but a phenomenon.

At the close of the Democratic Convention, Carter had seemed invincible. His normally fractious party had rallied behind him. The public opinion polls gave him a huge advantage over the incumbent President. With characteristic foresight Carter created a special unit of his staff to plan for the postelection transfer of power.

Then, circumstances began to change. Week after week the polls showed Carter's margin over President Ford dwindling. Under pressure, his campaign faltered and lost momentum. The pollsters pronounced the contest too close to call. Defeat, once deemed impossible, stared Carter in the face.

The strain showed in the final week. Everywhere he went the bands played FDR's old anthem, "Happy Days Are Here Again." At outdoor rallies balloons soared in the air and cheering thousands packed the streets. But the candidate's face was drawn, his words grim. "I want to talk to you," he told the crowd, "in a very quiet, very sober way."

On the night before the election, flying back to Plains from the final rallies, the reporters and staff joined in a lively rendition of "You Are My Sunshine." Carter made them sing it again, slowly, turning the cheerful tune into a lament. They held a mock election, voting Carter "most likely to succeed." They picked the campaign's worst hotel, worst speech, and so forth, and Carter broke in and said somberly that he hoped election day would not be the worst day of his campaign.

But the morning of election day brought reports of large turnouts, almost always a favorable omen for the Democrats. As the day wore on, early summaries of "exit polls," surveys of voters who had already cast their ballots, flowed in to Carter's headquarters, indicating he was running strongly in important areas. On board *Peanut One* that evening, en route to Atlanta, he was cocky and assertive. He told the reporters that the pollsters "took a dive" when they concluded that he and Ford were only a hairbreadth apart. "Pollsters don't like to go out on a limb," he said. "The safest strategy for them is to say that it's too close to call." He spoke of his Presidency as if it were an accomplished fact, mentioning the work done by his transition staff to help him select a cabinet.

His mind was easier than it had been for days when, about 7:00 P.M., he arrived at the Omni International Hotel, his election-night headquarters. The fifteenth floor was reserved for the Carter entourage, its Capitol Suite given over to the candidate, his family, close friends, and advisers. Carter took off his his jacket and loosened his tie. He had celebrated his fifty-second birthday on October 1, and with the fatigue lines etched in his face by the campaign, he looked his age. But he had kept his frame trim and wiry, making him seem taller than his five feet, nine inches. He stretched out on a small brown couch, one foot propped on a coffee table, and concentrated on the three television sets in front of him, complaining when someone blocked his view. Occasionally he took a phone call or made small talk. His wife, Rosalynn —a soft-featured, iron-willed woman who had helped carry much of the campaign burden—was close at hand. So were his three grown sons and their wives and his nine-year-old daughter, Amy, restless and tired, who spent much of the night napping on a couch.

Also present were two men who represented the contrasting strands of Carter's Southern background. The Reverend Martin Luther King, Sr., "Daddy King," father of a martyr, a man of great dignity, revered by the black community with whom he had done more than anyone else to vouch for Carter's credentials. And Charles Kirbo, senior partner in Atlanta's most powerful law firm, "an old-fashioned cracker" in the view of some of Carter's black supporters, cautious and unpretentious, an adviser without portfolio but with immense influence.

Down the hall from the Capitol Suite, in room 1536, the political staff established its situation room, presided over by Hamilton Jordan, who at age thirty-two had managed Carter's effort for the Presidency, just as he ran his gubernatorial campaign in 1970. In room 1536 Jordan's operatives and Patrick J. Caddell, chief of Carter's polling operation, manned a bank of phones on an L-shaped table along the wall, trying to make sense out of the numbers on the television screens. Caddell, at twenty-six, already had one Presidential campaign under his belt; he had been George McGovern's pollster in 1972. Jody Powell, thirty-three, Carter's press secretary, his spokesman and his alter ego, shuttled back and forth between the phone banks and the Capitol Suite, relaying information to the small group of reporters allowed on the floor.

The mood early in the evening, based on the turnout reports and exit-poll results, was confident, even buoyant. One member of Carter's youthful inner circle, Greg Schneiders, twenty-nine, the candidate's personal aide, who left the suite about 8:30 P.M. to dine with a group of reporters, was worried that the issue might be settled, the excitement over before he finished eating.

The early returns were encouraging. One by one the states of the Old Confederacy, the base of Carter's electoral strength, were falling into his column. The picture in the northern industrial states was promising. Massachusetts, the only state carried by George McGovern in 1972, predictably had gone Democratic again. Carter's margin in New York at first appeared disturbingly narrow. But then it was discovered that much of traditionally Democratic New York City had yet to report, and the Carter strategists realized that the state would be theirs. In Pennsylvania Carter quickly built up a comfortable lead, leaving little doubt he would win there. His advantage in Ohio was smaller, but he clearly had a strong chance to carry that state, which no Democrat except Lyndon Johnson had won since 1948.

At 11:15 P.M. Caddell slammed down a telephone receiver in the situation room, leaped from his chair, and shouted: "We've got it."

Much the same judgment prevailed in the Capitol Suite. Carter was already looking ahead. He placed a call to Representative Thomas P. "Tip" O'Neill of Massachusetts, majority leader of the House of Representatives and certain to be its next Speaker. O'Neill was a veteran of twenty-four years in the House, an influential fixture of the Washington establishment that Carter had made a prime target in his drive for the Presidency. Early in the battle for the Democratic nomination O'Neill had thrown his influence and prestige behind the candidacy of his House colleague, Morris Udall of Arizona. In the Massachusetts primary campaign, when the race still seemed wide open, O'Neill had belittled Carter's earlier victory in the New Hampshire primary over Udall and four other liberal candidates. "Carter got only 30 percent of the vote; the liberals got the rest," O'Neill had said.

But in late spring O'Neill had publicly conceded the inevitability of Carter's nomination and had given him his blessing and support. When he got O'Neill on the phone in the Capitol Suite, Carter told him: "I just want you to know that I will be able to work with you and the members of the Congress, and we'll get along great together."

Then another call, to Frank Rizzo, mayor of Philadelphia, satrap of that city's Democratic machine, one of the few remaining big-city bosses with real power. Rizzo and Carter had been bitter foes in April's Pennsylvania primary, a critical test for Carter. Rizzo had backed Senator Henry M. Jackson of Washington and Carter had publicly brought up Democrat Rizzo's support for Richard Nixon in the 1972 Presidential campaign. "I'm glad he doesn't think I'm in the same league," he had said.

"Mr. Rizzo doesn't feel comfortable with me. He wants a different candidate to become his next friend in the White House. And that is the way it should be, for Mr. Rizzo and I have very different ideas about who and what government ought to represent."

Carter's victory in the Pennsylvania primary cleared the path for his nomination. But Rizzo remained formidable. Philadelphia

County, which he controlled, was the only one of sixty-seven in the state that Carter did not carry.

So whatever differences there had been between the two men in April, Carter set them aside in October. On a visit to Philadelphia a few days before the election, he paid court to Rizzo, granting him a private audience aboard his plane. And on election day Rizzo turned out the votes in Philadelphia's Democratic wards, giving Carter his victory margin in Pennsylvania.

"I really appreciate what you did for me," Carter told him now over the phone. "You really knew what you were talking about."

But in the midst of the phone calls, the figures on the television screens began to temper the exultant mood on the fifteenth floor. As the vote count moved westward across the country, the trend to Carter tapered off. Ford still trailed in the popular vote by a substantial margin. But he had captured New Jersey in the East, and his own state of Michigan in the industrial Midwest. In the western reaches of the country—the Great Plains, the Rockies, the Pacific Coast—the President was ahead almost everywhere. Carter's electoral vote total, which had been climbing steadily toward the majority of 270 that would mean victory, was stalled, close to but still short of the mark.

Not long after midnight, Carter took in the sobering numbers on the TV screens and set the phone aside. "It looks like it's going to be a long night," he said. The press pool, which had been allowed into the Capitol Suite briefly, in anticipation of imminent victory, was ushered out by Jody Powell. Carter's candidacy was now in a state of limbo. After two years of unsparing effort, he could now do nothing but watch as his fate unfolded on the television screens.

The American political process provides no official agency to weigh Presidential election results and proclaim a winner, until long after the balloting. So it has fallen to the networks—with their vast capacity for gathering information and transmitting it instantaneously—to serve as the arbiter of Presidential contests.

It is no small responsibility. More than once Presidential candidates have won a majority of the electoral vote with a tiny plurality of the popular vote in key states. In the 1960 election, one of the closest, the switch of 5,000 votes in Illinois, out of more than 4.7 million cast, and 25,000 in Texas, out of 2.3 million, would have made Richard Nixon President instead of John Kennedy. Charges of vote fraud are common in Presidential elections; they were heard in 1960 and would be heard again in 1976. But a candidate faced with deciding, as Richard Nixon was in 1960, whether to challenge the result must consider the reaction of public opinion. The case against challenging, with all the divisiveness such an action would produce, is obviously much greater if the nation has already been told on television that the election has been decided.

The networks have tried to make their judgmental process scientific and rational. Their experts study the results from sample precincts selected in advance in each state and weigh them against the returns from past elections. But when the count is close, the element of "hunch" inevitably enters into their calculations. They work under severe pressure. They are competing against each other for the prestige of being the first to award major states and to designate the overall winner. But overriding even their competitive instincts, when the White House is at stake, is the fear of making a momentous mistake.

To Carter, as to many other viewers, the criteria by which the networks awarded states seemed at times mystifying and arbitrary. Early in the evening he was startled when CBS gave him Oregon, a state which he ultimately lost. Just as puzzling was CBS's failure to give him Hawaii, though its own figures showed him ahead with nearly every precinct accounted for, and Carter's campaign staff in Honolulu assured him the state was his.

The experts at CBS were having problems. Soon after they had consigned Oregon to Carter's column, they learned that some of the figures on which they had based their calculations were inaccurate and that their projection might turn out to be in error.

Still, they could not be sure either way, and they preferred to wait rather than make an embarrassing change. As for Hawaii, CBS's figures showed that Carter was, indeed, ahead. But the network had no set of sample precincts for this far-off state, and enough votes remained to be counted to give Hawaii to either Ford or Carter. So CBS held back, its splendid system of computers hampered by human error and uncertainty.

None of this, of course, was known to Carter and his people as they watched the returns flash across the screen. In a suite on the fourteenth floor, just below Carter's own command post, his chief issues adviser, Stuart Eizenstat, was entertaining twenty or so staff members and their wives with beer, soft drinks, and homemade cookies. Spirits had dropped with the long delay. Eizenstat's suite had only one television set, and it was switched frequently from channel to channel in the futile hope that one or the other of the networks would announce a break in the stalemate.

Some of the tense and weary people in the suite talked as if they believed the networks had the power to deprive them of victory. Eizenstat simply brooded silently. A slim, intense thirty-three-year-old Atlanta lawyer, he was something of an anomaly in the Carter organization. Unlike nearly everyone else, he had experience in the federal government and in national politics, having served in Lyndon Johnson's White House and in Hubert Humphrey's 1968 Presidential campaign. He was also set apart, in a staff marked by a spirit of carefree confidence, by the fact that he was a consummate worrier.

Three weeks earlier, with Carter ahead in the polls and his campaign exuding optimism, Eizenstat had told me in confidence that he expected the outcome to be just as close as the narrowly decided elections of 1960 and 1968. Now that the returns were bearing out his forecast, he was in agony. He tormented himself further by pointing to the undecided states on the television screen where a surge of votes for Ford could give the President victory.

In the fifteenth-floor situation room, Pat Caddell, Carter's

round-faced, mercurial chief prognosticator, was not in much
better condition. His assessment of the states that had been decided early was, in the words of his candidate, "unbelievably
accurate." Of the first twenty states won by Ford or Carter, he had
predicted all but one correctly. His sole mistake was Wisconsin,
which Carter won. Caddell had expected Ford to carry Wisconsin
because he had overestimated the vote for Eugene McCarthy. But
at 2:00 A.M. Caddell was exasperated. The later returns were not
following the patterns he had anticipated. "There must be some
logic to all this," he grumbled. "Maybe tomorrow I'll be able to
figure it out."

Down the hall, in the Capitol Suite, the candidate maintained
his vigil. The party's chairman, Robert Strauss, phoned to assure
him that he, Strauss, had been assured by Chicago's Mayor Richard Daley that Illinois would go Democratic, a forecast that
turned out to be overly optimistic.

Twice during the evening, Richard Moe, the manager of
Walter Mondale's Vice-Presidential campaign, called the suite
from Mondale's headquarters in Minneapolis, trying to reach his
counterpart in the Carter organization, Hamilton Jordan. Both
times Jordan was unavailable and, to Moe's surprise, Carter took
the calls himself, exchanged information, and then turned back to
the television.

Rosalynn Carter, who was not watching the screen as closely
as her husband, asked about his margin in the popular vote. "It's
still at three percentage points," Carter said. "We've been at three
points all night. It's held steady."

The electoral vote also held steady, irritatingly so. By 3:00
A.M. Carter appeared to have won twenty-one states, including
Hawaii. Together with the District of Columbia they gave him a
total of 265 electoral votes, five short of the majority he needed.
The network boards showed that Carter was leading, or trailing
by a close margin, in half a dozen other states, any one of which
would give him the Presidency. His best prospects seemed to be
Mississippi with seven electoral votes and Ohio with twenty-five.

Ohio was a sentimental favorite in the Carter camp. Carter's victory in the Ohio primary had assured his nomination, and the votes of the Ohio delegation at the convention had made it official.

"I wish Ohio would put us over," Rosalynn Carter told her husband.

"I do, too," he said. "That would make it three times."

But Mississippi was also a prize rich in symbolism for a Southern candidate for the Presidency. In the old days of the Solid South, no state had been more solidly Democratic than Mississippi. In 1944 it had given Thomas E. Dewey only 3,742 votes to 158,515 for Franklin Roosevelt.

Mississippi had also been Theodore Bilbo's state, the embodiment of Southern racism, the breach point of the South's estrangement from the national Democratic party. In 1948, the year of the Southern bolt from the Democratic convention, Strom Thurmond had carried Mississippi for his Dixiecrat party. Not since 1956 had any Democrat taken Mississippi in a Presidential election.

But now history was turning around again in Mississippi. An unlikely combination of the old bulwarks of segregation, Senators James Eastland and John Stennis, white liberals, and newly enfranchised blacks had strongly backed the Democratic Presidential candidate. Shortly before 3:30 A.M. Cliff Finch, governor of the state, one of its moderate new leaders, called the candidate with cheering news. "Jimmy, you're way ahead, 12,000 to 15,000 votes ahead. There's no way that enough votes can come in from these remaining precincts to turn it around."

Carter was holding his lead in the counties that were still reporting, Finch said. "You're not going to drop any more."

It was at this point, just at 3:30, that NBC made its announcement. After due deliberation and careful analysis, the network declared that Jimmy Carter had won Mississippi, and with it the Presidency.

"Tell everybody in Mississippi that they just put me over, and we're really proud of them," the jubilant candidate shouted into the phone.

"We did it, we did it!" Rosalynn cried. The President-elect hung up the phone, clapped his hands, and shouted: "All right!" Then he was engulfed by the people in the room, joyously hugging him and each other. Jody Powell broke open a bottle of champagne and poured for the pool reporters.

In Eizenstat's suite his guests cheered, shouted, and embraced. Eizenstat could barely speak. His wife handed him a towel and he wiped the perspiration from his face.

Downstairs in the ballroom of the convention center next door, the joyous crowd, which had been waiting since well before midnight, pressed toward the stage in anticipation of the victor's arrival.

In his suite Carter delayed only long enough to make a few obligatory calls of thanks and to take another call from Moe, who was again trying to reach Jordan.

Carter thanked Moe for Mondale's help in the campaign. "I love you all," he said.

"We love you, too, Governor," Moe replied, a response which drew startled looks from his companions in Minneapolis.

By the time Carter arrived in the ballroom, shortly after 4:00 A.M., the victory verdict was unanimous. All three networks and both major wire services had proclaimed him the winner.

His remarks were brief. He praised Gerald Ford, his defeated opponent but still the President. "As I've said many times throughout the nation, he's a good and decent man."

Then Carter touched on one of the major themes of his campaign: "We have a great nation, as you know, and sometimes in the past we've been disappointed in our own government. But I think it's time to tap the tremendous strength and vitality and idealism and hope and patriotism and sense of brother and sisterhood in this country to unify our nation and make it great once again."

There were cheers, mixed with rebel yells, and Carter sounded a populist chord: "I'm not afraid to take on the responsibilities of the President of the United States because my strength and my courage and my advice and my counsel and my criticism come from you."

He offered a traditional plea for unity "of all those in the United States whether they, like you, supported me or supported Mr. Ford or someone else." He closed on a characteristically personal note: "I want to thank all of you. I love everybody here. You've been great to me."

Then he was gone, to the cars outside for the ride to the airport and the trip home to Plains.

Given the hour, someone else might have decided to spend what remained of the night in Atlanta and make the journey to Plains with the benefit of a few hours' sleep. But Carter had determined days before that he would go home to greet the townspeople of Plains before he slept. His staff knew him too well to even try to change his mind.

When he boarded *Peanut One* at Hartsfield Airport, Powell and Schneiders told him the takeoff would be delayed until the reporters finished their stories and caught up with him. Carter wanted to know how long the wait would be. They told him forty minutes, and hoped for the best.

But by now he has waited about that long and the strain has begun to tell. In his shirtsleeves, he paces the aisle of the plane and badgers Powell and Schneiders. Where are the reporters? How much longer will he have to wait?

The information Powell and Schneiders have on the whereabouts of the press buses is sketchy, and they can only guess when the reporters will arrive. They tell Carter it will be soon. He retreats to his compartment in the front of the plane. But in a few minutes he returns, more adamant than ever.

"They've had their forty minutes," he growls. "Let's go." In Plains, he knows, a crowd has been waiting for him most of the night. It is past 5:00 A.M. and he wants to go home.

But Powell and Schneiders understand what the wrath of the reporters will be like if they find the President-elect gone when they arrive at the airport. They stall him again, promising the reporters will arrive at any moment.

Just before 5:30, when Carter's patience seems to be at the breaking point, the press buses arrive, the reporters scramble aboard the two planes, the doors slam shut. While some passengers are still searching for seats, *Peanut One* and *Peanut Two* take off for home.

In thirty minutes they are in Albany, the nearest airport of any size to Plains. First light is breaking when Carter leaves *Peanut One,* carrying his sleeping daughter. There is a crowd at the airport and he pauses to shake hands, then hurries to his car for the 45-mile drive to Plains.

The citizens of Plains had begun celebrating in the shank of the evening. A big throng, perhaps a thousand people, had gathered outdoors on the two blocks of Main Street, and stayed on for hours. By the time victory was announced, most had gone home, leaving behind a residue of beer cans, plastic cups, and empty film packs. But when word comes that the President-elect at last is on his way, volunteers hastily clear away the debris, and hundreds of people return to the scene.

It is moments after 7:00 A.M. when the motorcade arrives at the railroad depot that has served as Carter's hometown campaign headquarters. The timing is perfect for the television correspondents. The networks, having just begun their regular morning news shows, can bring their viewers live, from Plains, the homecoming of the President-elect.

"I told you I didn't intend to lose," Carter tells the crowd from the depot platform, using a standard phrase from his regular stump speech. The crowd laughs and cheers and Carter is suddenly caught by the sentimental moment. For the first time since he became a candidate, he loses his firm control over his emotions.

"I came all the way through, through twenty-two months," he says, his voice breaking, tears welling, "until I turned the corner and saw you standing there. And I said, 'People that are that foolish, we can't get beat.' " He smiles, regaining his composure, but his voice is still full. "All the others who ran for President didn't have people helping them who would stay up all night in Plains, Georgia, just to welcome me back."

Carter says it is time for each American to look within himself and ask: "What can we do to make our country great? What can we do to make our future brighter? What can we do to return laughter to the United States and hope?"

He has talked for about five minutes. The crowd is satisfied and he could leave now if he wanted to. But something nags at him.

"I just want to say one more thing. I had the best organization any candidate ever had. I had the best family any candidate ever had. I had the best home community any candidate ever had. I had the best support in my home state any candidate ever had.

"And the only reason we were close last night was because the candidate wasn't quite good enough as a campaigner. But I'll make up for that as President.

"I think the sun's rising on a beautiful new day, a beautiful new spirit in this country, a beautiful new commitment to the future."

To say he was "not quite good enough" was a striking concession for a candidate who had campaigned on the slogan "Why Not the Best?" This acknowledgment of imperfection might provide some reassurance for those who wondered whether he had sufficient awareness of his own limitations as a person and as a politician. In a way, his self-assessment seemed harsh. He had been good enough to win, in a field of endeavor where coming close counts for little. Whatever else he did, his success in getting his party's nomination had already won him a special niche in American political history.

And he had gone on to win the White House. But in the process of winning, as he may have sensed, he had nevertheless lost something, an opportunity he himself had helped create. Campaigning for the Democratic nomination, Jimmy Carter had touched a nerve in the electorate no candidate had even tried to reach. Unashamedly preaching the gospel of truth, trust, and love of country, he had offered new cause for hope in their government to citizens alienated by more than a decade of trauma and frustration. But somehow, during the weeks of his campaign against President Ford, the glowing promise of his early candidacy had been dimmed.

"I'll make up for that as President," he had said in that brief moment of humility in Plains. But what he did as President would depend in part on how he read the lessons of his campaign.

2

Campaign

───── ★ ─────

Off and Running

In the July heat of Miami Beach, at the 1972 Democratic Convention, ambition stirred into action. Gerald Rafshoon and Hamilton Jordan visited the Doral Beach Hotel, headquarters of George McGovern, the Democratic Presidential nominee. Rafshoon, an Atlanta advertising man, had been Jimmy Carter's media adviser in his 1970 campaign for governor; Jordan had been campaign coordinator. Their purpose was to urge upon McGovern's advisers the wisdom of selecting Carter as his running mate.

The mission was an exercise of Southern *chutzpah*. Carter and McGovern had last encountered each other in June at a Democratic governors' conference in Houston, where McGovern had made a belated effort to win support from the leaders of the state Democratic parties. Carter had been no help at all. To Gordon Weil, McGovern's executive assistant, it seemed that "Jimmy

Carter of Georgia had cast himself in the role of chief critic of McGovern. He had told reporters that McGovern's nomination would hurt the party's candidates across the South."

Carter's placement in the Democratic ideological spectrum, though not fixed precisely in anyone's mind, clearly was far to McGovern's right. Carter had been friendly enough toward George Wallace to have been asked to second Wallace's nomination for the Presidency. Instead, Carter had cast his lot with Senator Jackson, the most stubborn of McGovern's major rivals, whose hawkish views on the Vietnam War represented the antithesis of McGovern's position on that critical issue. Presenting Jackson's name to the convention, Carter likened him to John F. Kennedy.

At the Doral, Rafshoon and Jordan cooled their heels before they were allowed to see Pat Caddell, whose brilliant analysis of polling results had greatly helped McGovern's candidacy. Four years later Caddell would work alongside Rafshoon and Jordan to help make Carter President. But at the 1972 convention he had little time to squander on the agents of an obscure Southern governor.

To buttress their case that Carter would help the Democratic ticket in the South, the emissaries from Georgia had brought with them a public opinion poll of dubious significance. It suggested, unremarkably enough, that McGovern would run better in Georgia with Carter as his Vice-Presidential candidate than without him. Caddell glanced at the survey briefly, then sent his visitors packing.

This was not Carter's only approach to McGovern and the Vice-Presidency. He prevailed upon Andy Young of Atlanta, who that fall would become Georgia's first black congressman since Reconstruction, to press his cause in the McGovern camp. By Carter's account, "There was some vile language used and my name was immediately rejected. I never tried any more to have my name put forward."

McGovern was looking for a running mate whose views were

roughly compatible with his own. The only Southerner of note who met that criterion was Florida governor Reubin Askew, who had made clear he did not want the nomination. Besides, to the McGovern strategists, the South—which for four years had been intensively cultivated by Richard Nixon—seemed irredeemably lost to their candidates. They were more concerned with strengthening their campaign among the traditional Democratic constituencies in the North, a strategy which led them to the ill-fated choice of Senator Thomas Eagleton of Missouri, a Catholic, esteemed by organized labor.

The only immediate benefit Carter derived from the 1972 convention was the brief television exposure accorded him during his nominating speech for Jackson. But over the long run, the convention was a valuable learning experience, chastening but also in a way encouraging.

It brought home to Carter and his supporters the extent of his obscurity. "We have been rather provincial," Peter Bourne, the British-born psychiatrist who had been part of the Carter contingent at Miami Beach, wrote the governor afterward. At the convention Bourne realized "that very few people elsewhere in the country either knew who you were or very much about you." But as Bourne pointed out, this was an obstacle that could, with time and sufficient effort, be surmounted.

Having seen the national leaders of the Democratic party in action at Miami Beach, the provincials from Georgia felt they could be challenged. This feeling was reinforced in the summer and fall of 1972 by the clumsy handling of Eagleton's withdrawal from the ticket, and the bickering inside the McGovern organization. Watching the unraveling of McGovern's campaign, Carter could measure himself against other potential Presidential candidates and arrive at a judgment of his relative qualifications.

For politicians with egos normal to their calling, such comparisons are almost invariably favorable to themselves. In the fall of 1972, then Vice President Spiro Agnew—already much discussed as a 1976 Republican Presidential candidate—explained to me why he had no misgivings about his ability to handle the Presidency. "You have to evaluate, not yourself against the job as much as yourself against the people who can fill the job," Agnew said, less than a year before scandal destroyed his political career. "And I don't feel that I have any worries in that respect."

Carter's background in 1972 was roughly similar to Agnew's in 1968 when Richard Nixon selected him as his running mate. Like Agnew, Carter had been governor of a medium-sized state for two years and had no experience in the federal government. Like Agnew, he was not troubled by self-doubt. Once, he wrote later, he had viewed the Presidency with awe and reverence. "Then during 1971 and 1972 I met Richard Nixon, Spiro Agnew, George McGovern, Henry Jackson, Hubert Humphrey, Ed Muskie, George Wallace, Ronald Reagan, Nelson Rockefeller, and other Presidential hopefuls, and I lost my feeling of awe about Presidents. This is not meant as a criticism of them, but it is merely a simple statement of fact."

Consideration of the other alternatives for his future made a bid for the Presidency seem a risk worth taking. He was barred by the Georgia constitution from succeeding himself as governor when his term expired in 1974. He could then withdraw from the arena and retire, at the age of fifty, to his farm and warehouse in Plains. Or he could try to unseat the well-entrenched Herman Talmadge from the U.S. Senate, an effort which, even if it succeeded, would leave him a very junior member of that body.

His young associates began to prod him into action. Bourne was the first to commit himself to paper. In July 1972, soon after the convention, he sent Carter a nine-page handwritten letter. "I think you really understand what is going on in the country in a way that most people on the national scene do not," Bourne wrote. "I also believe that you have certain unique qualities which if adequately exploited would make you a major contender for the Presidency in 1976."

In October, Bourne, Jordan, and a handful of others met with Carter in the governor's mansion to present the arguments for his candidacy. Carter did not need much persuasion. A week after the meeting he flashed the green light, clearing the way for two years of quiet but intense preparation.

A joint memo, seventy pages long, from Rafshoon and Jordan followed. In one perceptive and significant passage Jordan noted that distrust of government was already a national issue of consequence. And he surmised that it would loom even larger by 1976.

But most of their advice had more to do with tactics than substance: Which newspapers to read and which journalists to cultivate, whom to hire for the campaign staff, and where to enter Presidential primaries. Rafshoon's counsel was couched in the argot of his trade. He talked of the need to develop a "heavyweight program" to project a "heavyweight image" and "to infect other Southern states and other regions with the Jimmy Carter 'good guy' brand of populism."

The memos contained no magic formula, and some advice— particularly the pointers on winning the favor of prominent journalists—was naive. Many of the suggestions could have been offered by anyone possessing common sense and a fair understanding of national politics.

The main significance of the memos is simply that they were produced, and acted upon, early in the game. "What is critical," Bourne wrote, "is the psychological and eventual decision to take the risk and to run for the Presidency to win, whatever the eventual outcome might be." Four years before the next Presidential election, Carter made that decision and started planning to implement it. He was off and running.

Carter's headstart gave him an advantage over rivals who moved with less speed and urgency. The recent history of both major parties has shown that the established leadership can be overwhelmed by insurgent forces with sufficient foresight and energy. In 1964 the adherents of Barry Goldwater captured control of the Republican party, largely because they worked harder and longer than anyone else. In 1972, in the Democratic party, which is far more open than the GOP, a similar outpouring of zeal by George McGovern's supporters carried him to the nomination over more prominent rivals.

In the wake of the 1972 election, conditions within the Democratic party were particularly favorable for another uprising by a candidate outside the traditional party structure. The reforms in party rules, which had aided McGovern's candidacy by breaking the control of party leaders over the selection of convention delegates, gained wider impact, making the delegate competition more open than ever. The pressure of complying with the new rules forced more states into adopting Presidential primaries. Winner-take-all primaries were abolished and formulas established for awarding delegates in proportion to voting strength. These changes were ideally suited to Carter's tactical plans. Not particularly strong anywhere, he proposed to run everywhere. Personal campaigning was his forte; in winning the governorship of Georgia he reckoned that he had given 1,800 speeches and shaken 600,000 hands.

Two successive setbacks in Presidential elections had left plenty of room at the top of the Democratic party. In view of the dimensions of his 1972 defeat, George McGovern was hardly in a position to claim the prerogatives and loyalties that might ordinarily be owed to the party's most recent standard-bearer. And McGovern's chief 1972 rivals all faced severe handicaps. Hubert Humphrey was shopworn. George Wallace was crippled. And even Henry Jackson's admirers acknowledged that he was numbingly dull.

Senator Edward M. Kennedy of Massachusetts, many believed, could have his party's nomination almost for the asking. Heir to the political dynasty his father and brothers founded, he was a compelling figure in his own right. But he had serious problems, too. His son had lost a leg to cancer, his wife's emotional difficulties were a matter of widespread gossip, and there was the tragedy at Chappaquidick, an open wound into which the press intermittently poked and prodded. Moreover, the risk of another Kennedy assassination was a specter that haunted his mother and others. In September 1974 Kennedy announced that because of his obligations to his family he would neither seek nor accept the 1976 nomination. Though some viewed his withdrawal with skepticism, Kennedy adhered to his decision, thus removing from the scene Carter's most formidable potential rival.

Another circumstance, unforeseen in 1972, also assisted Carter's candidacy. This was the enactment by Congress, in the wake of Watergate, of the 1974 campaign reform law, which imposed $1,000 limits on individual contributions to candidates for federal office. The law also provided federal subsidies, in the form of matching grants, to qualified Presidential candidates. The new ceilings helped Carter compete on a more nearly equal basis against such rivals as Henry Jackson and Texas senator Lloyd Bentsen, whose wealthy backers would otherwise have given them a significant initial advantage.

Meanwhile, Carter aided his own cause by prevailing upon Democratic National Chairman Robert Strauss to make him chairman of the party's 1974 congressional and gubernatorial campaigns. The post was considered to be little more than an honorary title, but Carter used it to great advantage. He traveled widely, often at party expense, to meet with local politicians, doing favors and making friends that would stand him in good stead when he launched his own drive for the Presidency. But Carter's occasional unorthodox utterances, aimed at generating publicity for himself, irritated Strauss, whose Presidential tastes ran to more conventional Democrats, notably Henry Jackson.

In the spring of 1974, at a Democratic governors' conference in Chicago, Carter expressed his concern about the impact of Richard Nixon's Watergate problems on that fall's balloting. By remaining in office, Carter said, Nixon would "seriously distort the political process" by causing the defeat of "a lot of deserving Republicans." He added that he doubted whether the Democrats were ready for the added responsibility that enlarged majorities in Congress would bring. Strauss fumed, and a close associate told

me later that the party chairman privately considered Carter to
be "the village idiot."

In his letter to Carter after the 1972 convention, Peter
Bourne had urged him to be "consistently on top of the issues.
Particularly in 1976 I believe the electorate will support candidates not for whom they represent but because they have taken a
clear, decisive position on the right issues."

As Carter surveyed the national scene before launching his
active campaign, no explicit issue of sufficient magnitude and
appeal offered itself to him. American involvement in Vietnam
had at last ended. The nation's economy was in trouble, but
Carter's differences with the other Democratic candidates on economic matters were neither strong nor clear.

There was abroad in the land, though, an increasingly perva-
sive mood that would ultimately endow Carter's candidacy with
the emotional appeal it required. The mistrust of government
which Hamilton Jordan had noted in late 1972 had, by the time
Carter formally announced his candidacy in December 1974, become the dominant fact of national political life.

The Flying Carpet

Chicago, March 14, 1975—More than one hundred liberal
Democrats have gathered here to take stock of themselves and
make plans for the Presidential campaign. They are meeting at a
motel near O'Hare Airport called the Flying Carpet, which boasts
an Aladdin's Lamp Lounge. In a way, the Arabian Nights setting
seems appropriate. In their present condition, the liberals could
use a magic lamp.

This is an impressive assemblage: leaders of half a dozen
powerful labor unions; intellectuals, such as Arthur Schlesinger,
Jr., and Michael Harrington; office-holders, past and present, including Bella Abzug of New York and John Gilligan of Ohio; and
a host of other less prominent toilers in past liberal crusades.

Many of them have been seasoned, and scarred, by the Presidential campaigns of Robert Kennedy, Eugene McCarthy, and George McGovern. United, they hold the balance of power in the Democratic party.

But at this point, with the first Presidential primaries less than a year away, the liberals are in disarray. The field for the Democratic nomination is already crowded, and none of the contenders has been able to attract more than a smattering of support from the people here. "As far as I'm concerned I'm against everyone in the race now," says Joe Rauh, the truculent elder statesman of Americans for Democratic Action. "And I don't need any more information to know that no one of them can do the job."

The problems run deeper than the perceived shortcomings of the declared candidates for the nomination. Most of the men and women at the Flying Carpet are children of the New Deal. Their politics, and the country's, have been shaped by a system of alliances and beliefs spawned by Franklin Roosevelt which are now tottering on the brink of collapse. The liberals are in danger of becoming political orphans.

Reality is forcefully brought home at the conference's opening session by three pollsters—Louis Harris, Patrick Caddell, and Peter Hart—who have been sampling the mood of the electorate. "The old political ground rules must be torn up," says Harris. "We are not likely to see elections run true to the old forms for the rest of our lives." Caddell declares that the basic attitudes of voters have altered greatly, "and probably changed for all time." Hart warns that "the old coalitions are breaking down." The powerful blocs that produced Democratic majorities can no longer be relied on to perform as monoliths. "Forget the old model and start to build anew," he advises.

The old model was founded on faith in the federal government, and designed to cater to a broad range of interest groups—union members, blacks, Jews, Catholics. Over the years it was expanded to meet increasing demands at home and to further the national interest abroad. This was the pattern by which the Democratic party dominated national politics for more than three decades. Its control of Congress was interrupted only twice; its hold on the Presidency was broken temporarily by Dwight Eisenhower but then resumed under Kennedy and Johnson.

But in the closing years of the Johnson Presidency the structure began to sag under its own weight and the pressure of expectations it had raised and changes it had fostered. The groups that had joined in the grand alliances of the New Deal, the Fair Deal, the New Frontier, and the Great Society developed new and competing interests. The commitments abroad aggravated problems at home, draining the economy and deepening divisions. The apparatus of government, which had been vastly enlarged to solve the nation's problems, became, itself, the biggest problem of all. Not only did it seem unreasonably costly and inefficient, but it had become alarmingly oppressive and, ultimately, corrupt.

Weary of racial upheavals and crime in its cities, and of the frustrations and divisiveness of the war in Vietnam, the country had turned the White House over to Richard Nixon in 1968. Nixon's immense reelection victory in 1972 stirred hopes among Republicans for a "new majority"—white, middle class, suburban, and respectable. But these hopes were undermined by the twists and turns of the economy and wrecked by the revelations of Watergate.

According to the pollsters at the Flying Carpet, the impact of these traumas on the Nixon majority, and on the rest of the country, has been devastating. "The great stable middle class is becoming unhinged," Caddell says.

With a mass of statistics drawn from their surveys, the pollsters outline the national mood for the liberals. Pessimism runs deep in what used to be a confident country. Only 10 percent of Americans are optimistic about the nation's future, compared with 75 percent ten years ago. More than 75 percent believe the country "is going in the wrong direction."

Cynicism has taken hold. Nearly 70 percent of those surveyed believe their government "consistently lies to the people."

Disbelief extends to political promises of all sorts, from the Left and Right alike. People believe that additional benefits from the government will have to be paid for several times over in higher taxes; they think that politicians who pledge a hard line against Communist aggression will, if elected, make concessions to Moscow and Peking. Confidence in public officials, and also in leaders of private institutions—businessmen, educators, and the clergy—is at the lowest point in a decade of measurement.

A sense of futility prevails. Only 38 percent of eligible voters went to the polls in the 1974 congressional elections, the lowest turnout in more than thirty years. And of those who did cast ballots, only a third thought their votes would make a difference. According to the poignant results of another survey, more than 60 percent of Americans feel that "what I think doesn't count anymore." The citizenry is so distraught, Caddell says, "there would be a movement to socialist action, except that the government is feared and disliked as much as big business."

The pollsters assert that if the Democratic party is to succeed it must become the vehicle for "radical and progressive change." But such words no longer have the meaning they did in Roosevelt's day. The old arguments of Left versus Right are forty years out of date, Harris says. "The politics of the easy promise is gone. What people want is not more quantity, but more quality in their lives."

The impact of the pollsters' statistics and conclusions on the conference is limited. "Nobody could come out of that discussion without being depressed and dismayed at the deep pessimism and cynicism of the country," says John Gilligan. But the liberals have difficulty accepting what the pollsters have said because it represents a rejection of what they have always believed. The pollsters have reported that the public no longer believes in political promises and government programs, but to the liberals progress still means more promises and programs.

Some people here are stubborn. The times demand radical remedies for the economy, says Congresswoman Abzug. "The candidate who presents honest, new programs will not be defeated." "Liberals don't care for personality and charisma," says Billie Carr, Democratic National Committeewoman from Texas. "We are waiting for someone to talk about issues."

The only consensus among those gathered here is that there is no consensus about whom they should support. They resolve to hold more meetings to learn more about the contenders for the nomination. "They are going to have to show me something more before I give another six months of my life to one of these characters," says Jerome Grossman of Boston, a veteran of the 1972 McGovern campaign.

"We're still waiting for our prince to come," says Billie Carr. But some sense that the times are out of joint, that they may already have waited too long. "We don't have a tiger," says Michael Harrington. "And if we don't think through the issues, we'll wake up and find out that the only tiger available is made of paper."

The Candidate

Jimmy Carter read the national mood better than the Democratic liberals did. He was fortunate that his background and character were well suited to the times, and he was shrewd enough to realize that public disaffection with the existing order would transform his apparent limitations into advantages.

When Carter declared his candidacy for the Presidency, scarcely anyone outside of Georgia had heard of him. But that made him a new face, at a time when all the findings of the pollsters and the instincts of politicians pointed to the public's weariness with old faces. Obscurity presented obvious problems. By the Catch-22 rule under which the press operates, only well-known politicians command much attention; unknowns tend to stay that way. But Carter had faced that problem in Georgia and overcome it by sheer personal effort, and would do so again.

Besides, though most of his opponents were better known than he was, they had managed to become just familiar enough to seem stale. In 1972 Henry Jackson had run for President and not even come close. Birch Bayh and Fred Harris had started to run and given up before the first primary. The record of their past failures undermined the credibility of their renewed efforts.

Carter had never served in Washington, another seeming handicap which the temper of the times converted into a plus. In the minds of many Americans, Washington had come to be identified with most of the country's ills. Jackson, Bayh, and Harris had all been there when things had gone wrong. The question hovering over their candidacies—which Carter did not have to answer—was why they had not done something.

The past positions of the Washington candidates were all publicly recorded and fairly well known. But Carter's activities in Georgia had been little noticed by the national press, and few people outside the state knew exactly what he had done there and what he stood for. He thus began his campaign with a clean slate, defining himself as he went along.

As his candidacy progressed, reporters and rivals checked back into this record, forcing him at times to explain past actions. But there were many major foreign and domestic issues he never had to deal with at all in Atlanta. This substantial gap in his experience naturally raised questions about his ability to govern the nation. Carter met that problem in part by taking what was in effect a cram course from scholars and former government experts which permitted him to discuss, with at least the appearance of knowledgeability, matters outside his personal experience.

More importantly, he contended that a firsthand grasp of the intricacies of public issues was not of great importance. Asked about his positions by Washington representatives of public interest groups, he said: "I don't care how much you talk about issues, or how many numbers of Senate and House bills you name." None of that mattered much, he said, "if the people don't believe that when you're in the White House, you're going to do something about the problem, and that they can trust what you tell them."

This rationale was central to his candidacy. It encouraged his supporters to overlook his unfamiliarity with the questions he would have to confront as President. By extension, it justified his insistent refusal to be labeled ideologically. Asked where he stood in relation to his Democratic rivals for the nomination, Carter said: "I never characterize myself as a conservative, liberal, or moderate, and this is what distinguishes me from them."

Occasionally, when pressed to define his views, Carter described himself as a "populist," a category which has become almost as popular among politicians as "pragmatist," probably because it is just about as hard to define. Usually, though, Carter liked to qualify his populism with some moderating adjectives such as "mild-mannered" or "modern." Rafshoon's memorandum had referred to "Jimmy Carter's 'good guy' brand of populism."

Carter claimed some family linkage with the South's populist tradition. He recalled that his maternal grandfather, Jim Jack Gordy, an astute local politician, had been an "avid supporter" of Tom Watson, the premier Georgia populist of his time. Near the end of his career Watson, like others of his kind, turned into a ranting bigot. But he was most celebrated for his earlier efforts to muster the resentment of the poor white farmers against the great business interests centered in Atlanta.

Carter followed a similar tack in his 1970 gubernatorial campaign against former governor Carl Sanders. Carter's first bid for the governorship, in 1966, after two terms in the state senate, had been marked by its relative earnestness and gentility. It failed. On his second try Carter worked longer, and hit harder. His invective was nowhere near as harsh as Tom Watson's. But he linked Sanders to the "establishment" in Atlanta and made much of his wealth and his ties to Hubert Humphrey. Sanders, it should be noted, set himself up for this attack by his flossy style; he wore electric-blue suits and his television commercials showed him water-skiing.

In his Presidential campaign, Carter's rhetoric exhibited intermittent reminders of the old populist strain as he inveighed against "big shots" and "powerful political figures." But neither in tone nor in substance did he ever try to match the gallus-snapping demagoguery of the old-time populists. In fact, his oratory lacked the vigor and color that enrich the public discourse of most modern Southern politicians. On the stump Carter was intense, sometimes emotional, but usually quiet and controlled. Time, breeding, and inclination had carried him a great distance from grandfather Gordy and Tom Watson.

Though Carter's boyhood on the family farm was physically rugged by modern standards, his family's circumstances were far removed from that of the hardscrabble rednecks who rallied behind Tom Watson. His father, James Earl Carter, Sr., "Mr. Earl", a strict disciplinarian and a demanding taskmaster, was also, his son writes, "an extremely competent farmer and businessman." He seems to have filled the role of squire in the community. His farm was relatively large and prosperous, he ran a general store and bought peanuts on a contract basis and sold fertilizer, seed, and other supplies.

Young Jimmy showed an early tendency to follow in his father's enterprising footsteps. By his early teens he had parlayed the proceeds from his sales of boiled peanuts on the streets of Plains into an investment in five houses, which he then leased to tenant farmers for a total rent of $16.50 a month.

His father's carefully nurtured friendship with the local congressman helped make it possible for Jimmy to fulfill a boyhood dream and enroll at Annapolis. He took well enough to the Naval Academy's engineering curriculum to graduate fifty-ninth in a class of 820 and ultimately won assignment to the navy's new nuclear submarine program. There he came under the command and influence of then Captain Hyman G. Rickover, who was at least as stern as Mr. Earl and singularly tactless. But Rickover was "unbelievably hard-working and competent," and Carter's admiration for him was boundless. It was Rickover, according to a story Carter told over and over in his campaign, who, when Carter acknowledged that he had not *always* done his best at Annapolis, demanded to know: "Why not?" Carter could not find an answer then, but the question eventually provided him with a book title and a Presidential campaign slogan.

His father's death in 1953 brought Carter out of the navy and back to the family farm and business in Plains. He freshened his knowledge of agricultural techniques, as he would later bone up on campaign issues, and in partnership with his mother branched out into sales of certified seed. The first year, when Carter was his own sole employee, the firm netted less than $200. But he kept at it day and night, with his wife's help, and the business grew and flourished. Running against Carl Sanders he called himself a redneck, and campaigning for President he described himself as a peanut farmer. But by the time he declared for the White House he was worth about $800,000 and his various agricultural enterprises grossed more than $2 million a year.

Jimmy Carter, when he entered the national scene in the 1970s, was a fairly typical representative of the new breed of entrepreneurs and managers who had emerged in the postwar era with the economic renaissance of the South. He was enterprising, ambitious, methodical, cautious but confident, and fundamentally conservative—all qualities characteristic of his class which, in his case, had been strengthened and disciplined by his upbringing and his navy background.

Unlike their better-established Yankee counterparts, the businessmen of the New South had been forced to scramble for what they had; they tended to be more aggressive and innovative. But the Southerners differed also from the new moneymen of the West, the plungers and wheeler-dealers of Texas and California. Resources in the South were not all that abundant, and optimism about the future was tempered by the memories and handicaps of past destitution.

On racial matters, the leaders of the South's new economy were relatively enlightened. They recognized that the bullwhips and bombings of the early 1960s, apart from their savagery and ultimate futility, created an atmosphere of instability harmful to business growth. They also realized that economic advance required a skilled labor force, which meant improved job training and incentives for blacks. When Carter declared, in his inaugural address as governor, that "the time for racial discrimination is over," and "we cannot afford to waste the talents and abilities given by God to one single Georgian," his words reflected not only humanitarian ideals but also the hard facts of Southern economic life.

Carter's racial liberalism in no way diminished his economic conservatism, an attitude deeply ingrained in him. "He's conservative on money," Charles Kirbo, himself one of the staunchest conservatives around Carter, once told me. "He's efficient and careful with money, very careful with money. He's careful about his own money. He doesn't have any interest in showing how big a car he owns. You might say," Kirbo added, "that he's a little tight."

Other Presidential candidates could appeal to harassed businessmen and overburdened taxpayers by promising economies in government. But when Carter spoke out against excess government spending and budget deficits he spoke from the heart, and from personal experience. Such profligacy reflected, he said, "the kind of improper management that really grates on the consciousness of a businessman. I know what it means to meet a payroll. I know what it means not to waste my own. I never have known an unbalanced budget in my business or my farm or as governor of Georgia."

To citizens weary of government programs and regulation, Carter defended free enterprise with the fervor of a successful practitioner: "Whenever there is a choice between the government performing a function and the private sector performing a function, I believe in the private sector having responsibility."

But the sophisticated new capitalists of the South had learned that they must live with government. If they were clever they could perhaps influence its policies; but this was best done quietly.

What they could publicly demand was that the government work better, much as they would like their own enterprises to function.

In the governor's office Carter's devotion to economy and efficiency was evident even on the smallest matters. He complained that the bathrooms at the executive mansion were overstocked with toilet tissue; and he ordered the thermostat turned down to 65 degrees, until he found out that doing so automatically turned on the mansion's air-conditioning system, which sent the electricity bill soaring.

More constructively, Carter made his first priority as governor a massive reorganization of the state government. The struggle to enact his proposals consumed much of his political capital and energy. Though the scope and benefits he claimed for the reorganization were somewhat exaggerated, it was a significant achievement, curbing waste and duplication and expediting the flow of services.

It was also a big help to Carter's Presidential candidacy, bolstering his promise to end "the horrible bureaucratic mess in Washington" by reorganizing the government and establishing "tight businesslike management." "This is not a job for the fainthearted," Carter said. "It will be met with strong opposition from those who now enjoy special privilege, those who prefer to work in the dark, or those whose personal fiefdoms are threatened." But as Carter almost unfailingly pointed out, he had met those same adversaries in Atlanta and prevailed.

Ultimately, though, the appeal of Carter's candidacy rested less on his experience in business and government than it did on his character. The voters he met, usually in small groups, were struck by his forcefulness, determination, and sincerity. And they were especially impressed by his expressions of religious faith. In the jaded political world, Carter's well-advertised devoutness struck a refreshing and, for many, an inspiring note. His avowals of trust in God greatly reinforced his efforts to persuade voters that they should trust him.

In the Hand of God

Concord, New Hampshire, May 14, 1975—The New Hampshire Presidential primary, the first in the nation, is still nine months off. But Jimmy Carter has already been a frequent visitor to this state, and he has come here again today to officially open his campaign headquarters in Concord, the capital.

Carter's major test in next year's primaries will come in the Florida primary—which follows New Hampshire's by two weeks —where he plans to challenge George Wallace. But he knows he needs to do well in New Hampshire if he is to have much chance against Wallace.

So far as the public is concerned, Carter's candidacy is only another blur in the crowded field of Democratic contenders. But he has attracted some attention among political professionals who think his Southern Baptist background might help him win votes, particularly among members of the country's growing evangelical movement.

When I asked Carter about this, on the plane coming up here from Washington yesterday, he seemed surprised at the question. It was clear, though, that he had thought about the subject. He said the evangelical movement now included about 40 million persons, people like himself "who are deeply committed to establishing government as moralistic and decent."

His sister is a full-time evangelist and religion had long been a major part of his own life, he told me. "That doesn't mean I'm anointed," he said carefully. "It means I have an obligation to try to discern the best qualities of the American people in government and put them into effect."

I reminded him that at a Democratic governors' conference, two years earlier, when the full dimensions of the Watergate scandal were emerging, he had introduced a resolution for national prayer, including prayers for Richard Nixon. The resolution was tabled by the other governors, who were more interested in backing the creation of an independent prosecutor to investigate Nixon.

Carter nodded. "I thought then that Nixon was guilty," he said, but had felt obligated to pray for him anyhow.

"Religion is part of my life, part of my consciousness," he said. "It may or may not be politically significant."

It certainly seems to be a significant part of his candidacy. At his first appearance today, at the mayor's prayer breakfast in Manchester, the state's largest city, Carter was very much at home. "The most important thing in my life is my belief and my commitment in God," he said. "And this provides a stabilizing force, and also a standard of excellence for which I, and I know all of you, feel committed to strive."

He left the breakfast guests with the advice that they should try to do their best in all things. "It is important for us always to be striving," he said. "We should never deviate from recognizing our own unworthiness, but also our absolute strength when our hand is in the hand of God."

Carter does not confine his references to religion to prayer breakfasts. He also talks about God to the forty or fifty people who have gathered here for the reception marking the opening of his state headquarters on the second floor of a run-down office building. After sandwiches and homemade cookies are passed around, he says: "I'm running for President because I'm a deeply religious person." It is an article of his faith, he explains, "that every experience or opportunity we have, ought to be devoted in the maximum possible way to bring about changes in the things that concern us."

The candidate is soft-spoken and uses no rhetorical flourishes. The cadence of his speech is uneven and his voice rises and falls in a distracting way. But he is believable and persuasive, and he holds the attention of everyone in the headquarters.

"I have told every support group with whom I have met during the campaign this," he says. "I don't have to be President.

There are a lot of things I would not do to be elected. I would never tell a lie, make a misleading statement, betray a trust, or avoid a controversial issue. I have a deep commitment to my principles that are based on my religious beliefs that would be unshakable.

"I ask you to give me your support on a tentative basis. I want to be continually under the influence of trying to measure up to your own expectations. If I ever should betray a trust, don't support me."

On the flight up, Carter claimed he had an important advantage over his rivals because he could attract volunteers more easily than they. Listening to him here, I can understand why. The blend of trust and God is powerful medicine in a country starved for some source of inspiration.

But Carter has set a high standard for himself, one that will be hard to maintain in the rough and tumble of the campaign. He is hard to fathom and hard to predict. He has a tendency to blurt out comments better left unsaid. Yesterday word came that the Cambodians had seized the United States merchant ship *Mayaguez* in international waters. Reporters asked Carter for his reaction. At first he said only that the matter should be handled with "great restraint." But then he was told that Lloyd Bucher, skipper of the *Pueblo,* which the North Koreans had taken at sea in 1968, had urged that the United States retake the *Mayaguez* immediately.

"I don't have much respect for Bucher, in fact almost none," Carter said. "He is the last person to talk, having abandoned his own ship when challenged by a small force at sea."

But Carter can also be just as slippery as the average politician. On a visit to New Hampshire last month he told a reporter there was "no way" he could support George Wallace, if he won the nomination. But today, asked the same question, he said "some circumstance" might arise which could cause him to back Wallace.

Following his speech at the campaign headquarters, Carter

goes to a nearby factory to shake hands with the workers changing shifts. Gerald Rafshoon, who has been Carter's media adviser and friend since Carter ran for governor of Georgia in 1970, comes along to take pictures for Carter's campaign brochures. Rafshoon unintentionally parks his car in a spot reserved for a truck driver who works at the plant. This causes a fuss when the driver arrives with his truck. Rafshoon apologizes and moves his car, but the driver is still angry and determined to make a scene.

"Your man took my parking place," he shouts at Carter, who is shaking hands at the plant gate. Carter tries to ignore him, but the driver keeps shouting, and some of the other workers begin to pay attention.

Finally, Carter glances at Rafshoon, who has a camera dangling from a strap around his neck. "He doesn't work for me," Carter tells the driver. "He's a photographer."

The confused driver gives up and wanders off. Carter might just as easily have apologized to the driver and given him a few dollars for his trouble. But he evidently does not like to give anyone an inch if he can avoid it.

It is a trivial incident, but it suggests something about the character of this candidate for President. Everyone is more conscious of Presidential character traits now because of Richard Nixon. And Carter seems to be basing his campaign on the strength of his own character. He has asked to be watched closely and it is clear that he bears watching.

Themes and Variations

In January 1976 no fewer than ten Democrats were running for President, and an eleventh, Hubert Humphrey, seemed only to be waiting for an opportune moment to enter the race. It was hard for reporters and voters to keep track of them all, or to tell them apart. Among those struggling for support and recognition was Senator Birch Bayh of Indiana, who was asked at a reception for local party leaders in Lowell, Massachusetts, what distinguished him from his rivals for the nomination.

Bayh, close to being the model of a modern liberal Democrat, was stumped for a moment. "I wish I could say I was head and shoulders above the rest," he said. But, he acknowledged, other candidates held much the same views he did. "There are a number of people running who I frankly would be very comfortable with as President." Then Bayh, who had announced his candidacy less than three months earlier, brightened. "But they've been running for a year," he said, "and none of them are getting anywhere."

Bayh was not getting anywhere either. By March, after two dismal primary defeats, he would drop out of contention.

One candidate was getting ahead, though, and he was Jimmy Carter. No one had to ask how he differed from the rest. With the exception of George Wallace, who it was generally assumed could not be nominated, Carter's competitors were running on updated versions of the old New Deal platform. Carter had broken with the Democratic party's past. By doing so, he set himself apart and, to the surprise of nearly everyone but himself, moved out front.

Instead of addressing himself to the divergent demands of interest groups, he set forth broad themes, appealing to common concerns. The traditional promises Democrats had made relied on faith in the federal government. Carter's major themes, of competence and trust, reflected the loss of faith in that government. He promised "to make the government work," efficiently and economically. He promised a government that would be "decent and honest and trustworthy, a source of pride instead of shame."

These were certainly not brand-new ideas. When he announced his candidacy for the 1972 Democratic Presidential nomination, George McGovern lamented "the loss of confidence in the truthfulness and common sense of our leaders." Edmund Muskie, campaigning for the 1972 nomination, adopted as his main slogan "Trust Muskie." But McGovern was distracted and damaged by controversies over such matters as welfare and Vietnam. Muskie, once he had asked voters to trust him, could not offer persuasive reasons why they should.

By the time Carter became a Presidential candidate, Watergate had made trust a far more important concern than it had been in 1972, and Carter responded more simply, directly, and convincingly than any of his rivals.

He talked of the war in Vietnam, "which the people didn't support," and its cost in lives and money. He talked of Watergate and the President who had lied and subverted the agencies of government. "In the last few years we've been hurt," he said. "We've seen some precious things slip out of our hands. We've lost a lot of respect for our government."

Lacking the support of existing Democratic constituencies, Carter sought to build a consitituency of his own, on a highly personal basis. He spoke of forging a bond with the voters that was "intense" and "intimate." He told his supporters they should consider his candidacy tied to "the hopes and dreams and aspirations" of their own lives, calling upon them to seal the alliance by making, on behalf of his candidacy, nothing less than "a sacrificial effort."

Carter's message was not altogether different from the message George Wallace tried to send to Washington in 1972. Wallace was perceived by his supporters, George McGovern pointed out in 1975, "as the voice of the little man." His main strength came, McGovern believed, not from racism but from his assaults on the establishment. "He has a reputation for letting the chips fall where they may."

Carter's listeners could hear echoes of Wallace's rhetoric. "It's like a wall has been built around Washington," Carter told the voters. "A lot of us are outsiders. We don't see why these strange things happen in Washington." Like Wallace, Carter sought to capitalize on his differences with established political leaders. "I never have depended on powerful political figures to put me in office. Most of the time they're against me, because I don't yield to them and I don't trade with them. My obligations are to tens and hundreds of thousands of folks just like you all across the country."

But even when he was seeking the redneck vote against Carl

Sanders for governor of Georgia in 1970, Carter never resorted to the blatant appeals to bigotry which had made Wallace an infamous figure to blacks and liberals. Probably the most basic difference was that Wallace's message was primarily negative, shaped by resentment, fear, and hate. As Garry Wills wrote: "Wallace offered neither palliative nor real cure; just a chance to scream into the darkness."

Carter looked into the darkness and proclaimed there was light. The failures of government, he contended, could be corrected if the government could be made as good as the American people—honest, compassionate, and even filled with love. Not many politicians could have made that pledge sound credible. But Carter's evangelical fervor, bolstered by the testimony of his religious faith, drove his message home. His stump speeches were essentially sermons, and the medium embodied the message of morality.

An aura of religion surrounded his early campaign and gave it a distinctive tone. Carter drew his favorite definition of politics from the writings of the Protestant theologian Reinhold Niebuhr: "The sad duty of politics is to establish justice in a sinful world." At a time when he had few endorsements from other politicians, he managed, without of course actually saying so, to leave some of his listeners with the impression that his candidacy had the blessing of God.

In March 1976 Richard Reeves, in an influential article in *New York* magazine, compared Carter to William Jennings Bryan and Mohandas Gandhi. "Carter has figured out a couple of very important things," Reeves wrote. "What national leaders and other candidates perceive as a political crisis is actually a spiritual crisis, and that more symbolic communication is the best way to reach Americans drifting in an atmosphere saturated with instant communication."

But the drawback to symbolic communication is that some people take the symbols literally. Carter's early proclamations of his faith caused acute discomfort among Catholics and Jews, whose perception of Southern Baptists was influenced by primordial memories of night riders and burning crosses. These groups had to be assured of the candidate's aversion to bigotry and his belief in separation of church and state. Others worried that Carter might be prone to mysticism or priggishness or both. And the effort to set these fears to rest led to Carter's foolish attempt to demonstrate his tolerance of sin through the medium of *Playboy* magazine, an adventure which only raised broader questions about his judgment. Ultimately, as his campaign progressed, Carter decided on the prudent and simple course of talking less about his religion.

Truth was another potent symbol which helped Carter's cause. "Lying is *the* issue in this campaign," said Charles Morgan, the Southern civil liberties lawyer and one of the first prominent liberals to back Carter's candidacy. "And Carter is the only candidate who speaks to that issue."

Inevitably, though, Carter's oft-repeated promise never to tell a lie drove the press and his rivals to try to catch him in one. Their efforts led to a continuing series of often tedious arguments which sometimes dominated the coverage of his campaign and served mainly to demonstrate the suppleness and swiftness of Carter's intelligence.

If the candidate did not flatly lie, or avoid controversial issues, he certainly had a knack for drawing fine semantic distinctions which helped to cover his tracks and soften controversy. When, after publicly declaring that he never asked for political endorsements, he sought and gained Birch Bayh's backing in the Indiana Presidential primary, Carter explained: "I asked for his support, I didn't talk about an endorsement."

Though the dictionary gives "pardon" as a synonym for "amnesty," Carter managed to read between the lines enough of a difference to serve his purposes in dealing with the touchy issue of Vietnam draft dodgers. In the Iowa campaign, caught between opponents and proponents of a constitutional ban on abortions, Carter said he might support a "general statute" prohibiting abortions, a remedy so ill-defined and esoteric that he ultimately discarded it.

As the campaign developed, it became harder for Carter to avoid specifics by relying on the broad themes of trust and competence. This had been the hallmark of his early candidacy and had greatly contributed to his broad appeal and initial success. But success had focused attention on him, spurring demands from various interest groups that he declare himself on matters that concerned them directly. The press and his opponents accused him of being "fuzzy on the issues," and the charge caught on, becoming his most serious problem.

Reluctant to commit himself, but unable to ignore the pressure, Carter began issuing more specific statements, often then qualifying and elaborating what he had said, shifting from one carefully formulated stand to some other redefined middle ground. His staff responded to the charges of vagueness by citing the stack of position papers they had produced, covering almost every public question of consequence. The critics replied that Carter's fault was not that he had too few positions on issues—but rather that he had too many positions on each issue. "He has more positions than the *Kama Sutra,*" Mark Shields, one of Morris Udall's advisers, wisecracked.

Many of the major promises Carter made were cautiously and sometimes artfully phrased, to avoid antagonizing important voting blocs, and to give him maximum room to maneuver, as candidate and as President. He pledged to overhaul the income tax system, but he did not say how or when. Unemployment would be reduced, but in a way that would not aggravate inflation. He favored mandatory national health insurance, but could not yet say what role private insurance companies would play in the system. The Pentagon budget would be cut, but the United States would not weaken its defenses.

Yet if these views left questions unanswered, they also left room for those who wanted to support Carter for their own reasons, to make their own interpretations of his candidacy. Carter had acquired early important support from some blacks and liberals who saw his candidacy simply as a vehicle for defeating George Wallace in the Florida primary. Prominent in this group were Martin Luther King, Sr., Representative Andrew Young, and Leonard Woodcock, president of the United Auto Workers.

Their strategy was designed to avoid the error of 1972, when the liberal vote was divided among a number of primary candidates and Wallace won a smashing victory. Young, who took every opportunity he could get to speak to Democratic groups in Florida, offered them all the same advice: "Don't bring all the good guys down here and let Wallace chew them up. Let's make Florida a referendum on the South."

Carter was the logical candidate of the anti-Wallace forces because he was a racial moderate, but also a Southerner. Beyond these qualifications, Carter's liberal supporters did not think much about his record, or where his campaign might take them and him afterward. As the Florida primary neared, one of Carter's liberal rivals for the nomination, Morris Udall, became uneasy about the backing Carter was getting from liberals. "Most of them don't think he's really a threat to get nominated," said Udall, who by this time took Carter very seriously. "If Jimmy wins Florida," Udall warned Leonard Woodcock, "he doesn't expect to go back to raising peanuts." But Udall was in a poor position to complain. He himself had stayed out of the Florida primary and advised his supporters there to back Carter. In the end, only Henry Jackson, among Carter's major rivals for the nomination, joined the Florida competition between Wallace and Carter, and Jackson was not strong enough to prevent Carter's victory.

The Florida primary had sweeping impact. It finished Wallace as a major force in the Democratic party. It gave Jimmy Carter first claim to all the Southern delegations. And coming on the heels of his victory in New Hampshire, it made him the front-runner for the nomination.

Carter's liberal supporters realized they were too deeply committed to him now to change, even if they wanted to. They were, in effect, stuck with a winner. Andy Young suddenly found himself involved in Carter's New York campaign, where he dealt with a flood of phone calls from across the country. "These were people who saw Carter and liked him and just wanted to make sure that he was all right on race," Young later recalled.

"Yeah, he is all right on race," Young told the callers. "There are lots of other questions I may have, but you know . . ."

For the liberals Young talked to, that reassurance was enough. They did not trouble themselves or him about the "other questions." These liberals, who not long before had been heavily oriented to issues, were now more oriented to winning. In 1968 their opposition to Hubert Humphrey's nomination had divided their party and contributed to Humphrey's narrow defeat. In 1972 they had seized control of the party with George McGovern, but he had been overwhelmed by Nixon. For the past three years they had looked for another candidate who would speak to the issues that mattered most to them. They had considered Morris Udall, Birch Bayh, Fred Harris, and others, but none seemed to have much prospect of winning the nomination, let alone the election. They decided to settle for success and for Jimmy Carter.

Their attitude was summed up by Harold Willens, an active fund raiser and supporter of Eugene McCarthy and George McGovern. "In 1968 and 1972 it made sense to support McCarthy and McGovern despite their unelectability because they were banner carriers in an anti-war crusade," Willens wrote friends in May 1976, urging them to support Carter. "In 1976 it strikes me as little more than personal luxury for us to insist on some kind of purist perfection rather than rally around a decent American to whom citizens across the political spectrum have responded in primary campaigns as well as public opinion polls."

As Willens noted, what was impressive about Carter was not just his success but the breadth of support that made it possible. In New Hampshire, where he was facing four liberal opponents, Carter drew most of the conservative and moderate vote. In Massachusetts, though he ran behind Jackson, Wallace, and Udall, he won the black vote. In Florida, against Jackson and Wallace, he won most of the liberal vote.

His early victories and his distinctive personality made Carter a media hero. The week after the New Hampshire primary he was on the covers of both *Time* and *Newsweek*. He survived setbacks in Massachusetts and in the New York primary in April to confront Jackson in Pennsylvania. The scenario could not have been more favorable if Carter had written it himself. He was the outsider, pitted against the big shots, Mayor Rizzo and the labor bosses. And even the big shots had lost their enthusiasm for Jackson, whose campaign faded. Carter won a decisive victory. Election night, Pittsburgh mayor Peter Flaherty, an early Carter supporter and later to be named his deputy attorney general, joyfully recalled John Kennedy's 1960 campaign for the nomination. "Pennsylvania is the West Virginia of 1976," he said.

For all practical purposes the contest was over. But Carter's rise was so swift and unexpected that not everyone in the party was yet prepared to concede him the nomination. Nineteen Presidential primaries remained, and some still hoped that the front-runner could be overtaken.

Morris Udall stayed in to the bitter end, finishing a close second here and there, but never coming in first. He was the last of the traditional liberals in a year when the liberal tradition was dying.

Two late starters, Idaho's senator Frank Church and California's governor Edmund G. Brown, Jr., provided most of Carter's competition in the closing weeks. They defeated him in nine of the final primaries, mostly in Western states, but also in New Jersey, a record that should have served as warning of Carter's vulnerability in those areas. But Carter's advisers explained the setbacks on the grounds that Carter was contesting almost every state—he entered every primary except West Virginia—while his opponents could concentrate their resources. Besides, Carter was gaining delegates even in the states in which he was defeated. His total was climbing—"inexorably," as he put it—toward the majority he needed, and party leaders were coming to regard his nomination as inevitable.

On June 8, the last day of the primary season, Carter lost California and New Jersey. But he won a sweeping victory in Ohio, and that ended any lingering doubts about his prospects. Before the next day was over, he had pledges of support from Mayor Richard Daley of Chicago, Senator Jackson, and Governor Wallace, and the nomination was as good as his.

Most misgivings within the party about his lackluster showing late in the campaign were swept aside by the widespread relief that for the first time since 1964 the Democrats could hold their nominating convention in an atmosphere of harmony and by their prospective nominee's high standing in the polls. The first Harris poll after the primaries showed that Carter's campaign themes had established him as "a new, positive national figure." People liked the fact that he was not from Washington, and he was considered to be "a man of high integrity." Some had doubts, though. A fair number of those surveyed thought he had ducked taking stands on the issues and suspected that, behind his smile, he was tough and cold-blooded. But by margins of about two to one, voters admired him for having the courage not to make promises in order to get votes and believed he had conducted his campaign so as not to be obligated to any special interest.

All that remained was the ceremony of the convention. This Carter carried off in fine style, with the adroit assistance of Chairman Strauss, who suppressed whatever lingering resentment he may have felt toward Carter in the interest of unity. Carter turned his selection of a running mate into a suspenseful drama and then won acclaim from many on the left who had held out against him, by choosing Senator Walter Mondale of Minnesota.

His acceptance address was an elaboration of his standard stump speech, rambling and moralistic. Sparks from the old populist flame kindled its most provocative passage. "Too many have had to suffer at the hands of a political and economic elite who have shaped decisions and never had to account for mistakes nor to suffer from injustice," Carter declared. "Too often unholy, self-perpetuating alliances have been formed between money and politics, and the average citizen has been held at arm's length."

The convention finale was a tableau of unity. Leaders of every Democratic faction—George McGovern and George Wallace, Hubert Humphrey and Edmund Muskie—crowded onto the stage at Madison Square Garden while Daddy King delivered the benediction with stunning force. His voice rising and falling, his hands waving, the old man cried out: "Surely the Lord sent Jimmy Carter to come on out and bring America back where she belongs." And armed with that blessing, the candidate set out to finish the Lord's work.

Last Lap

Carter left New York trailing glory and euphoria. He had made it from the governorship of Georgia to the Democratic Presidential nomination, roughly the political equivalent of a trip from the earth to the moon. He had been almost alone when he started, and now every faction of his party had rallied to his side. The hardest part of his journey to the White House seemed behind him. But, as it turned out, the last lap was strewn with pitfalls that almost wrecked his candidacy.

The polls made complacency a problem. Immediately after the Democratic Convention, Carter had a lead of about 30 points over both President Ford and Ronald Reagan, who were then still struggling for the Republican nomination. The candidate and his advisers told themselves that the margin was inflated, that it was bound to narrow as soon as the Republicans held their convention and made their choice. But it was hard to conceive of the possibility of defeat and difficult to recapture the urgency of the campaign for the nomination.

The candidate pointedly set up his headquarters away from the Washington scene, in Atlanta. He himself withdrew to his home in Plains, where he and his running mate hosted gatherings of experts on the economy, foreign policy, and defense, held press conferences, and pondered strategy. Activity was limited because nothing demanded immediate action. Members of the campaign staff assembled in Atlanta, found their offices, and puzzled over exactly what was expected of them. The candidate was 140 miles away, and the impetus of his leadership was lacking.

As the summer drifted by, the most obvious question facing Carter and his advisers was how best to allocate their resources, particularly the candidate's time, for the fall campaign. The shortest cut to victory was to concentrate on the South and the industrial North. These were the areas of greatest strength for Carter personally and for the Democratic party; the states they contained were enough to assure a majority of the electoral vote.

But Carter and some advisers looked at the polls and the map and saw the possibility of a sweep that would come close to matching Nixon's forty-nine-state landslide in 1972. More than pride was involved. Carter himself talked earnestly to reporters about the broad governmental reforms he proposed and said: "The mandate that's crucial to me in carrying out quickly my promises to the people can only come from a wide-ranging success among the electorate." Hamilton Jordan, his chief strategist, agreed. "We're in too good a shape everywhere to start giving away states," he told me. "We haven't gotten this far by being supercautious." Later on, if necessity demanded, Jordan said, the focus could be narrowed. So as Labor Day and the start of the fall campaign neared, the priorities of time and money were left unsettled.

But a more fundamental uncertainty prevailed in the Carter camp, and this boiled down to the question of how the candidate should address the nation. The issue was complicated by Carter's relationship to the Democratic party. He had won the nomination by running against the Democratic grain. He had made capital of the fact that he was not beloved by party regulars, and he had tried to put some distance between himself and the party's dominant liberal ideology.

But, as Carter noted later, his status automatically changed with his nomination. "All of a sudden, whether I wanted it or not," he said, "I inherited the Democratic party." The legacy was a mixed blessing, its most evident liability for Carter being the party's pronounced liberal bent. As George McGovern, who had reason to know, pointed out, the Democratic party is more liberal than the rest of the country. To accommodate that liberalism and to help unite the party, Carter had selected Walter Mondale, perhaps the best and the brightest of its liberal leaders, as his running mate. He had also accepted, in broad outline, the party's platform, which embodied most of the principles of traditional Democratic liberalism. His own statements, during and right after the convention, seemed to support the overall thrust of the platform.

Thus, a few weeks after his nomination, Carter's candidacy had taken on a somewhat different complexion. Listening to the oratory at the Republican Convention, and reading their private polls, Carter and his advisers began to fear that in the electorate's view Carter had shifted from the roomy grounds of the center into a corner on the left. He was risking the loss of the conservatives whose support had helped him gain the nomination. Perhaps more serious, he was in danger of being branded as an over-promiser, the stigma which skeptical voters have come to attach to traditional Democratic candidates. Carter had fought against that image from the earliest days of his candidacy, and he was determined still to avoid it at all costs.

Just before the official start of the fall campaign, Carter, who had previously said that attacking unemployment would be his top priority in office, now announced that his first goals would be to curb inflation and to balance the budget. He claimed that he was only reasserting the basic commitments of his campaign for the nomination. But the shift was such a pronounced lurch that it revived criticism of the candidate's ambiguity and inconsistency on issues.

The conflict between Democratic liberalism and Carter's concern with retaining the broad, nonideological constituency he had established during the primaries plagued him throughout the campaign. It was no easy matter to disown the traditional philosophy of his party, particularly when unions, blacks, and other groups whose support was essential for his success still adhered to the old shibboleths. And it was even harder to develop a new ideology, to translate the themes of his preconvention campaign into terms sharp and clear enough to sway the electorate during the brief span of the fall campaign.

Carter was not ready for this task, either intellectually or politically. So he temporized and compromised, giving Ford grounds to jeer at his opponent: "He wavers, he wanders; he wiggles, he waffles."

Carter's efforts to deal with the strategic and tactical problems that faced him were hampered by his relative isolation from the mainstream of the party whose nomination he had won. Carter and his intimates were strangers to the traditional Democratic leaders, notably the union officials whose effective cooperation was vital to his candidacy. But coordination between the Carter campaign and the powerful unions around the country became such a problem that in the last two weeks of the campaign, the AFL-CIO assigned one of its most experienced political operators, William Du Chessi, to travel on *Peanut One* as labor's liaison man with the candidate. "It wasn't that they wanted to give us trouble," said Du Chessi. "They just didn't understand us. They didn't know the people in the labor movement, and they didn't know how we function."

Having waged and won a lonely battle for the nomination, Carter's team of Georgians was reluctant to grant influence or access to outsiders. Ted Van Dyk, who had been a top adviser in the Presidential campaigns of Hubert Humphrey and George McGovern, was summoned to Atlanta to help prepare Carter for his televised debates with President Ford. Van Dyk helped assemble the briefing books. But when it came time to drill the candidate on the material just before the debates, Van Dyk was told he was not welcome. Carter might be embarrassed by the presence of outsiders, Eizenstat explained, and would accept coaching only from a few members of his old inner circle. Van Dyk stayed on the job, but concluded that it "just pains them to take help from anybody."

For the most part Carter relied on the same advisers who had guided him to the nomination. Under the stresses and strains of campaigning against an incumbent President, they behaved, in the harsh characterization of Greg Schneiders (who was one of them), "like a lot of stupid kids. It was the first national political campaign for most of us. There were very few veterans. And there were mistakes made that undoubtedly caused doubts and loss of support."

Awkward situations seemed to pursue Carter. In August he met with a group of Catholic bishops, hoping to placate traditionally Democratic Catholic voters who were disturbed by his unwillingness to support a constitutional ban on abortions. For his trouble he was publicly rebuked by the bishops and picketed by right-to-life groups.

Pressed for details of his tax reform proposals, he blundered into an answer which suggested that he intended to boost the rates for half the nation's taxpayers. The Republicans, hungry for an opening, made charges, headlined around the country, that Carter intended to soak the middle class. Carter struck back by contending that the Republicans had nurtured loopholes for the privileged few. But he had been put on the defensive, a posture which he found himself in too often during the campaign.

As the first of the televised debates approached, Carter's advisers, mindful of the candidate's natural intensity and aggressiveness, cautioned him not to be overly rough with the President. Gerald Rafshoon, one of the coaches, explained the strategy to me a few days before the confrontation. "If we told him: 'Jimmy: win debate. Win debate and you don't have to campaign anymore, you can spend five days a week in Plains,' he might demolish Ford. We want him to be cool. We don't want a sympathy reaction for the President."

But when the debate began, Carter seemed subdued and overly restrained. He lost the test against Ford, in his own view, because he had shown "excessive deference" to the President.

Like any candidate challenging an incumbent, Carter sought to convince the country that, in the well-worn phrase, it was time for a change. But the public's willingness to accept this proposition was tempered by anxiety. A Johnny Carson gag summed up the dilemma, labeling the Ford-Carter campaign as a contest between fear of the known and fear of the unknown. Voters understood Ford's limitations; they were uncertain about the risk they would run with Carter.

Carter had tried, with some success, to avoid being labeled ideologically or hemmed in by issues. But the consequence of this was that attention focused, as he said, "to an extraordinary degree on my character. Who am I, what do I stand for, is there a secret there?" Rafshoon had considered Carter's character his greatest asset. But in the campaign he was subjected to an examination so intense that any candidate would have had difficulty withstanding it without injury or embarrassment.

In the midst of this public scrutiny the *Playboy* interview burst into print, catering to prurient and psychological interests. It was a vast distraction, throwing Carter off stride, forcing him into convoluted explanations and ultimately into a public apology for characterizing Lyndon Johnson as "lying, cheating and distorting the truth." Said Pat Caddell: "It was the worst kind of thing he could have done."

The candidate was harried and frustrated. His press secretary, Jody Powell, was even more distraught, so much so that he persuaded Carter to summon the members of the writing press who traveled with him for a heart-to-heart, off-the-record talk. We gathered in a San Diego motel room where Carter, seated on a hassock, his sleeves rolled up, described the *Playboy* interview as "a disaster," confided that he was deeply depressed about the progress of his campaign, and asked for advice. When some of us told him it was no part of our job to counsel candidates of either party, the session trailed off into complaints by Carter and Powell at what they considered to be the unfairly gentle press treatment accorded the incumbent President. The meeting did Carter little good. When news of it leaked out, as he should have known it would, it provided another embarrassing indication that his campaign was in trouble and that he was unsure of how to handle it.

Every week Carter's lead in the polls slipped a bit. His advisers, fighting off panic, met to survey the situation and recommended a shift in emphasis: Carter should stop paying so much homage to the Democratic party's traditions and past leaders and resume his identity as an outsider. Carter took that advice for a while and seemed more comfortable.

But then he was distracted by Ford's assertion, in the second television debate, that Eastern Europe was free from Soviet domination. This was a gaffe of such grand proportions that Carter needed to say little about it. But he could not let it alone. Perhaps driven by resentment at his own embarrassments, Carter abandoned discretion and punished the President mercilessly. He suggested that Ford had been "brainwashed," and asserted that Ford had been more secretive, less informed, and generally worse as President than Richard Nixon. His aides, fearful that he would damage himself more than Ford, finally persuaded him to drop the subject.

"The general consensus was that I was overly strident and overly aggressive," Carter said later. "Had I let him stew in his misstatement about Eastern Europe and not made an issue of it, I think I would have been much better off."

Carter returned to the familiar themes of his early candidacy. He was moralistic and optimistic. Despite all that had gone wrong with the government, the *system* of government, he insisted, was still the best in the world. He made that point over and over again, stressing it so broadly that he invited ridicule.

"Richard Nixon didn't hurt our system of government," Carter declared at an outdoor rally in Tampa in mid-October.

"Watergate didn't hurt our system of government," he continued with the familiar litany.

"The CIA revelations didn't hurt our system of government," Carter added.

"It didn't help," a young man standing near me shouted.

Those around him laughed. But if Carter heard, he gave no sign. He plunged ahead: "Our system of government is still the basis, that doesn't change, that gives us a way to correct our mistakes, to answer difficult questions, to bind ourselves together in a spirit of unity and to look at the future with confidence."

Carter's approach, however reassuring, lacked focus and clarity. He did not really explain why and how the best system of government had gone wrong. Nor did he address in any detail the "difficult questions" facing the country.

Ford, having recovered from the furore over Eastern Europe, was pressing ever closer on the heels of his challenger, as Carter's own polls showed. In the campaign's closing days Carter returned to the Democratic tradition. Seizing upon bleak new economic reports, he warned, as Democratic candidates had always done, that another Republican administration would make the economic picture even darker. He called upon the old party mainstays, the big city machines and organized labor, to turn out the Democratic vote.

On election day it was the old New Deal coalition, what remained of it—the South, the blacks, the big cities—that helped win him the White House. But in scope and dimension his victory fell far short of matching Roosevelt's triumphs, or of fulfilling Carter's own hopes for a broad mandate.

Carter's major achievement was in restoring the South to the national Democratic party; of the eleven states of the Old Confederacy he carried ten, all but Virginia. This was the broadest sweep of the South for a Democratic Presidential candidate since FDR's day. For Roosevelt the Solid South was just an appendage to a huge national majority; all eleven Southern states could have gone Republican in the four Roosevelt elections without affecting the outcome.

But for Carter, the almost Solid South was critical, contributing proportionately more to his success than to any Democratic Presidential candidate in modern times. The ten Southern states Carter carried, together with the border states of Missouri, Kentucky, and Maryland, provided him with 149 electoral votes, just over half his total of 297. In popular votes Carter carried the Deep South and border states by 1.9 million votes; he trailed in the rest of the country by 150,000 votes. Among the Northern industrial states he failed to carry New Jersey, Illinois, and Michigan. In the farm belt he won only in Minnesota, Walter Mondale's home state, and neighboring Wisconsin. In the West he lost everywhere except Hawaii.

The shape of his victory left the President-elect with obvious problems, but also with substantial opportunities. Carter's base in the South was shaky. It was built on an uneasy alliance of blacks and of whites, whose conservative tendencies were offset by regional pride. Carter could not be a regional President. Nor could he depend too heavily on the remnants of the old New Deal coalition. The support he won from some of its components, such as urban Catholics and Jews, was below the standard for a Democratic candidate. Moreover the coalition itself was shrinking, mainly because its urban strongholds were losing population.

On the positive side was Carter's strength in small towns, among white Protestants and better-educated white-collar workers. These groups made up Carter's own constituency, attracted by his personality and the faith he had revived in the country. Their support offered the potential for a new majority, built on the framework of the old Roosevelt coalition, but broader and better adapted to the demography of the last quarter of the twentieth century. Carter had begun assembling this alliance in the campaign, but he would need to solidify it as President.

Immediately after his victory, Carter asserted that he felt free to pursue his own course. Many groups and individuals had helped him, he acknowledged, but none so much more than the others that he owed any of them a special debt. "I've never promised a person a position in government to this minute," he said.

"I feel deeply obligated to people, but I'll do what I think is best for the country. I don't have any strings on me."

But if he had not committed himself on appointments, he had made a flock of other promises. The most important was to restore rationality and trust to the Presidency. And his own fortunes, and the health of the political system, depended on his keeping his word.

3

"The Sweetest White People on Earth"

Plains, Georgia, November 14, 1976—The Plains Baptist Church is a seventy-year-old white clapboard building with stained-glass windows on the corner of Paschall Street, two blocks from the Carter family peanut warehouse and the center of town. It has been part of the fabric of Jimmy Carter's life as far back as he can remember. His parents took him here every Sunday when he was a child; his father taught in the Sunday school. Carter has been a member of the board of deacons for years, though he was placed on inactive status when he began running for President. When he is in town he still takes his turn teaching the men's bible class on Sunday mornings.

In Plains, as in other small Southern towns, the churches are major social as well as religious institutions. There is not much else to do. Plains Baptist maintains a heavy schedule of activities. Its members attend choir practice, and church suppers and services on Wednesday night and Sunday night, in addition to Sunday morning.

Twelve days after Carter's election to the White House, his church has confronted him with a test of his leadership and character. The basic issue is whether the church will change a whites-only policy it overwhelmingly adopted eleven years ago and admit blacks to membership. The question is mainly symbolic; there is no evidence that the black Baptists of Plains, who have their own church nearby, are clamoring to worship with the white Baptists. But the symbolism goes to the heart of Carter's candidacy and the promise of his Presidency. As a white Southerner whose political success has been fostered by black support, he has come to be viewed hopefully in some quarters as a healing force. This hope has a mythic quality and strength, drawn from the imagery of a son of the South, with its racist history, emerging to lead the entire nation, blacks and whites, toward a resolution of the American dilemma.

And so on this dreary Sunday morning—it is raining and the temperature is in the low 40s—several hundred people, tourists and reporters, are waiting outside Jimmy Carter's church. No one will worship here today. The regular service at 11:00 A.M. has been canceled so that members of the church can hold a business session, or conference, to deal with the controversy over the membership rules. But the men's bible class is still scheduled to hold its regular 10:00 A.M. session. And the reporters and other onlookers have been gathering since well before then, hoping to catch a glimpse of Carter, who is expected to attend the bible class, and of the Reverend Clennon King, who is expected to try.

King is the black minister of the Divine Mission Church in Albany, 40 miles south of Plains, who precipitated this drama two weeks ago by seeking admission to the church. He appears today about 9:30 with several companions and goes to a back door. Last Sunday this door was open and King managed to get into the bible class. But now the door is locked and King is told firmly that he will not be allowed to enter. He and his friends, surrounded by reporters, huddle under a passageway near the door to await the outcome of the conference.

Carter and his family arrive soon after and are escorted by the Secret Service into the church through the front entrance. Then the other members of the congregation begin entering the building. Some are irritated by the crowd outside and the cordon of Secret Service agents and state highway patrolmen.

One man is determined to push through the group surrounding Clennon King to use the back door. "All right, get moving now," he shouts. "I'm going into my own church if I have to knock somebody down. Everybody get out of the way."

Suddenly there is an ugly tension in the air. I notice a black man in a business suit with some sort of security insignia on his coat. He is Ozell Sutton, head of a five-man team from the Atlanta office of the Community Relations Service of the U.S. Department of Justice. The job of the Community Relations Service is to conciliate racial disputes before they turn into violence. Sutton, who is an old hand at civil rights demonstrations in the South, says he and his men are there mainly to observe, for the present. Right now, he says, the controversy is an internal matter within the church. If it should spread to the rest of the community, the CRS might step in.

While Sutton waits, he chats with three other official-looking men who are sitting in a patrol car. They are agents of the civil disturbance section of the Georgia Bureau of Investigation. This section was created by Carter, when he was governor of Georgia, with a purpose similar to Sutton's Justice Department unit. Like Sutton's men, the state agents are keeping an eye on the crowd.

One reason for their concern is the presence at the church of a man named Bill Wilkinson, who hands out business cards identifying him as Imperial Wizard of the Knights of the Ku Klux Klan. Wilkinson tells reporters that "thousands of Klansmen" around the country "will send any support the congregation desires" to maintain segregation.

So far as is known, no one in the congregation has asked for the Klan's support. But it seems bizarre that Wilkinson is here, and that a meeting of the President-elect's church should require the attention of federal and state government agencies concerned with civil disorder.

For the time being, though, order prevails. Secret Service agents clear a path to the back door for the church members. As they file past King and his companions, waiting under their shelter, King calls to them: "Please vote for me," and "Vote for open doors." A black minister with King, named J. W. Williams, cries out: "I'm going to tell you people today that God will come down to this city. God is going to set an example for every man in this church."

A reporter asks King and his friends if they believe the congregation will vote to let them in. Elder Thorpe, the minister of a church in Washington, D.C., and the most belligerent member of the group, says: "Yeah, if we change the color on our faces, they'll let us in."

King himself says the matter is in the hands of God. He tells of an anonymous phone threat received this morning in Albany. "The man said: 'It's against the law to shoot deer today, but coons is okay.' "

King shrugs his shoulders. "The thing I'd say is if God wants you to die soon, it's nobody can stop you from dying. If God wants you to live, it's nobody can stop you from living."

Clennon King is fifty-five years old, a husky man with white hair; he has a rich, musical voice, he speaks softly, and his manner is gentle. One of his companions says that King has discouraged black residents of Plains from joining him at the church because "he doesn't want anybody to get hurt."

But King's eyes have a zealot's glint, remindful of the portraits of old John Brown. And he is determined. As he waits near the door, Charles Hicks, owner of a tavern in Plains and a prominent figure in the local black community, tries to persuade him to leave. Hicks is afraid that King will cause problems for the blacks in town.

"Why don't you go back to Albany?" Hicks demands.

King nods at the church door. "When you go inside, I'll go back to Albany."

Hicks goes away, leaving King at his post.

Since the controversy started, two weeks ago, King's motives and his background have been the subjects of considerable attention and speculation, none of it very illuminating. He is a difficult man to sort out.

Even his name adds to the confusion. He is not one of *the* Kings, having no direct relationship to the illustrious family headed by the Reverend Martin Luther King, Sr. But Clennon King's brother, C. B. King, is an attorney and prominent black political leader who ran for the Democratic nomination for governor in 1970. By some accounts King's advertising in that campaign was partly subsidized by Carter's organization, which hoped he would draw black votes away from Carter's chief opponent, Carl Sanders—but this story has been denied by Carter's aides. At any rate, C. B. King has a far more respectable reputation than his brother Clennon.

The word most often used to describe Clennon King's background is "checkered," and it seems to fit. He was arrested once for deserting his wife and was later imprisoned for four years in California, for failure to support his six children.

He is reported to have a history of mental illness. But the only firm evidence of this is that in 1958, after he tried to enter the then segregated University of Mississippi, state officials had him committed to a mental institution, from which his brother obtained his release after about ten days.

His political activities have been varied and generally futile. He supported a back-to-Africa movement for American blacks and once ran for president on the Afro-American ticket. In the 1976 Georgia Democratic primary he ran simultaneously for three state and local offices, losing all three.

Carter and his people consider him an eccentric and a crank. His record clearly is a far cry from the standard of sober probity set by most black leaders during the great civil rights revolution of the 1960s. But the champions of controversial causes cannot be preselected. Respect him or not, those who favor desegregation of the church are stuck with Clennon King. Without him, there would not now be any controversy.

The puzzle is why the issue has taken so long to come to a head. The policy of the church has been widely known since Carter came to national attention. Carter himself wrote about it in his campaign book, *Why Not the Best?* The racial record of the Plains Baptist Church is similar to that of many other Southern churches. In the years right after the Civil War, blacks and whites had worshiped there together. But with the end of Reconstruction and the subsequent establishment of segregation throughout the institutions of the South, the black and white Baptists of Plains split into separate congregations.

Segregation remained the unchallenged rule in Southern churches until the 1960s, when black leaders sought to break down the barriers there, as everywhere else. They had the support of some white clergymen who were troubled by the painful truth of Martin Luther King, Jr.'s assertion that "11:00 A.M. on Sunday is the most segregated hour of the week." In 1965 civil rights groups staged demonstrations at churches in Atlanta and in Americus, only a few miles from Plains.

Alarmed at the prospect of black intrusion, the deacons of Plains Baptist Church, meeting in Carter's absence, proposed that the congregation formally bar blacks from worship services. After pondering the impact of the situation on his political future, Carter, then a state senator, spoke out against the proposal. But the deacons easily carried the day. Of the six votes cast against segregation, five came from Carter and members of his family.

Since then, racial attitudes in the South have softened. In 1970 the Southern Baptist Convention passed a resolution expressing "gratitude to God for the progress being made by an increasing number of our churches where persons of other races are welcome into all areas of church life and fellowship." "Hopefully," Carter wrote in *Why Not the Best?*, "not many churches in the United States today would forcibly exclude any worshiper because of race."

By summer, when Carter's nomination was assured, his churchgoing in Plains had become a public event. Black reporters occasionally attended services, along with their white colleagues. Black Secret Service agents sometimes sat near Carter's third-row pew. The reaction of the congregation was mixed. Some members still harbored prejudice against blacks. Others simply resented the fact that their worship services and bible classes had become a spectacle. In August it took the intercession of Jody Powell to get church authorities to agree to admit women reporters to cover the meetings of the men's bible class. Meanwhile, the 1965 ban on black members remained on the books, and no one pressed the point.

Then, on October 24, three Sundays ago, one of the reporters clustering around Carter after the bible class asked him if blacks could join the church. "If they wanted to," Carter replied. He said that any person seeking to join the church would be judged individually. "But I think the church's attitude is to receive blacks now."

Coincidentally, in his sermon that day, Pastor Edwards reinforced what Carter had said. He noted that some churches "make race a criterion of fellowship" and declared he believed that to be wrong.

The next day Clennon King read in the local paper what Carter and Edwards had said and, for reasons that are still not clear, but no longer seem to matter much, decided to force the issue. He visited the motel in Americus where most of the Carter press corps stayed and left word of his intentions. And he left a note at Pastor Edwards' home, telling him that he would be at the church on Sunday, two days before election day.

But when King arrived at the appointed time he learned that the deacons had voted to cancel the services rather than admit him. The Reverend Edwards sent him away, but urged him to return. The pastor made clear to reporters that he opposed the deacons' action and would fight to change the church policy. Whereupon the deacons, in their wisdom, voted to fire the pastor.

The ensuing public furore broke over the Carter campaign in the closing hours of the election. The candidate, campaigning feverishly in Texas and California, tried to fend the problem off as best he could. He still held to his position of 1965. He said: "Anyone who lives in our community and who wants to be a member of our church, regardless of race, ought to be admitted." But he would not resign from the church. "I can't resign from the human race because there's discrimination," he said. "I think my best approach is to stay within the church and try to change the attitude which I abhor."

But no matter what Carter promised, the deacons' ruling stood as an affront to the blacks whose support he had diligently sought all year long. His private polls registered a negative reaction in some black precincts and alarm spread in his already edgy Atlanta headquarters.

But the damage was probably lessened because King's choice of the Sunday before election to appear at the church engendered suspicions which King himself did little to allay. "There's no timing at all, but God times things," he said. "I don't know why God timed it this way."

Carter's supporters contended that the Republicans had put King up to it, and President Ford's aides lent credibility to this theory by their own heavy-handedness. They sent telegrams to four hundred black ministers around the country, calling attention to the episode, as if it might otherwise have escaped notice.

But whatever force had moved King to act originally, he was now self-propelled, and determined to press his case. On the Sunday after election he was back at the church. This time the worship service was held as usual, but King, though he had slipped into the bible class, was jostled by the deacons and denied admission.

"Don't you tell me these doors aren't going to open," King insisted when he left. "They're going to open."

On St. Simons Island, off the Georgia coast, where President-elect Carter was on a working vacation, Jody Powell let it be known that Carter was "concerned and disturbed" by the events at the church. Carter had talked with the Reverend Edwards and with some of the deacons. He "hopes and believes," Powell said, that the controversy will be resolved amicably, and in a way that will permit all the right to worship, without regard to race. So the lines have been sharply drawn. Carter has publicly acknowledged his concern and involvement, and his prestige is at stake.

To win the election he has already endured a series of grueling tests. Now he had to prove himself once again, to reaffirm his claim on public faith and confidence, without which he cannot govern effectively. The issue Clennon King has forced upon him is intensely personal. But because it is so personal, it has drawn the attention of the country and the world.

In national politics, Carter's Southern origins are a potential weakness but also a potential strength. As a Southerner seeking the Presidency, he was always vulnerable, always under scrutiny for a telltale sign of bigotry. The greatest crisis of his primary campaign stemmed from his remarks favoring "ethnic purity" of neighborhoods. Actually, his opposition to "forced integration" in housing, whatever its merits, was not substantially different from the views of his non-Southern rivals. Underlying the uproar was the suspicion that Carter, by his ill-chosen phrasing, had given himself away, exhibited his true Confederate colors. It took a public apology by Carter, and the reassurances of his prominent black supporters, to quell the outcry against him.

The other side of the Southern coin is that Carter has benefited disproportionately from his support of civil rights legislation and his endorsement by blacks. Because he is a Georgian, these aspects of his background have been taken as signs of particular enlightenment, even by sophisticated observers.

"There is no good man like a good white Southerner," Eleanor Holmes Norton, New York City's black Commissioner for Human Rights, told me during the New York primary campaign. "You can talk about a born-again Christian, but a man who's been born again to civil rights, who speaks with a Southern accent and is good on civil rights issues, is the best form of civil rights advocate."

The black voters Carter won in the primaries were significant, not just for their numbers, but for the impact they had on white liberals. Carter's black support was, in the phrase of political analyst Richard Scammon, "his passport to liberal acceptance." In the general election Carter's black support was critical, particularly in the South. Surveys taken right after the election indicate that Ford won a majority of the white vote in the South; black voters, about 95 percent of whom supported Carter, gave him his victory margin in the states he needed to win the Presidency.

The blacks understand this, and they will not let Carter off the hook. Elder Thorpe, Clennon King's friend from Washington, tells reporters outside the church that he campaigned for Carter in the election. "Now that he has made it almost to the seat, has he forgot the people that put him in office, the black people?" Thorpe says blacks "want to know how the President is going to do. Is he going to sell the people out, or is he going to go for justice?"

The rest of the world also wants to know what the President-elect will do. Reporters are here from half a dozen or more foreign countries. During the campaign Carter talked a great deal about morality in foreign policy. A Japanese journalist tells me that the decision at the church will affect Carter's ability to exert the moral leadership in international affairs that he has promised. It will be difficult, he contends, for Carter to help negotiate the differences between blacks and whites in southern Africa if he cannot erase the color lines in his own church.

The significance of the controversy at the church is heightened by the general realization that his church and his religion loom large in Carter's life. No Presidential candidate in modern times has placed such stress on his religion. His regular attendance at the church and his role in the bible class have been widely reported and have molded the country's image of the man it has just elected President.

Carter's position that he will not leave the church would be hard to maintain if the vote should go against him. Coretta Scott King, a prominent Carter supporter, has already declared that he should quit if the congregation refuses to change its ban against black members. Other black leaders are likely to feel the same way. Certainly Carter's promise to work within the church for racial tolerance would have a hollow ring if, eleven years after he first spoke out against segregation, a majority of the congregation still opposes him.

But quitting the church would not be a satisfactory alternative either; it would be a severe personal wrench. Moreover, it would be a concession of defeat that probably would be considered an ill omen for his Presidency.

But most church members, on both sides of the issue, are not concerned with Carter's political problems. Those who support desegregation talk in religious terms. Tim Lawson, one of the deacons, believes that "anyone who wants to worship God, not to cause a disturbance or anything else, should be allowed to do so." James Ethredge, who is training to be a missionary, says there is no basis for prejudice in the Bible. "Jesus taught in the parable of the Good Samaritan what prejudice is all about, and we just ought not to have it."

The opposition to Carter is not based entirely on prejudice; some of it reflects small-town rivalries and resentment of the dominant role the Carter family has played in Plains. The leader of the group determined to maintain segregation is said to be Albert Williams, Carter's chief business competitor in town.

Many in Plains are proud of Carter's success. But others are disturbed by his fame and the changes it has wrought on their community. "I'm sick of hearing it called Carter's church," one woman tells Fay Joyce of the *Atlanta Constitution.* "It's God's church. Carter's not going to have to live with integration like we will."

"We don't feel like swapping a church for a President," one of the deacons complains. "You all have made our Sunday into a spectacle. The service has been broken up by the press."

For all the complex emotions involved, the problem here for Carter boils down to a test of political skill. But it is a different sort of test from those he is used to. He has been reckoning with voters by the tens of thousands, and ultimately by the millions. Today in the church there will be no more than two hundred votes to count.

This is small-group politics; tactics and strategy must be adjusted to the size and sensibilities of this electorate. It is hard, even for a President-elect with all the resources he can summon, to overpower this constituency. Each individual vote looms large. The situation calls for tact and compromise.

Before he left on vacation last week, Carter met with the Reverend Edwards to make plans for the conference. This week, since his return, he has been on the phone to the pastor and to some of the deacons. Outside the church, Jody Powell tells reporters that Carter is reasonably confident of the outcome. But no one can be certain how the congregation will react once the discussion begins.

The press and the public must wait outside the church during the conference. But some members of the congregation take notes, and afterward reporters learn what happened in the meeting.

Hugh Carter, the President-elect's cousin, a deacon and the clerk of the church, makes the first move. He has opposed desegregation in the past, and he voted with most of the other deacons to fire the Reverend Edwards two weeks ago. But Hugh has since talked matters over with his cousin and changed sides. With tears in his eyes he says: "I think we've all acted too hastily—both the pastor and the deacons. I ask Brother Edwards to forgive me." Then he moves to table the proposal to fire Edwards.

It is a parliamentary maneuver, designed to avoid a showdown vote on the pastor. It fails by a vote of 100 to 96.

Now the President-elect and his allies rise to defend Edwards. The pastor has done a good job, Carter says. It is unfair to hold against him Clennon King's effort to join the church. The vote comes on the motion to fire Edwards, and the tide turns. The tally against firing the pastor is 107 to 84. It is a victory for Carter, but the margin is disturbingly thin.

Next, before debate begins on the ban against black members, Carter and his allies unveil another part of their strategy. They propose the creation of a "watch care" committee of deacons who will screen applicants for church membership over a period of time. The committee will judge the sincerity of prospective members and report back to the full congregation. No one can find good reason to object to this idea, and it is approved unanimously.

So the way has been paved to deal directly with the motion to open membership of the church to all who wish to worship there, depending, of course, on the recommendations of the watch care committee. The President-elect speaks in favor of the motion. He makes clear he is not advocating Clennon King's membership. "King is here to disrupt the church," he says. "His brother knows it. The blacks know it. We know it. He's crazy. I could not vote for this man under these circumstances, and I don't think anyone else could either."

Despite the official policy, Carter points out, blacks have worshiped in the church. "No one said anything about it, and I felt good about it because they came here not to disrupt but to worship, and the key to the whole thing is to open the doors."

Next Carter makes his central point, aiming at the distress the church members feel at the turmoil surrounding them. "I have been on the telephone talking to people the last two days, to leaders of groups," he says. "The Ku Klux Klan wanted to have a rally on the church grounds. The Southern Christian Leadership Conference would bring people by the busloads. Groups such as the Black Panthers would come. If the church continues to lock the doors, next Sunday you might have two thousand people demonstrating or wanting to come in.

"People all over the world are looking at this church now," he says. "It's because you're locking the doors that people want to come in."

Carter breaks the solemn mood for a moment with a small

joke about his brother Billy, who does not attend the church and who sells beer at his gas station. "If you were to have a rule that anyone who sells beer cannot come to church, then Billy would be here next Sunday."

He underlines the reason for the watch care committee. It would allow the congregation to rescind its ban on blacks and still control its membership.

Falling back on one of the standard devices of political oratory, Carter tells the congregation how important this vote is. "The world is looking at this church. This situation we're in—and the decision that will come from the situation—is more important to me than being elected President."

At the moment he says it, he may believe it to be true. At any rate it is a masterly performance, and the congregation is impressed. The vote is 120 to 66 to admit all Christians, regardless of race. When the results are announced, many in the sanctuary weep. Some of the deacons rush to the front to hug the pastor they had tried to fire. Crying with joy, Rosalynn Carter turns to a neighbor and says: "This is the greatest day of our lives."

The conference of the Plains Baptist Church concludes, nearly three hours after it began. Carter walks out into the rain, Rosalynn on his arm. He looks emotionally drained, but greatly relieved. He quickly summarizes for the reporters the decisions of the conference.

"I was proud of my church," he says.

A reporter asks how much influence Carter had on the decision. "I was just one of the church members and they all know that," he says.

Does the new policy mean that blacks can become members?

"Yes it does," Carter says. "There will be no exclusion of anyone from either worship or membership on the basis of race."

He walks past the reporters toward the crowd of tourists, shaking hands and accepting congratulations.

On the church steps, Hugh Carter, fulfilling his responsibility as clerk, is reading the text of the resolutions to the press.

Clennon King, standing nearby, shouts: "What shall I do, Mr. Carter?"

"I can't tell you," Hugh Carter says. "Our doors are open to anyone who wants to worship."

King is delighted. Someone asks if he feels vindicated. "I think it vindicates the church," he says. "It vindicates the people of Plains. It shows you how beautiful Southern people are. They may growl and grimace, but they're the sweetest white people on earth."

The new policy gets its first test at worship services that evening. A black tourist named Roger Sessoms, who had been outside the church that morning, enters midway through the services and sits near the President-elect. When the service is over, Carter walks over to Sessoms and shakes his hand. "Thank you for coming," he says. "I'm glad you came tonight."

So Carter's triumph is confirmed. It is a famous victory, heralded on the Sunday evening newscasts and in the Monday morning papers.

But the real significance of what happened here is by no means clear. It seems certain Clennon King will never be a member of the Plains Baptist Church.* Carter called him crazy and said he would not vote to admit him. That leaves the principle of the congregation's decision. But this is diminished by the main argument Carter used in advocating the abandonment of the racial ban. He did not so much urge the congregation to open their hearts to a black brother in Christ as recommend the best way to end a public nuisance.

It may be that a loftier approach would have failed. If this is true, then Carter misjudged the congregation when he said, a

*On January 9, 1977, Clennon King's application for membership was rejected by unanimous vote of the congregation, including the President-elect. The watch care committee had recommended against admitting him. On February 20, the Reverend Edwards announced he was quitting as pastor, blaming a "backlash" against his support of King. Jody Powell said the church members should be allowed "to return to running their own affairs." Carter had by this time transferred his membership to the First Baptist Church in Washington.

few weeks ago, that he believed its attitude now would favor the admission of blacks.

Carter will face many more tests of principle over the next four years, and no one knows how he will meet them. But it was evident today that rather than risk defeat in his own church he took the safest and most expedient course. Expedient solutions are very popular in politics, but Carter's candidacy had given reason to expect something more from him, particularly in matters of race and religion.

4

The Best Laid Plans

---------------- ★ ----------------

"We are people who plan ahead," Hamilton Jordan remarked a few weeks before election day. "That's one reason why Jimmy Carter has succeeded politically. "He started in 1966 planning for the 1970 governor's campaign, and in 1972 planning for the 1976 Presidential campaign."

It was in keeping with Jimmy Carter's character, then, that in May 1976, two months before his nomination and six months before his election, he began planning for his Presidency. As time went on, the preparations exceeded anything previously attempted. "No one has ever done this before," Jack Watson, the chief planner, told me in October. "No candidate for the Presidency, post nomination, has ever undertaken as an organized effort to plan precisely what he would do in detail if he is elected."

Carter himself had great faith in this undertaking. On election day, in a confident mood as he flew to Atlanta on *Peanut One* to monitor the returns, he talked proudly of what had been accomplished by Watson's group, including the preparation of "a working list" of seventy-five names from which he would pick his cabinet-level advisers. "We've made a lot of progress, in an unpresumptuous way, of course," he said.

The transition period between election day and inauguration day is inevitably a time of turmoil and disorganization, as other Presidents-elect had learned to their sorrow. But Carter seemed better equipped than any of his predecessors to deal with these problems. A few days after his election he was presented with a 20-foot stack of briefing books intended to lay the groundwork for a successful transition. By contrast, after his election, John Kennedy was provided only with a handful of memorandums prepared by Clark Clifford and Richard Neustadt. Richard Nixon, according to one chronicle of his Presidency, had little more than "a short list of notions" when he set up his transition headquarters in New York's Hotel Pierre. Moreover, Carter knew that the planning could continue with plenty of financial support. Congress had set aside $2 million to pay for the postelection transition, more than four times what had been available in federal funds to President-elect Nixon.

Given these considerable advantages, Carter determined to use the seventy-eight days before he was sworn in not only to prepare for the responsibilities of power but also to publicly demonstrate his qualities of leadership. Ford's campaign tactics, and Carter's own erratic utterances on the stump, had left the country uneasy about its newly chosen Chief Executive. In the President-elect's own judgment, rendered shortly after his victory: "A lot of people still feel a question about what is going to happen when Jimmy Carter gets in the White House."

Carter's transition moved forward to a drumbeat of publicity. He talked to reporters about the "superb staff" which had been working in the midst of the campaign on dozens of major transition questions. "When the nation, through the news media, realizes the amount of work we've already done to prepare for the transition period," he said, "it will be recognized as an unprecedented effort." In the next few weeks, at a series of televised press conferences, he underlined the point, stressing the painstaking efforts being made to recruit the senior officials of his administration. He introduced the members of his governing team to the country as they were selected, offering their imposing credentials as evidence that the ship of state was in reliable hands.

But the President-elect's vaunted transition apparatus was beset by rivalry and confusion. Critics complained that the cabinet-level choices Carter made, for all their competence and experience, were not the new faces the country had been led to expect. Despite the time, money, and attention lavished on it, the Carter transition raised as many questions about the Carter Presidency as it answered.

Some of the internal difficulties were inevitable; others could be traced to the way the preelection transition planning had been organized and conducted. In the past, Hamilton Jordan had always been the point man in Carter's planning operations, "the guy who looks ahead," as he put it, "and lays it down on paper." But in the midst of the campaign Jordan had little time for anything but politics. The task of supervising the preparations for the Presidency was delegated by Carter to Jack Watson, a thirty-eight-year-old ex-marine, educated at Vanderbilt and Harvard Law. Watson had come to know Carter through Charles Kirbo; he was a Kirbo law partner and, some believed, his protégé. He had worked in Carter's 1970 gubernatorial campaign, helped to draft Carter's plans for state government reorganization, and had been Georgia finance chairman of the Presidential campaign before taking charge of the early transition planning in May, soon after Carter's victory in the Pennsylvania primary.

Watson had a $140,000 budget and a large view of his job, which he described as "policy planning." By this he meant "the actual movement from one administration and its philosophies and priorities to another administration with different priorities and in many cases different philosophies." He organized his staff of fifty into task forces to deal with government reorganization, foreign affairs, budget analysis, economic planning, and other issues. Along with the work on policy development he collected a mass of names of potential job applicants to serve as a talent pool for the future Carter administration. "We're looking for people aged thirty to forty," he said, "people who have made decisions and had to live with them and know how that rubs."

Watson's work suffered from one basic handicap. It was taking place in a political vacuum. Some separation between Watson's operation and the campaign organization headed by Jordan was, of course, necessary. The campaign staff needed to concentrate on winning the election while the transition staff had to be shielded from undue publicity, to avoid giving the impression that the candidate was taking victory for granted. Accordingly, Watson's policy coordinators and synthesizers, as they were called, were based in a bank building in downtown Atlanta, a few miles from the campaign headquarters.

Ultimately that distance became a no-man's-land separating two rival camps. Part of the problem was personal. Relations between Watson and Jordan, as one colleague drily observed, "were never terrific." They are two very different men: Watson, with his Ivy League manners and suits, his earnest discourse and memorandums, his serious demeanor, is what Jack Armstrong might have been like if he had gone to Vanderbilt and Harvard Law. Jordan is what Huckleberry Finn might have been like if he had gone to the University of Georgia and pledged Phi Delta Theta. Chubby and cheerful, he ran the campaign in windbreaker and old slacks, with a folksy nonchalance that only partly concealed his forceful ambition and shrewd judgment.

The campaign seemed to Watson to be "a cauldron of activity and frenetic movement. Everybody was going off in all directions at once. Hamilton and the others didn't have time to think about post–November 2." Still, Watson conceded, "I could have structured more contact, more communication with Ham, and with the other people in the campaign." But he was absorbed in his own work. And he was conscious that many people in the campaign organization felt that too much stress was being placed on planning, diverting energies that ought to be concentrated on winning the election.

Jordan's staffers grumbled among themselves that Watson was trying to isolate their leader and themselves from the transition planning and from the future administration. From what they could tell of what Watson was up to, he seemed overly ambitious and unrealistic. In midsummer the campaign staff learned that Watson was pushing ahead with plans for developing relatively explicit policy options on major issues. That prompted a sharp critique from Stuart Eizenstat, head of the campaign issues staff, which set Watson back on his heels.

"You can't refine proposals in the middle of a campaign," one of Eizenstat's deputies argued later. "When Jimmy Carter is out there on the stump, giving his four-point formula for welfare reform, which is general as hell, you can't have some guy back in Atlanta reviewing a very specific proposal with various interest groups. Because if you do," he said, "the idea will get out that Carter is basically lying."

Both sides made conciliatory gestures. Watson called a joint meeting of his and Eizenstat's staffs ostensibly to foster cooperation. But Peter Bourne came away from the meeting with the feeling that Watson's message to the campaign staff was: "Your job is to win the election. Our job in transition is to put together the government," a viewpoint that seemed to confirm the campaign staff's worst suspicions. Jordan assigned one of his political coordinators, Jim Gammill, to serve as liaison between the campaign headquarters and the transition office. But Watson's colleagues tried to keep their work out of Gammill's reach because, as one put it, "we didn't want it to get back to the campaign."

By late in the campaign the estrangement between the Watson and Jordan forces had come close to outright hostility. But the pivotal figure in the struggle, the candidate himself, was preoccupied with his battle for the White House and oblivious to the tensions between his aides. Jordan and Watson, despite their differences, had a common interest in keeping their disagreements from Carter. "No matter how much Watson and Jordan hurt each other," said Joseph Browder of the transition staff, "they knew they would only get hurt worse if Carter realized what was going on."

Inevitably though, after the election, the behind-the-scenes conflict led to a confrontation. The prelude was a meeting of Carter's aides in his home in Plains, a few days following his victory. Watson arrived bearing his voluminous gift of briefing documents and also a plan for conducting and staffing the transition. He nominated himself to be general overseer, in charge of cabinet nominations, policy development, and federal budget analysis. Jordan was to be relegated to the job of assembling the White House staff and given one assistant.

This was not what Jordan had in mind for his future and he set out to change matters. That process took about ten days and was an unequal contest from the start. Watson, without really meaning to, had pitted himself against Jordan, who had known Carter longer and understood him better. Moreover, the work Watson had produced for Carter was vulnerable to criticism. The seven thousand names yielded by the heralded talent inventory program amounted, in the view of the campaign staff, to a mishmash of the obvious and the obscure, lacking political or other standards for winnowing out the most likely job candidates. Trade associations, labor unions, and other groups had been queried on a shotgun basis and their suggestions, in most cases, automatically stashed away. Among the more prominent, and incongruous, names that wound up in the file was that of John Connally, renegade Democrat and vigorous campaigner for Ford, whose folder included a recommendation from his sponsor that he be given "a high position" in the Carter administration. Also recommended was a woman banker from the Midwest who, the Democratic senator from her state subsequently informed a Jordan aide, was a conservative Republican "who probably has never in her life talked to anyone who makes less than $40,000 a year."

Watson later claimed that he had never intended to submit names of potential cabinet nominees to the President-elect. Instead, he said, he was concentrating on providing Carter with the criteria he could use in making choices. But Carter, judging from his remarks aboard *Peanut One* on election day, evidently expected a list of candidates.

As for Watson's policy-planning work, it was, as might have been expected, uneven in quality. Some material was first class and ultimately proved to be useful, but some of it was superficial. At any rate Jordan and his people saw no point in trying to formulate policy for the incoming administration until the new cabinet had been selected. This task, they contended, in view of the condition of the personnel files, would have to start from scratch.

Carter agreed, and to all intents and purposes the skirmish between Jordan and Watson was over. Jordan created a personnel advisory group, staffed mainly by campaign veterans, with himself in charge to assemble names and credentials of potential cabinet choices. Stuart Eizenstat was placed in charge of policy development. Watson was left with the title of transition coordinator, with responsibility to develop supplementary proposals for the federal budget, a job ultimately taken over by the President-elect's choice as budget director. Although Watson was depicted in some quarters as having been victimized by Hamilton Jordan, he was also a victim of his own zeal and naiveté, and the unrealistic assignment Carter had given him.

The episode produced a spate of embarrassing publicity, particularly unwelcome when the President-elect was striving to demonstrate his sureness of grip and clarity of purpose. Jody Powell complained that the press exaggerated the importance of the story, and it is probably true that the internal differences of the Carter organization held little interest for the vast majority of Americans. But in Washington it gave Congress, the press, and the bureaucracy—who were trying to take the measure of the incoming administration—an intriguing first impression.

The shuffling for position was a delay and a distraction, a

period of about ten days during which, as one transition staffer conceded, "basically nothing was happening." Even after the original plans had been reordered, an atmosphere of tension and uncertainty prevailed among those charged with carrying on the process. It is hard to tell how much more might have been accomplished under other circumstances, but the bumpy beginning robbed the incoming administration of some of the early impetus its leaders had hoped to build.

Perhaps more significant in the long run is the light cast on Carter's managerial style. During the summer lull in his campaign marked by softball games and other leisurely activities, he might have made clearer to Watson what was expected of him, and urged greater communication between him and Jordan. But his tendency is to give subordinates broad, hazy, and sometimes overlapping assignments, leaving them to work out the details among themselves. This technique, which personnel experts like to call creative tension, is supposed to spur the individuals involved to greater achievement, but it also can have bruising and wasteful results.

Once Jordan's differences with Watson had been settled, Carter could belatedly focus his attention and energy on the major task before him, the selection of his cabinet and his senior advisers with cabinet rank. In a press conference on November 15, two weeks after his victory over Ford, the President-elect outlined the process for the nation. Understandably, he did not mention Watson's efforts at recruitment during the summer and fall. Instead, he said that a list of candidates for each position "is already being developed." Some of the possibilities would be obvious to him, from the campaign and before. Nevertheless, "an intensive search" would be conducted nationwide to collect the names of all qualified persons. He had asked a group of prominent citizens to assist his own staff in the search for talent. As a sort of practical test, some prospects would be asked to evaluate possible programs for the next administration. He and Mondale would interview the contenders for the top jobs, congressional leaders would be consulted, and then the country would be informed. "We will be careful and thorough and deliberate in making these major decisions," he said.

It was an impressive plan, but there was one catch in it from the beginning. To the extent that this orderly process depended on firsthand contact with the President-elect, it was hindered by his decision to sequester himself in Plains, Georgia. Carter's hometown was served by no airline, railroad, or bus company. It was without any motel, hotel, or even a restaurant, except for a sandwich shop which, as a sign posted behind the counter informs its patrons, lacks a rest room.

The logistical problems presented by Plains were pointed up in early December when Carter summoned sixteen of the nation's most prominent businessmen, financiers, and economists to confer with him there. Though the stated reason for the meeting was to discuss economic policy, the occasion also gave the President-elect a chance to view some prospective nominees in action. Three of the economic advisers would ultimately get cabinet-level posts.

"It's an elimination contest," Jody Powell joked with reporters after the meeting got underway in the Pond House, Carter's mother's summer cottage. "Every fifteen minutes they take a vote and everybody who gets less than three votes leaves."

Most of the guests were an hour late because the plane they had chartered from Washington had to stop for refueling. The plane chartered by Bert Lance, Carter's friend and banker from Atlanta, landed at the wrong airport, and he had to hitch a ride to the Pond House in a pickup truck. The discussion went on for nearly five hours with no refreshments served, not even a cup of coffee. At one point A. W. Clausen, chairman and chief executive officer of the Bank of America, quietly asked Hamilton Jordan for something to drink. Jordan beckoned him into the kitchen and hunted for soda or fruit juice, but the refrigerator was bare.

Clausen would have been happy to settle for a glass of water. But Jordan couldn't find a clean glass.

"You could drink from the spigot," Jordan suggested.

Clausen declined. He pointed out that the kitchen sink could be plainly seen from the living room, where the meeting was still in full swing.

The only remaining option was the bathroom, across the living room from the kitchen. Clausen entered there and got his drink. But Jordan forgot to tell him that the lock on the bathroom door tends to stick. The head of the nation's largest bank tugged and pushed on the door until Jordan hurried over and released him.

Clausen subsequently asked that his name be withdrawn from consideration for appointment for personal reasons that presumably had nothing to do with this experience.

No matter what hardships the trips to Plains may have caused his advisers and potential appointees, Carter was content there. He viewed its isolation as an advantage. "Here," said Jody Powell, "he is not besieged by people who want to see him." He spent most of his waking hours in the wood-paneled den, comfortably clad in a sweater, jeans, and sneakers, talking on the telephone which plugged directly into the White House switchboard. Occasionally he would tramp in the fields hunting for arrowheads, alone or with Rosalynn. He talked publicly of his dependence on his Vice President elect for advice, but on matters that concerned him most, he made his own decisions. He stayed away from Washington as much as he could and in private conversation referred caustically to the team of advisers assembled there. Some three hundred people were working full time on the transition on the dreary fifth floor of an HEW office building near Capitol Hill. But the President-elect's aides came to believe that the transition process that mattered most was confined to the corridors of Carter's own mind.

Carter had run for President as an outsider, pledged to clear the capital air of the establishment's stodgy notions, and had led the country to expect he would bring along a team of other outsiders to help him. "I think my inclination would be to go toward a new generation of leaders," he told the *National Journal* shortly before his nomination. "I can't say I would never use somebody who has served in a previous administration. Obviously I will use some. But my inclination would be to go to a new generation."

His campaign manager, Hamilton Jordan, was even more specific. If Cyrus Vance were named Secretary of State and Zbigniew Brzezinski head of National Security in the Carter administration, Jordan told Robert Scheer of *Playboy,* "then I would say we failed, and I'd quit. But that's not going to happen."

Shortly before the election, Jordan told me he should not have singled out Vance and Brzezinski for exclusion. But he remained firm on the basic point. "If you look at the top twenty people in the Carter administration, whether they're cabinet officials or White House advisers or whatever, fifteen of them will be people you've never heard of before, people that are not big names nationally. There'll be a lot of new faces and young blood."

The terms "new generation" and "new faces" and "outsider" were vague and ill-defined. After his election, Carter suggested that "sometimes an outsider is just someone who has never had his name in the newspapers before." Landon Butler, who worked with Jordan's personnel group, contended that "when people talk about new faces, they mean *their* new faces."

Nevertheless, to many liberals, the meaning of these words was fairly clear. It had less to do with obscurity than it had to do with a record of opposition to the established order. "A characteristic that troubles me very often," said Ralph Nader, whose own name and face were not unfamiliar, "is that the people who first point out the abuses are the people who become the pariahs. We will watch this administration to see if it shuns these people simply because they were right too soon."

But Carter did not know many such leaders of protest, nor did he appear eager to make them his friends. Nader himself had been one of the exceptions. He had been invited down to Plains during the postconvention summer lull to confer with the President-elect on consumer issues and had been photographed umpiring one of the softball games in which Carter pitched. But after Carter had been persuaded that Nader's much-publicized visit had caused him political damage, their relationship had gone into eclipse.

As he pondered his choices for the cabinet in his den in Plains, Carter was in no mood to entangle himself with controversial figures or unknown quantities. The rhetoric of the campaign was set aside. Said one member of Jordan's personnel group: "There never really was any emphasis on getting new faces." Confronted with the burdens of the Presidency, mindful of public uncertainty about his character and beliefs, Carter followed the customary pattern of Presidents in making his cabinet-level appointments. He selected people with experience, people with established reputations, and, when possible, people he knew.

No President has ever known enough people personally to staff his administration. John Kennedy, after serving fourteen years in the Congress, is said to have complained during his transition: "I don't know any people, I only know voters. How am I going to fill these jobs?" Carter was more handicapped than Kennedy or most of his other modern predecessors because of his limited experience on the national scene. But he made the most of the relationships he had.

The President-elect "knew from the beginning" that for Secretary of the Interior he wanted Governor Cecil Andrus of Idaho, "a close, personal friend." The choice helped him keep a promise to Democratic governors that one of their number would be in his cabinet. From Georgia he recruited two even closer friends: Bert Lance, who had been Carter's state highway commissioner, to head the Office of Management and Budget, and former federal circuit judge Griffin Bell as Attorney General. Bell was a Carter boyhood chum and, like Jack Watson, a law partner of Charles Kirbo.

From among his campaign advisers Carter chose Cyrus Vance—lawyer, diplomat, and former Pentagon official—to be Secretary of State, and East European scholar and former State Department policy planner Zbigniew Brzezinski to be National Security Adviser. Despite Hamilton Jordan's ill-considered comments, both men were all but inevitable choices because of their prominence and rapport with the President-elect.

Carter had met Vance and Brzezinski through the Tri-Lateral Commission, to which Mondale also belonged. This private organization, founded by David Rockefeller to strengthen the economic ties linking the United States, Japan, and Western Europe, had been a useful source of information and advice to Carter during the early stages of his candidacy. He made two more major appointments from its ranks, Harold Brown as Defense Secretary and Michael Blumenthal as Treasury Secretary.

One of Brown's major attractions, aside from his experience as Air Force Secretary under Lyndon Johnson and as president of California Technological Institute, was that he represented a compromise of sorts in the long-standing debate over United States military strength. James Schlesinger, President Ford's former Defense Secretary, was the choice of hardliners for the Pentagon post. Paul Warnke, former Assistant Secretary of Defense and adviser to George McGovern, was the favorite of the doves. Carter ultimately named Schlesinger as his energy adviser and picked Warnke to be chief arms negotiator and head of the disarmament agency.

Blumenthal's chief competitor was Charles Schultze, who had been Lyndon Johnson's budget director and had the strong endorsement of many of his fellow economists. But the reports to Jordan's staff on Blumenthal, the chairman of Bendix Corp., depicted him as a rare combination—"a tough manager but also a liberal Democrat committed to social causes"—and gave him the edge. Schultze was named chairman of the Council of Economic Advisers.

Walter Mondale, whom Carter had designated as his chief adviser in the selection process, was a major influence on two choices. One was Joseph Califano, former domestic affairs adviser to Lyndon Johnson, who was named Secretary of Health, Education and Welfare. The other was Bob Bergland, a congressman from Mondale's home state of Minnesota and a longtime friend, who was chosen Secretary of Agriculture.

In another bow to Capitol Hill, Carter selected Representative Brock Adams as Transportation Secretary. Adams, the former chairman of the House Budget Committee, had campaigned hard for the Transportation post.

The process of picking a Labor Secretary stirred a bitter dispute among important supporters of Carter's candidacy. The AFL-CIO strongly backed John Dunlop, who had been President Ford's Labor Secretary. Feminist and black groups opposed him because of what they contended was his poor record in combating job discrimination. Irritated by the public pressure from labor leaders, Carter bypassed the controversial Dunlop and instead chose F. Ray Marshall, a University of Texas economics professor who got along well with the union movement and was also highly regarded by women and black leaders.

Of course, that decision by no means satisfied the women and the blacks. Immediately after his election, Carter had pledged to give "a heavy representation" to minority groups and women in his cabinet, echoing promises he had made during the campaign. These groups now intended to hold him to his word. Hamilton Jordan's personnel group was given a goal of placing two women and two blacks in cabinet-level jobs. Carter interviewed a number of women and blacks, but had difficulty matching slots with people.

His aides talked of appointing Representative Barbara Jordan of Texas as Ambassador to the United Nations. But she was interested in becoming Attorney General, a post for which the President-elect thought she lacked the experience. Besides, one Carter aide said: "The idea of a black woman heading the Justice Department was enough to make Charlie Kirbo apoplectic."

The Housing and Urban Development post was discussed with Franklin Thomas, head of the Bedford-Stuyvesant redevelopment project in New York, and with Congressman Andrew Young. Both turned it down. Many blacks considered the job to be a dead end in which they would be caught between the pressures of urban needs and the limitations of the economy and the federal budget.

Ultimately, the President persuaded Young to become Ambassador to the United Nations and named Patricia Roberts Harris, a black woman lawyer, as HUD Secretary. That gave him two blacks, one of them a woman, but still left him one short of the quota. The search concentrated on a candidate for Secretary of Commerce, which from the beginning had been set aside as a woman's job. The post was offered first to Jane Cahill Pfeiffer, an IBM vice president, who turned it down for personal reasons, and then to Juanita Kreps, vice president of Duke University. Mrs. Kreps accepted the job and in return gave the President-elect a piece of her mind. "In the case of the search for women, it was the men who did the searching," she said. "And I do think that we simply have to do a better job of searching in the case of both women and minorities."

Other critics of the selection process were less restrained. Ralph Nader characterized Carter's choices as "conservatives with high integrity," who, he predicted, would "follow the wrong policies straight instead of crooked." In a long, bitter critique in the *Washington Post*, William Greider cited the number of major positions given to men who had been in government "when the big lies were told in the sixties" about the Vietnam War. "None of them spoke up, at least not so they could be heard by the public," Greider wrote. "The last laugh is on those who thought Carter might have the nerve or the political vision to break cleanly from the past. Instead, he has revived it."

For his part, Carter brushed aside whatever sins of omission or commission his appointees might have committed in the past. "I think that working with me," he said, "their major commitment will be toward world peace, and I think they like myself will be eager to be judged on performance."

Even more fundamental than Carter's promise to recruit new leadership was his pledge to restore honesty and trust to government. The Watergate revelations and other disclosures of official lawlessness had made this promise particularly relevant to two positions, the heads of the Justice Department and the Central

Intelligence Agency. Carter's choices to fill these jobs were the most controversial he made, though for quite different reasons.

Early in his campaign Carter had said it was "a disgrace" that during the Watergate era the public had come to believe that "the Attorney General was not fair enough and objective enough and nonpolitical enough to pursue the enforcement of the law." The remedy he proposed at the time was to remove the Attorney General not only from politics but also from the cabinet; the AG would serve for a fixed term and be selected solely on the basis of merit.

Carter's choice for the post, Griffin Bell, had resigned from the bench early in 1976 and had not taken a prominent role in Carter's Presidential campaign. But he had quietly helped raise money and had given advice. Moreover, his long association with the President-elect, and with Charles Kirbo, hardly squared with the impression Carter had fostered that objectivity and independence would be major criteria in his selection of an Attorney General. Consequently, when Bell met with Carter in December, in the company of Kirbo and of Senator Eastland, the archconservative chairman of the Senate Judiciary Committee, it was widely assumed that he was there to give advice on other prospects for the Justice Department, rather than to discuss his own candidacy. The subsequent announcement that he was Carter's choice startled many of the President-elect's own advisers and stirred a wave of protests.

Apart from his relationship to Carter, Bell's attitudes on race disturbed and angered many of the black leaders who had backed Carter's candidacy. They complained about his membership in segregated clubs, his wholehearted support of Richard Nixon's nomination of G. Harrold Carswell for the Supreme Court, and his judicial rulings on desegregation cases, which could most sympathetically be described as moderate.

Responding to the criticism, Carter claimed that he had searched all over the country to find the best man for the job. "Quite often when I would call someone in California or Chicago or somewhere else and ask for recommendations, they'd say, 'Well, you've got the best man in the United States right there in Atlanta—Griffin Bell.' "

But members of Carter's transition staff received no such input from their canvassing. Bell's name was not even on the list of potential nominees they submitted to Carter. Asked who the persons were who had urged the President-elect to nominate Bell, one of Carter's close aides told me: "I can think of two—Jim Eastland and Charles Kirbo."

In selecting a trusted friend as Attorney General, Carter was following the practice of many of his predecessors. The reasons are easy to understand. No other official is in such a critical position to harm or protect the President's political welfare as the head of the Justice Department. In his book *Kennedy Justice,* Victor Navasky refers to "the tension between law and politics" underlying the Department of Justice. To ease that tension for themselves, John Kennedy chose his brother as Attorney General, Richard Nixon picked John Mitchell, and Jimmy Carter selected Griffin Bell.

Carter noted the analogy with Kennedy by making a joke about his own brother, Billy. "Since he doesn't have a law degree," he said, "I've asked Attorney General Bell to serve until Billy can become qualified."

The promise to remove the Attorney General from politics had not been broken, only postponed, he said. "I intend to go forward with my campaign commitment to remove the Attorney General and his immediate subordinates, including the FBI director, from the political realm, and to assure that all the appointments are made on the basis of merit and merit alone."

The Senate confirmed Bell's nomination by a 75 to 21 vote, with 16 of the nay votes coming from Republicans. Most liberal Democrats who had zealously opposed Republican nominees with questionable civil rights records were not prepared to challenge the choice of the incoming Democratic President. Birch Bayh, who had led the successful fights against Nixon's Supreme Court nominations of Carswell and Clement Haynsworth, was floor

manager for Bell's nomination. After the vote, James Flug, who
as an aide to Senator Kennedy had helped to defeat those nominations, told me: "If Bell was a Nixon nominee, we would have
beaten him."

The battle over the nomination of Theodore Sorensen to head
the Central Intelligence Agency was fought on much different
grounds and to a much different conclusion. Like the Justice
Department, the CIA had become a subject of increased public
concern since the last Presidential election, as a result of a series
of newspaper disclosures and government investigations, including a Senate inquiry in which then Senator Mondale had par-
ticipated. This probe had revealed, Mondale later said, "the use
of bribery, corruption, and violence in almost every corner of the
world . . . aimed at our friends as well as our foes."

In some ways, Carter's ill-fated choice of Sorensen to head
the agency came closer than any other major nomination to fulfilling the expectations of new leadership in government. In view of
his service to President Kennedy, and later to his brothers, Sorensen was certainly not a new face on the Washington scene. But
so far as the intelligence community was concerned, he was an
outsider. This, many outsiders believed, was just what the intelligence community needed, but also what many insiders did not
want.

Whether Carter had this in mind when he selected Sorensen
is unclear. He said little publicly about it to explain his reasons for
the nomination. He may have been concerned mainly with dis-
charging a debt to someone who had given important support at
an early stage in his candidacy, whose abilities he generally admired, but who did not readily fit any other prominent position
in his new administration. Sorensen, a man not lacking appreciation for his own assets, wanted, according to friends, nothing less
than a cabinet post. He would have preferred to have been Secretary of State, or perhaps Attorney General. But these jobs were
given to others and finally, after twice turning it down, he agreed
to take the intelligence post.

Opposition surfaced immediately. The most obvious criticism was Sorensen's lack of direct experience in intelligence, which was just the quality that commended his selection to others. John Connally called the choice "mystifying." Conservatives complained about Sorensen's distaste for covert operations and his previous criticism of intelligence operations.

They spread their attack into more personal areas, recalling Sorensen's attempt to get noncombatant status in the draft and his help to Ted Kennedy in preparing his explanation for the Chappaquidick tragedy. Then, just before the Senate Intelligence Committee was to hold hearings on his nomination, more damaging information came to light. Sorensen had filed affidavits in the Pentagon Papers case, stating that he had used classified White House material in writing his book about the Kennedy administration.

The opposition was now transformed into what one transition adviser called "a firestorm." Warned that the nomination was in serious trouble, Carter publicly reiterated his confidence in the nominee. But when he called several senators on the committee, his support seemed only lukewarm. To Senator Joseph Biden of Delaware, who told the President-elect he did not believe the committee would approve the nomination, Carter replied: "I'll be talking to Ted and whatever Ted wants to do, I'll do."

When the committee hearing opened, Sorensen read a ten-page statement defending his record, then abruptly announced his withdrawal. "It is now clear," he said, "that a substantial portion of the United States Senate and the intelligence community is not yet ready to accept as Director of Central Intelligence an outsider who believes as I believe." It was the first time since the Coolidge administration that a President had been rebuffed on a nomination by a Senate controlled by his own party.

Sorensen's pacifist leanings, his ties to the Kennedy family, and finally his controversial affidavits made him vulnerable to his foes. But Griffin Bell also was vulnerable on his record. The difference in the outcome of the two nominations reflected mainly the relative strengths of their opposition. The intelligence officials and their allies who spearheaded the drive to stop Sorensen were more resourceful and influential than the civil rights leaders who opposed Griffin Bell. But it is also true that the President-elect fought more vigorously for Bell than he did for Sorensen. No one knows whether a more determined effort by Carter might have saved Sorensen's nomination, but it was clear that he was not prepared to risk his prestige in such a confrontation on the eve of his inauguration. Three weeks after Sorensen's withdrawal, Carter submitted a much safer choice for the CIA, an Annapolis classmate, Admiral Stansfield Turner, who had been serving as NATO commander in Southern Europe. Turner was easily confirmed.

The withdrawal of Sorensen, three days before the inauguration of the new President, was the last significant event of the transition, an interval which most members of the incoming administration were glad to see end. "It was a bummer," said Landon Butler. Another White House staffer, Mark Siegel, called it "a monumental disaster."

"Transition is by definition a period of intense and extreme uncertainty," Jack Watson said after it was over. "Nobody knows what they are going to be doing in two or three months. Everybody wants a good job in government, but nobody knows if they are going to get it. All these stresses and strains existed, and sometimes I felt them all converging on me." As Watson pointed out, these pressures were highly personal and difficult to avoid, but they were magnified by the friction between Watson and Jordan.

Carter was fortunate in that several outside factors helped to ease the strains of his interregnum. He was the first President-elect to have substantial financial support for planning and recruitment. In fact, the $2 million allocated by Congress turned out to be more than enough; about $350,000 was returned to the Treasury. Members of the Ford administration overcame their disappointment at being turned out of office and made a good-faith effort to assist in the transfer of power. Moreover, no great crisis at home or abroad intruded to exert premature pressure on the incoming Chief Executive.

Largely for these reasons, Stephen Hess, a Brookings fellow who served in the White House under Eisenhower and Nixon, wrote in *The Wall Street Journal* that Carter's transition was "the best in history." Hess added, though: "This of course can be interpreted as faint praise. The standards are not very high."

Carter and his aides set higher standards for themselves than had previous administrations. "We are not doing this for the beauty of doing it," Jack Watson said in October. "If we don't enable President Carter to act with better information, earlier, and to accomplish more, earlier, then this will have been in my judgment a largely academic exercise."

Some of the criticism directed at Watson right after election day was probably too harsh. Of the policy options and legislative analyses developed by his staff, a number would prove helpful as reference points for the new agency heads. Most of his best staff members went on to take important posts in the new administration. The talent inventory program, carried forward after the election by Mathew Coffey, provided a helpful bank of names for use in staffing the agencies after inauguration day.

But in only one area, economics, did Carter have a major proposal ready by the time he entered office. Some administration officials argued that the policy-making process cannot move any faster. "The President does not want to, or should not want to, impose judgments on his new cabinet," said Orin Kramer, of the White House Domestic Council staff. "If you look at how far we went in policy against the standards set by the transition people in August, then the transition failed. But if you want to evaluate it against standards that other people would believe proper, then it didn't fail."

The clearest lesson provided by the Carter transition was in the difficulties of planning for the Presidency, difficulties which the new team in Washington appeared to have underestimated during the campaign. "There is no easy way to take over the government, to have everything fall into place neatly and quickly," Jack Watson acknowledged after inauguration day. "No matter how careful and methodical and comprehensive you are, there is still an incredible, almost incomprehensible amount of work and pain that must be endured in the transition period and beyond to get your government in place."

Expectations for the appointment process also were overinflated. The talk by Carter and Jordan of new faces led to disappointment in the cabinet choices, and cost Carter some of the credit he would otherwise have received when he later made more imaginative appointments at the subcabinet level.

The picture of the new President that emerged from the transition was rather different from the impression he gave during the campaign. He had depicted himself as an apostle of order and efficiency, but he often seemed to rely more on his own instincts than on the procedures for decision making that his aides devised. He had talked vaguely of bringing in a new breed of leaders to Washington. But his choices for the highest positions in his administration were mostly familiar figures, a number of whom had served in previous administrations and most of whom might have been selected by any other Democratic President. Carter praised them highly for their managerial skills, but in most cases it was not clear what commitment they had to the spirit and thrust of his campaign.

To some, Carter's behavior during the transition was a pleasant surprise. He seemed more human, more flexible, more traditional, and less given to making disturbing changes than had been expected. But he was committed to change of some sort. And it would be one of the first tasks of his Presidency to determine at what speed and in which direction he would move.

5

The New Beginning

─────────── ★ ───────────

Walking Home

January 20, 1977—Leontyne Price is singing "He's Got the Whole World in His Hands," and her rich voice warms the cold morning air at the Lincoln Memorial. Some five thousand people have gathered here for what the inaugural committee has called a "people's prayer service." This is Jimmy Carter's day and it seems appropriate that the first public event should be an occasion for worship.

The Reverend Bruce Edwards, pastor of Carter's church in Plains and his ally in last fall's segregation controversy there, speaks first. "It is fitting that we gather for prayer because the man for whom we pray is himself a man of prayer, a man who seeks God's leadership and direction," Edwards says. But "prayer is more than a hope, prayer is a commitment. Thus when we pray that Jimmy Carter will be a good President we are pledging to

96

support him by doing all that is morally right to make him a good President." Edwards begins to sound more like a civics teacher than a preacher. "Citizens should do more than vote," he says. "We can become involved in solving the problems of state, local, and national government by becoming part of the political party process. We can help because we are the government. As we pray this morning, we come pledging ourselves to be part of the renewal of this government."

A hymn follows and then Ruth Carter Stapleton, clad in a red cape, takes the podium. The evangelist sister of the President-elect, she has become something of a celebrity in her own right. By her own account, she helped guide Carter through one of the bleakest emotional periods of his life, following his defeat in the 1966 Georgia gubernatorial campaign. She reads briefly, from the Book of Kings in the Old Testament, the verses in which Solomon pleases God by asking from Him not riches "but an understanding heart," or, as she phrases it: "Father, give me the wisdom that I need to rule Your people with justice." No sooner is she finished than she is hurriedly escorted from the platform and out through the crowd to a waiting car.

Martin Luther King, Sr., delivers "The Message." Bundled up in a black overcoat, his brown fedora jammed down almost to his ears, King begins by recalling that "upon these hallowed grounds, fourteen years ago, my son stood and delivered his great speech on 'I have a dream.' "I do not know if the President-elect is here or not," King says, "but if so I do highly greet him and his family, and all of the official family of this country."

Carter is not here, and Mrs. Stapleton, who was presumably representing the First Family to be, is now gone. During the campaign Daddy King was Carter's patron saint among the blacks, rallying to his side during the "ethnic purity" controversy, delivering the memorable invocation at the Democratic Convention. There is no immediate explanation for Carter's absence here this morning, but later an aide says he did not want to turn the services "into a circus."

But the people who are here seem sufficient unto themselves. They cry out "Yes sir," and "Amen," and "Praise the Lord" as King rumbles on. He takes his text from the Gospel according to St. John. "Lovest thou me?" Jesus asks Peter, and then commands him: "Feed my sheep."

"The sheep must be fed," Daddy King says, hunched over the podium, his fist thrusting into the air. "That's what it's all about. That's what the President-elect is all about. That's why he's up here. Because we sensed that he was concerned about the least of these, more than all the rest."

Rocking back and forth, King admonishes the crowd: "Guard the sheep. Be sure we're willing to share in feeding the sheep, insteading of fleecing the sheep." The crowd laughs and the old man grins and rubs the point in. "In many instances the sheep is being fleeced. Instead of being fleeced, they need to be fed."

When King is through, Pastor Edwards leads everyone in a prayer for the next President, asking the fulfillment of Isaiah's prophecy: "They that wait upon the Lord shall renew their strength; they shall mount up with wings as eagles; they shall run and not be weary, they shall walk and not faint."

In the silence that follows, someone shouts out in the crowd, loudly enough to be heard in the press section near the speaker's platform: "The Attorney General is a racist." It is a discordant reminder of the bitterness over Carter's selection of Griffin Bell to be his Attorney General and, in a small way, recalls the protests that marked the preceding two Presidential inaugurations. But it is an isolated note. There are no angry signs or banners, and no one else takes up the heckler's cry.

The crowd joins the choir in singing the President-elect's favorite hymn, "Amazing Grace," and stands while Edwards delivers the benediction. Then the thousands stream away from the Memorial, many heading for the Capitol Plaza, where in little more than three hours Jimmy Carter will take the oath of office.

At Blair House, where Carter spent last night, across Pennsylvania Avenue from the White House, he has been up since 6:30

A.M. He, Rosalynn, and Amy breakfasted on scrambled eggs and watched the prayer services on television. At 8:45 the family drives to the First Baptist Church, a few blocks away. The Reverend Charles Trentham, the minister of the church, who is eager to have Carter become a member of his congregation, welcomes the President-elect with a prayer that leaves no doubt about his allegiance. "I believe in Jimmy Carter," he says. "I voted for him. On the day he was nominated, I thanked God for the emergence of a new leader."

The inaugural sermon is delivered by the Reverend Nelson Price, from Marietta, Georgia. Price and Carter met at a Jaycee convention some years ago, according to Price, and "covenanted to pray together." In 1973 Carter asked Price to visit him at the Governor's Mansion in Atlanta and told him he was thinking of running for President. Price advised the as-yet-undeclared candidate: "Dear brother, you'd better get prepared because the Lord may have a hand on your life." Then, as Price recalls it, both men got down on their knees to pray.

This morning Price quotes a line from John Adams, written on his second night in the White House and carved above the mantel of the State Dining Room. "May none but Honest and Wise Men ever rule under this Roof." What this nation needs, Price tells the congregation and the President-elect, are leaders who can live up to the description of James Monroe offered by Thomas Jefferson: "Monroe was so honest, that if you turned his soul inside out, there would not be a spot on it."

After services the Carters return to Blair House briefly and then, at 10:30, walk across the street, holding hands, to the White House. A reporter asks Carter how his new home looks. "Beautiful," he says, beaming. Jerry and Betty Ford greet Jimmy and Rosalynn Carter at the front door and escort them inside to the Blue Room for coffee. It is a scene that, with slight variations, could take place in any upper-middle-class neighborhood. The older couple moving out, looking forward to a comfortable retirement, welcoming the younger couple moving in, with years of striving ahead. The two couples chat for a while and then, a few minutes after 11:00, the President and the President-elect get into one black limousine, their wives into another, and they head for the Capitol.

Both the incoming and outgoing Presidents are wearing business suits, instead of the traditional morning clothes. This was Carter's choice and it was not casually made. It is part of the broad effort by Carter and his aides to use the inaugural to signal a new, unpretentious tone for the Presidency. The contrast they are drawing is really not with Ford, probably one of the most unprepossessing of Presidents, but rather with Ford's immediate predecessor and sponsor, Richard Nixon. In keeping with protocol, Nixon, who at the moment is our only living ex-President, was formally invited to the inaugural. He did not choose to come. Yet the impact of his Presidency is much in evidence.

By pardoning Nixon, for whatever Watergate crimes he might have committed, Ford dramatized his ties to Nixon and caused himself political damage he could never fully repair. It is a reasonable if unprovable assumption that, absent the pardon, it would be Gerald Ford, not Jimmy Carter, taking the oath of office today.

More broadly, Nixon's tenure in the White House, marked by pomp, privilege, and remoteness, is remembered and resented as the culmination of the Imperial Presidency. That memory is the counterpoint for the theme of Carter's inaugural.

Right after the election, Bardyl R. Tirana, the young lawyer picked to run the inaugural committee, announced that this would be a "people's inaugural." Invitations would be mailed to more than three hundred thousand Carter campaign workers—the largest guest list in the history of these occasions. Anyone who did not get an invitation should feel welcome to come anyway, Tirana said. "President Carter will be everyone's President, and the city of Washington is everyone's capital."

Tirana took as his model the inauguration in 1829 of the country's first populist President, Andrew Jackson. Old Hickory invited all his supporters to a postswearing-in celebration at the White House, and nearly everyone came. Women fainted, men fought, and the President himself nearly suffocated in the throng. The White House was left a mud-spattered shambles. Tirana said he hoped to capture the spirit of the Jackson inaugural but avoid its confusion.

But heroes are not made running inaugurals. Tirana's phone has been ringing off the hook for days with calls of complaint from Democratic leaders, campaign officials, and others who did not get tickets to inaugural events. One Democratic state chairman has been quoted as saying that "only a blizzard" can save Carter from being damaged politically by the way the inaugural has been run. Tirana, according to the people who have dealt with him, is well-intentioned and pleasant, but naive politically and ineffective as an administrator.

This week, though, the resentment over the confused arrangements has been overshadowed by a sense of anticipation and excitement. The critics have been drowned out by the sound of music. Yesterday, for example, an inaugural visitor could choose from among a bluegrass concert at the Hirshhorn Museum, a classical concert at the Renwick Gallery, a jazz concert at the Smithsonian, the Army's Singing Sergeants at the Air and Space Museum, and a Trinidad Steel Band at the Martin Luther King, Jr., branch of the public library. The Folger Shakespeare Library had James Dickey reading his poetry, the Kennedy Center offered a children's show, and for anyone who wanted to look back, the National Archives presented film highlights of inaugurations since 1929. These were some of the more than three hundred events, nearly all of them free and open to the public, arranged by the much-maligned inaugural committee.

The tens of thousands of visitors to Washington include a substantial contingent of Southerners celebrating the inauguration of the first self-acknowledged Southern President since the Civil War. Some may have felt some trepidations about their visit to the Union capital. A few weeks ago, a Carter transition staffer prepared a mock memorandum offering guidance to Georgia residents planning to attend the inaugural. Among the tips: "Before leaving for Washington, clean red mud from windshield. Leave soda crackers, viennas, RC Colas in car or pickup. First-class tourist homes do not take kindly to guests who prepare food in their sleeping rooms. And this above all—don't let any Yankee show you up. Constant screaming of '*HE'S A GOOD OL' BOY*' will make it difficult for them to engage you in conversation on their intelligence level."

But the visitors from Georgia and elsewhere in the South seem to have been readily assimilated. The inaugural committee has given them and everyone else plenty to do. Out-of-towners and Washingtonians alike have had a chance to participate in the inaugural, in one way or another, and this has helped to create an atmosphere of good feeling.

The broad impact of the inauguration on the country, though, will depend of course on what the new President says and does. He and Ford arrive at the Capitol Plaza at 11:40 A.M. and the red-coated Marine Band strikes up "Hail to the Chief." In the invocation, Methodist Bishop William R. Cannon calls upon the Almighty "to save us from the arrogant futility of trying to play God." Noting that Carter's administration will open the third century of American independence, Bishop Cannon says: "Let this be the beginning of a new era." Then a massed choir of black Atlanta college students stirs the crowd at the inauguration of this Southern President with a stunning rendition of "Battle Hymn of the Republic," the Union's Civil War anthem.

The oaths of office follow. House Speaker O'Neill does the honors for Mondale. Chief Justice Burger, Earl Warren's successor, whose conservative leadership of the Supreme Court Carter spoke of approvingly during the campaign, swears in Carter. He takes the oath not as James Earl, his given name, but as Jimmy, and this is how he will sign all official documents. The nickname which has been a talisman and the hallmark of his style is now formally incorporated into his Presidency.

Now, for the first time as Chief Executive, he speaks to the nation. He begins slowly and deliberately. "For myself and our nation, I want to thank my predecessor for all he has done to heal our land." Applause sweeps the plaza, from the congressmen and senators on either side of the platform, and from the thousands of spectators in front. Ford rises and bows. The clapping is strangely muted, because nearly everyone is wearing gloves, but it is sustained and spontaneous. Ford bows again. He is deeply moved, and it is a poignant moment also for many of those watching here and on television around the country. Not since his first month in office—the honeymoon period he abruptly terminated by pardoning Nixon—has Ford been so popular and so well thought of by his fellow citizens. His faults have been overlooked and the appreciation of his virtues—solidness, predictability, openness—heightened by the inevitable comparisons with Carter, who seems far more complicated and self-contradictory. Yet the voters chose Carter, perhaps with their fingers crossed, partly because he possesses a certain vitality, a flair for dramatizing himself that Ford lacks.

After paying his respects to his predecessor, the new President launches into the body of his speech. The first draft was prepared by Patrick Anderson, Carter's chief speech writer during the campaign, but has been substantially revised by Carter himself. James Fallows, who was Anderson's assistant and now will be Carter's chief Presidential speech writer, told me two days ago that he had read the final version, though he had not contributed to it. "It is pure Jimmy Carter," he said.

It is clear to me now, following the prepared text in the press section as Carter reads, what Fallows meant. Carter's inaugural address is, like the foundation of most of his campaign speeches, essentially a sermon, resting on faith in time-honored American verities. An axiom borrowed from his high-school teacher, Miss Julia Coleman, provides a down-home touch and an overall theme: "We must adjust to changing times and still hold to unchanging principles." The obligatory biblical quote, from the Old

Testament prophet Micah, helps set the tone of simplicity and humility: "And what doth the Lord require of thee but to do justly and to love mercy and to walk humbly with thy God."

The prose is spare, the allusions cryptic. One aphorism is balanced off against another. Much is left to each listener's interpretation.

Carter says his inauguration "marks a new beginning . . . and a new spirit among us all." Then he quickly cautions: "I have no new dream to set forth today, but rather urge a fresh faith in the old dream."

A moment later he looks boldly to the future: "But we cannot dwell upon remembered glory. We cannot afford to drift. We reject the prospect of failure or mediocrity or an inferior quality of life for any person. . . . Our commitment to human rights must be absolute, our laws fair, our natural beauty preserved, the powerful must not persecute the weak, and human dignity must be enhanced."

This sounds like a large order, and the President promptly qualifies it: "We have learned that 'more' is not necessarily 'better,' that even our great nation has its recognized limits and that we can neither answer all questions nor solve all problems."

Under his leadership, Carter says, the nation will maintain "a quiet strength, based not merely on the size of an arsenal, but on the nobility of ideas. . . . We will fight our wars against poverty, ignorance, and injustice . . ."

These lines draw considerable applause. Seated with the House members, to the President's right, Representative John Burton of California needles Representative Mendel Davis of South Carolina. "There goes the Charleston Navy Yard."

But then Carter says: "Let no one confuse our idealism with weakness. Because we are free, we can never be indifferent to the fate of freedom elsewhere."

Burton leans over to Davis again: "You just got your Navy Yard back."

When his Presidency concludes, Carter says, he hopes it will be said that the country created more jobs, strengthened family relationships, bolstered respect for the law, and fostered pride in the government. "These are not just my goals. And they will not be my accomplishments, but the affirmation of our nation's moral strength and our belief in an undiminished, ever-expanding American dream."

In just under fifteen minutes he is finished. It was a dignified, serious talk, but bland. The loudest applause was for the praise of Ford. The speech was like Muzak, intended to create a mood, rather than as a call for action. Carter's arhythmic delivery added to the blurry effect. The written text was stronger than the spoken words.

Given past precedents, perhaps it is just as well that Carter has not tried to electrify the nation. In 1961 John Kennedy delivered the most stirring inaugural address since Franklin Roosevelt's time, promising the world that Americans "would pay any price, bear any burden to assure the survival and success of liberty." His three years in the White House were marked by the Bay of Pigs misadventure, the nuclear showdown with the Soviets over Cuban missile sites, and the deepening entanglement in Vietnam.

Richard Nixon, at his inaugural in 1969, called on Americans in statesmanlike tones to "lower our voices" and pledged: "For its part, government will listen . . . to the voices of quiet anguish, the voices that speak without words, the voices of the heart—to the injured voices, the anxious voices, the voices that have despaired of being heard. Those who have been left out, we will try to bring in." His service as President was marked by the most intense effort by the federal government in modern times to stifle and repress the voices of dissent.

Both experiences suggest that rhetoric can be a trap. Kennedy led us into peril; Nixon grossly misled us. It may be that we are fed up with eloquence and are prepared to settle for ambiguity.

Immediately after his speech Carter goes to a small office in the Capitol to sign the formal nominations of the cabinet-level officials he has already chosen. Someone asks how it feels to be President. "It feels very gratifying, very sobering, I'd say to some degree, humbling," he says. "I want to be sure that I do a good job."

He has his first meal as President—ham and cheese sandwiches and stuffed avocados—and is ready to leave for the parade to the White House. Jim Wright, majority leader of the House, glances out the window at the clear, sunny skies and says: "It looks like the Lord is smiling on us all."

"The Lord has been smiling on me for a long time," Carter replies.

He and Rosalynn drive away from the Capitol at 1:30 P.M. in an open car. When they leave the Capitol grounds and reach Constitution Avenue, at the beginning of the parade route, the car stops. The President and the First Lady get out, he takes her hand, and without further ado they begin walking to the White House, waving and smiling.

If Carter had been walking on water instead of Constitution Avenue, the watching throng could not have been much more surprised. No one can remember a President walking in his inaugural parade before. "He's walking, he's walking," people shout to each other as if to confirm the evidence of their eyes. Robert Freeman, a University of Maryland faculty member who has seen nearly every inaugural since Eisenhower's, hears the sounds of astonishment rippling through the crowd and says to a friend: "This must be what it's like at Lourdes when the cripples are healed."

Later Rosalynn Carter tells me that her husband had asked her on Monday of inauguration week: "How would you like to walk from the Capitol to the White House?"

"How far is it?" she asked, half-seriously.

"No, I mean it really," Carter said. "How would you like to walk?"

"Well, I think it might be nice," she said.

He had already cleared the idea with the Secret Service. But

Carter cautioned his wife that their approval was contingent on secrecy. "If one person finds out about it, we won't be able to do it." So Carter's plans have been a well-kept secret, adding to the drama of the moment.

Richard Nixon considered walking in the parade after his second inaugural, it is subsequently reported, but dropped the idea because the Secret Service objected. In the Nixon years, which were also the Vietnam years, the atmosphere was much different in Washington. During the 1969 inaugural, the press car I rode in, which followed the President's limousine to the White House, was hit by stones, thrown by Vietnam demonstrators aiming at Nixon. In 1973 fruit and garbage were hurled at the President's car.

Carter's inaugural is not without its protestors. The Youth International Party had a smoke-in this morning, demanding among other things "the liberation of marijuana" and unconditional amnesty for all war resisters. Some of the Yippies show up along the parade route, carrying banners reading "The Ku Klux Klan Loves Carter" and "Impeach Carter Before It Is Too Late." But they are few in number and relatively subdued, and no one seems concerned by their presence.

Attention is focused on the new President and his wife, now joined by their daughter, Amy, skipping between them, as they walk the mile and a half to the White House. It is already clear that this is what will be remembered most about Carter's inaugural, far beyond anything he said in his speech. Carter is no great shakes as an orator and must realize that. He has chosen to make his major statement about his Presidency by the simple physical act of walking home.

The walk enthralls the crowd, and millions watching on television, not just because of its novelty, but because it seems natural and appropriate. Carter is a healthy, vigorous man who lugged his own garment bag around during the campaign, and even after his election. He has said time and again that he wants his to be an open Presidency, that he intends to keep in touch with the people who elected him. Out there on the street, with his wife and their child, he is trying to show that he means what he said.

At 2:00 P.M. the First Family arrives at the White House reviewing stand to watch the parade. The stand is warmed, more or less, by some newfangled solar heating contraption. But the parade itself is the traditional hodgepodge of floats, bands, military units, and national graffiti. American Samoans and American Indians, bagpipers and hoedowners, roller-skaters and unicyclists, and, perhaps inevitably, a 40-foot-long inflated peanut proceed down the historic route for two hours. When the Carters walk through the northwest gate into their new home, the President tells a reporter: "It's been just about a perfect day."

But it is not quite over yet. After an inspection of the White House living quarters, a round of meetings with job prospects, and dinner, the President leaves with Rosalynn and Amy for a rapid tour of the various inaugural parties.

Shortly after 9:00 P.M. the band in the grand ballroom of the Mayflower Hotel strikes up "Dixie," and the Carters march onto the stage and wave. The President is wearing a tuxedo, Rosalynn the pale blue satin gown she wore at his inauguration as governor.

"Hello, everybody," the President says. "Is everybody having a good time? Is this the greatest country on earth? Does everybody like my wife's old dress?"

The crowd cheers and applauds after each question.

"I'll try to do a good job," Carter says. "It's your country as much as mine. We want to make the greatest country even greater."

Then he asks: "Does the band know something slow?"

It does. The President and Rosalynn swirl around the floor to the strains of "Love Makes the World Go Round" and "Moon River." Amy sits on the edge of the stage, holding a small bouquet of roses, looking bored. Her parents return to the stage, wave good-bye, and head for the next party on their itinerary.

By 1:00 A.M. Carter is back at the White House. The first day of his new beginning is over, and he has given a lift to the country's spirits. After a few hours' sleep he will have to begin presiding over what Pastor Edwards called the renewal of the government.

Strategy of Symbols

Right after Christmas, and three weeks before his inauguration, Jimmy Carter had summoned his cabinet-level nominees to the resort island of St. Simons, off the Georgia coast. He brought them all together for the first time on the morning of December 28, in the sunlit, spacious living room of a friend's vacation home. Carter, in sweater and slacks, sat near the picture window, Mondale on his left, the others grouped around them. In this casual atmosphere Carter called the meeting to order and then laid out for the guidance and comment of his senior advisers an agenda for the first months of his Presidency.

The agenda had been prepared, at Carter's behest, by members of his and Mondale's staff, under the supervision of the Vice President-elect. "Fritz has done some good work," Carter remarked. Each guest was given a copy of a twenty-nine-page memorandum, ranging broadly over the next half year, along with a more detailed calendar that blocked out on a weekly basis a schedule of Presidential activities in fourteen categories through the end of March. The stated purpose of this combined prospectus was to "suggest a strategy for leadership during the crucial first few months of the Carter administration." The Mondale agenda incorporated recommendations from another planning memorandum ordered up by the President-elect, called "An Initial Working Paper on Political Strategy." This sixty-page document had been prepared by Patrick Caddell, pollster-in-chief for the Carter campaign, who had been asked by his victorious client to continue to serve him in the White House as a political adviser outside the government. Presumably, Caddell's advice would be bolstered by his polling for the Democratic National Committee.

The weight which Carter attached to these guidelines was

evident during his first month in office, as he moved to establish himself in the White House. He sent his Vice President on a ten-day tour of Western Europe and Japan to lay the groundwork for a spring summit conference. And he dispatched Clark Clifford —Washington lawyer, elder statesman, and troubleshooter for every Democratic President since Truman—to make a fresh assessment of the long and tangled dispute over Cyprus which still divided the nation's Greek and Turkish allies. At home, the new President swiftly kept his controversial promise to pardon Vietnam draft violators. He moved to stimulate the economy, by submitting to Congress a two-year $31 billion recovery package. And he also sought to pave the way for his promised reshaping of the bureaucracy by asking Congress for revival of the Legislative Reorganization Act.

These were only some of the steps taken during Carter's first thirty days which emerged from the broad blueprint sketched by Mondale and Caddell. Not all their recommendations were accepted, and some were modified as to timing and other details. Nevertheless, their work, which had the new President's overall approval, represented a remarkable if not unprecedented effort to set down in advance the goals and guidelines of a new administration.

But the idea for the planning was in a way more ambitious than the plans themselves. They had been prepared for an insurgent leader who had performed something close to a political miracle. He had overcome the hierarchy of his own party, then unseated an incumbent President. He had promised to "rock the boat" in Washington once he got there. He was considered so prone to activism that two of his closest advisers, Jordan and Kirbo, had each separately mentioned to me that their chief concern about his Presidency was that he would attack on too many fronts at the same time.

Given that background, the plans for Carter's early Presidency were notable for their modesty and caution. This approach reflected a sobering assessment of the nation's political and economic condition and the President's own position, shared by the planners and evidently by the President himself. "We have been operating on the assumption that because of the nature of his Presidency, before you can lead the country, you have to have the credibility to lead the country," Caddell explained to me a few weeks after inauguration day. "And all of this is a step-by-step process, not done overnight."

Looming large among the circumstances that both defined and circumscribed Carter's Presidency was the residual impact of Watergate and Richard Nixon, and also of Vietnam and Lyndon Johnson. Ford had helped alleviate the public's darkest suspicions and deepest resentments of the White House by creating, as Caddell put it, "an atmosphere of civility in the Presidency." With Ford's help, and with the passage of time, the country had now progressed to a stage which Caddell called "cautious stability." Most of the poison had been drained from the atmosphere, but skepticism still prevailed. "Americans have no real expectations that government is willing or able to solve most of the country's major problems," Caddell had advised the President-elect. "Voters are no longer willing to grant authority to leadership, no longer willing to follow because the government suggests that they do so."

Carter's sphere of immediate action was also limited by the flimsiness of the mandate he had won at the polls, with its slim electoral vote majority and its concentration in the East and South. Moreover, even after two years of campaigning, Carter was still a relative stranger on the national scene, the least familiar person to emerge as President since the 1920s.

Carter, in the view of his advisers, faced a conundrum. To build faith in his own leadership, and restore credibility in the governing process in general, he had to make the government work, he had to fulfill his commitments and the public's expectations. "Any democracy functions only on the belief that your vote and my vote and everyone else's will be translated at least in some vague way into public policy," Caddell contended. "The failure of that to happen is what leads to a breakdown in government."

But Carter, at the outset of his Presidency, lacked the broad support required to gain approval for fundamental solutions to the divisive problems of economics and energy, or to carry out his promised sweeping reforms of the bureaucracy and tax structure. Even under the best of conditions, with the strongest of mandates, such achievements would take months, perhaps years. "Without trust," Caddell warned the President, "the country won't wait that long."

The urgent imperative for Carter was to build trust and buy time. Caddell's memorandum pointed to "the need for small sets of promises and projects that we can accomplish quickly to provide evidence that longer-term goals can be realized." The President, his advisers believed, was in a precarious position, needing to take action, but unable to take risks. The Mondale agenda suggested that "effective executive leadership be demonstrated through a series of early legislative victories, projecting the image of a 'can-do' President who has taken charge in Washington." But the report quickly added a caveat: "As a corollary to this, the new administration cannot afford any major early legislative defeats."

The President would also be handicapped, his advisers pointed out, by the troubled state of the economy, which they expected would impose strains on the federal budget well into 1978. The Mondale agenda assumed that at least for the time being, these economic problems "will permit little if any overall increase in current policy expenditures for actions not directly tied to the recovery. Reform-oriented proposals are therefore given priority and emphasis is placed on the initiation of long-term planning for those campaign commitments that would have major budgetary impacts."

Carter's strategists viewed the beginning of his Presidency in large measure as an extension of his candidacy. "Events and activities suggested in the early months are intended to reinforce and build upon successful themes established in the campaign and during the transition," the Mondale agenda stated. "The intent is to convey a clear impression that the President and his cabinet will provide a leadership with well-defined priorities which are designed to carry out the President's campaign commitments in an orderly and efficient fashion."

For the new President it was almost like being a candidate again. After campaigning for the Presidency for two years, he in effect resumed the campaign on taking office, still seeking the mandate that had eluded him. Once again he concentrated on image-making and mood-setting, or, in the language of the Mondale agenda, themes and impressions. Once again public attention focused on his personality more than on his policies. The difference now was that he was the President. Every gesture he made was cloaked with the prestige of his office. He held unchallenged possession of center stage and he exploited that advantage to the fullest.

The first test came immediately after his inauguration, from a source none of his advisers could have anticipated. A mass of frigid air swept in from the Arctic and clamped an unrelenting grip on much of the nation. Polar winds piled up snowdrifts in the North and lashed even the Deep South. In Atlanta, in Carter's own state of Georgia, the temperature plunged below zero, and in Miami, for the first time that anyone could remember, it actually snowed. The *Miami News* brought out a souvenir edition headlined: THE DAY THAT COULDN'T HAPPEN.

But the winter was no frivolous matter. It created the nation's worst energy crisis since the Arab oil embargo of 1973. This time it was natural gas, the heating fuel for half of all homes and a good share of industry, that was in desperately short supply. Schools closed and so did factories, laying off tens of thousands of workers. Cars, trucks, and trains froze to a standstill; rivers clogged with ice. The cost in lost production and wages, and in ravaged crops, ran into the tens of millions of dollars and threatened efforts to revive the economy.

The frustrating truth was that the President could do little about the winter's afflictions except to provide some emergency assistance and pray for the weather to turn warmer. But the crisis had its political advantages. No one could blame it on the President, or expect him to solve it. While it lasted it presented a chance to dramatize one of the major themes of his Presidency set forth in the Mondale agenda: "Carter as a leader who is close to the people, who cares about their problems and is determined to give them a government that is courteous, compassionate, helpful and cares about human needs."

The President took personal charge of the energy crisis, signaling his concern at every opportunity. On his first full day in office he called upon everyone to lower their home thermostats, a plea he reiterated time and again. He drafted special legislation to spur shipments of natural gas to areas hardest hit by the cold. And he talked about shifting to a four-day work week to save fuel in factories and offices.

Luck assisted his efforts. He was photographed slipping and almost falling on the ice outside the White House. The incident, Carter remarked, "shows how nimble I am." But it also helped to make the point that the President himself was not immune to winter's inconveniences.

Nine days after his inauguration, on January 29, he summoned members of his cabinet to a special Saturday session and called in the press to witness his urging them to muster all the resources of their departments to combat the cold. He wanted everyone to know, the President said, "that we are available to help them, that we're not waiting to be begged, that we're taking the initiative to meet them more than halfway."

Early the next bleak morning, which was Sunday, Carter put on a sweater under his suit jacket, boarded a helicopter, and flew off to Pittsburgh, one of the cities most beleaguered by the weather. He took with him a pool of reporters and some Pennsylvania congressmen, one of whom, William Moorehead, remarked: "This is the first time I have ever done this."

"You mean flying a helicopter?" Carter asked.

"No," said Moorehead, "taking off from the south lawn of the White House."

"Me, too," the new President said.

The two-hour flight, during which the helicopter sometimes dipped only 200 feet above the mountains, was turbulent enough to make one of the reporters airsick and to force the President to give up reading the Sunday *Washington Post.*

In Pittsburgh, Carter told workers at a Westinghouse turbine plant which had been forced to cut back production because of the cold that he had come "to give the people of our country some feeling of assurance that the federal government mechanism, working with state and local governments and private industry, can deal with the energy shortage." The country needs "a comprehensive energy policy," he said, and promised to have a plan ready within three months.

He made his now-familiar plea for lowering home thermostats and said he was setting a good example. "I have got on heavy underwear, and the White House is cold inside."

The crowd laughed and the President added: "My wife—when I told her that we were going to lower the thermostats drastically in the White House—she shed a few tears, because she is really cold-natured." The First Lady, he explained, was tired from the exertions of the campaign and the inaugural activities. "She said, 'I just can't do it.' But we have gotten accustomed to it. I hope that all the people in this country will realize that we are in it together."

After answering a few questions and offering a parting bit of advice, to wear "heavy underwear and sweaters," Carter left in time to return to Washington for lunch. It had been a good morning's work. His trip dominated the news on that typically quiet Sunday, giving the country a picture of a President eager to look at problems firsthand, energetic, caring, open, and human enough to discuss his underwear and his minor domestic squabbles.

Just as important as the attention gained by the trip itself was its effectiveness in setting the stage for the President's first address to the nation, two days later, which had been listed in his agenda as "a fireside chat." The idea had been much discussed during the transition as one means for the President, as Caddell put it, "to build a sense of personal intimacy with the people." It was a gambit borrowed, of course, from Franklin Roosevelt, who had employed it brilliantly. FDR's first fireside chat, given a week after his inauguration, dealt with the banking crisis in such plain language that, as Will Rogers observed, he made everybody understand it, even the bankers. One of the strengths of Roosevelt's chats was that they usually focused on a particular problem. Now the cold wave and the energy crisis provided Carter with a focus, or at least a peg for his talk.

But the television age gave Carter a substantial technical advantage over Roosevelt. While the term "fireside" had merely been a felicitous metaphor for FDR's radio talks, Carter had a three-log fire blazing in the hearth when he went before his viewing audience. The setting was the White House library, rather than the Oval Office, which was deemed too formal for the occasion. A debate among White House aides over what Carter should wear —a suit coat or a denim jacket—had been settled with the compromise choice of a sweater and tie. Caddell had favored the sweater, contending it would help to frame Carter's remarks as a conversation, not a speech. "It's a failure if it's a speech," he said.

It was not a failure. Dressed in a beige cardigan, self-assured and knowledgeable, the President discussed his efforts to develop a comprehensive, long-range program to deal with the shortage of energy. He spoke of harsh realities: "We must face the fact that the energy shortage is permanent. There is no way we can solve it quickly." But he took care not to paint too grim a picture. The sacrifices called for would only be "modest. . . . We need not sacrifice the quality of our lives."

Though the energy crisis was the most timely aspect of the talk, it took up only one page of the seven-page prepared text, which the President carefully followed from a teleprompter. His main point was more general, and went back to the promises of his campaign. "One of the things we need to deal with is the feeling that you overpromised," Caddell had advised Carter beforehand. "The idea is to give a sense that you are committed to promises, that they are things you are going to do, but that they are going to take a long time."

Seated in front of the library fireplace, under a Gilbert Stuart portrait of Washington, Carter recalled that he had made "a number of commitments" during his campaign for the Presidency. "I take them very seriously. I believe they were the reason that I was elected. And I want you to know that I intend to carry them out." One by one he reviewed his major pledges—to cut unemployment, curb inflation, reorganize the bureaucracy, revise the tax code, and reform the welfare system—and reported on his plans to fulfill them.

But he added a cautionary note that was in keeping with an admonition from Caddell "not to overbuild expectations on things that can't be delivered quickly." In his two weeks in office, Carter told the nation, he had already learned "that there are many things a President cannot do. . . . As President I will not be able to provide everything that every one of you might like. I am sure to make many mistakes. But I can promise you that you will never have the feeling that your needs are being ignored, or that we have forgotten who put us in office."

The twenty-four-minute talk reinforced for the millions of viewers the impression of a President in command of his job, confident but not cocksure, realistic but committed to keep his word. Still, this favorable impression had to be supported by action. The memorandums from his advisers offered guidance on timing, tactics, and tone. But in a sense, as Carter acknowledged in his fireside talk, his work was already cut out for him by the promises he had made during the campaign.

Right after election day Carter had directed Stuart Eizenstat to compile all the pledges he had made in his run for the White House. On November 30 Eizenstat completed the assignment and delivered to the then President-elect a document whose size and scope seemed to lend support to the suspicion that candidate Carter had overpromised. Although it ran on for 111 pages, covering ten major areas, from the economy and natural resources to foreign and defense policy, subdivided into fifty-two sections, Eizenstat reported that it was "certainly not exhaustive." He had drawn on all the material in the files of the issues staff, Eizenstat said, but "undoubtedly there are certain speeches or statements which were not recorded and thus not available to us." Moreover, the compilation did not include promises made by Mondale during his Vice-Presidential campaign.

On second glance, though, the document was not quite so burdensome. "The strength of the various promises naturally varies," Eizenstat pointed out. The candidate's tendency to draw fine semantic distinctions, which had made him the target of charges of fuzziness during his campaign, now served to ease the obligations on his Presidency. "Some promises indicate only that you will 'consider' taking a certain action; others indicate that you 'support' a certain action; and others indicate that you will definitely initiate or take certain action," Eizenstat wrote. "In many instances the full context of your speech or statement must be reviewed to determine the exact strength of your promise."

So far as is known, Carter was the first President in history to take the trouble to collect his campaign promises after his election. But Carter and his aides were reluctant to share the fruits of their research, and so their apparent act of good faith led to a dispute with the press.

The trouble started after inauguration day, when reporters learned about the Eizenstat document, which they promptly dubbed "Promises, Promises," and asked for copies. The White House refused, taking the position that the reporters could collect the promises on their own. Perhaps they could, but without Eizenstat's files it would be a long and tedious task. Besides, reporters argued, if the book was based on public statements, why should it not be made public?

The wrangling over "Promises, Promises" gained the attention of *The New York Times*'s op-ed page. NBC correspondent John Hart wrote that one White House staffer told him, "Release of the book might open the way to caricature. . . . In six months somebody might take the book and say, 'Look, he made 129 promises here, and so far has kept only 25.' "

A few days later Jody Powell announced that the White House had decided to release "Promises, Promises" after all. "It did not seem worth getting into a tiff over," he told reporters. "Maybe if you have it, there will be much less interest in it." When the document was finally distributed, on February 17, it included a disclaimer from Eizenstat, who contended it should be considered merely as "a rough approximation of some commitments made during the campaign." Since Carter had never personally certified the accuracy of the statements, "it would not be correct to regard this document or its release today as a statement by the President of his campaign promises. The compilation is properly viewed only as a historical document. . . ." But Eizenstat's lawyerly niggling could not change the fact that the book was a statement, drawn from Carter's own words by his own staff, of what the country had been led to expect from him as President.

The urgent question facing the new President and his advisers was which of the many pledges could be kept during his early days in the White House. Some, as Caddell pointed out, would take years to fulfill completely; they required the agreement and support of diverse interest groups and the Congress on complex matters. But other actions the President could take on his own; he could demonstrate his commitment to his word and help to establish the themes of his Presidency.

Carter had promised he would pardon all Vietnam draft violators in his first week in office. As it turned out, he acted on the first day. Using the same Presidential authorty by which Gerald Ford had pardoned Richard Nixon, Carter issued a "full, complete, and unconditional pardon" for anyone who had violated the Selective Service Act during the Vietnam War. This brought relief to some 10,000 young men, mostly white and middle class, who had either fled the country or refused to be inducted into service. It was of no help to a much larger group, more than 400,000 Vietnam-era veterans, many of them black and poor, who had received less than honorable discharges for desertion and other violations of military law. Action on these cases was postponed pending further study, the President said.* He had promised nothing more during the campaign; indeed, if he had promised anything less, he might not have won his party's nomination.

Criticism filled the air. Peace groups said the President had not gone far enough. Veterans groups called the pardon an insult to the millions who had served. A Harris poll indicated that the public disapproved by a margin of about 46 to 42 percent. But the survey also suggested that the President had been wise to act when he did. "With the passage of time, public opinion in this country is hardening against draft evaders," Harris concluded.

At any rate, no one could fault Carter for not keeping his word on this issue. In time, the administration hoped that criticism of the pardon would fade. Meanwhile, the President's prompt action gave substance to one of the major themes listed in the Mondale agenda: "Carter as a President who will unify the country, healing past divisions, so that we can bet on with meeting the problems of the future, rather than debating those of the past."

Just as important to the Carter Presidency was another agenda theme: "Carter is an outsider who intends to shake things up." The biggest and most important prospective shakeup was the President's much-heralded pledge to reorganize the bureaucracy. Carter had taken the first step in this direction on February 4, in his third week in office, by asking for revival of the Executive Reorganization Act, first passed during the Truman Presidency. This law, which Congress had allowed to expire when Nixon was in the White House, would permit Carter to shift around existing federal agencies, subject to congressional veto. Chances for approval seemed good, but that would be no more than a beginning. It would take months to work out details of which agency would

---

*At the end of March the President approved a Pentagon program that made it possible for about 60,000 deserters to have their discharges quickly upgraded and established a procedure for about 350,000 other Vietnam veterans to apply for upgrading of their discharges by military review boards.

go where, not to mention the difficulty of avoiding major opposition within the bureaucracy and the Congress.

In the interim, the President could make the existing bureaucratic framework more responsive and efficient—or at least he could try. "We will cut down on government regulations and make sure that those that are written are in plain English," he announced boldly in his fireside chat. Every regulation would bear the author's name, and each cabinet member would read every regulation before it was issued by his department. In his days as a state senator, Carter had imposed a similar discipline on himself, keeping a campaign promise that he would read every piece of legislation before he voted on it and becoming in the process, as he said, "an expert on many unimportant matters." Looking back on it, Carter had termed his legislative promise "unfortunate," and the bureaucracy took an equally dim view of his edict on regulations.

The rulings promulgated by federal agencies are often drafted by whole squads of specialists. For example, John Snow, head of the National Highway Safety Administration, pointed out that twenty or thirty lawyers and engineers had prepared a recent ruling on anthropomorphic test dummies, making the question of which one should bear the responsibility of authorship difficult if not impossible to answer.

Moreover, the output of the federal regulation writers was several magnitudes greater than the Georgia legislative docket. At HEW an official estimated that for Secretary Califano to regularly scrutinize the masses of rulings spawned by his far-flung department would be the equivalent of reading *War and Peace* once or twice a week. "Of course we're going to do what the President said," Snow told the *Washington Post.* "But if he's serious, he'll bring the federal government to a grinding halt." Before very long Carter quietly dropped his sign-all, read-all order. A press aide said the President believed his point had been made.

But some parts of the bureaucracy seemed to have a built-in resistance to the Carter White House. When some three hundred former Carter campaign workers were referred to federal agencies for ninety-day trial jobs, many were scornfully turned away. One applicant rejected by the State Department reported being told: "We don't have anything for political hacks." Another campaign veteran was advised: "If you had any brains, you'd have never worked for Carter."

Most of the applicants were young people who had poured their energies into the campaign for little pay and now wanted a chance to prove themselves in middle-level posts in government. They returned from the agencies "terribly demoralized," according to Jim King, the White House personnel director. King, a former aide to Ted Kennedy and a normally affable man, was furious. "It was like hitting Tarawa Beach," he told me. "The tide is running out, the boats are stuck, and we're being shot to pieces. This government employs almost three million people and I'm being told there's no room for three hundred people."

King complained to Secretary of State Vance and HEW Secretary Califano, whose departments were the two worst offenders. Carter brought the problem up at a cabinet meeting. He did not necessarily expect that all the applicants would be hired, the President said. But he did want them treated with courtesy and civility. Ultimately, most of the campaign workers found jobs, either on their own or with the grudging compliance of agency personnel directors, but only after King's steady nagging.

The one place where the President could carry out his will and implement his style with relative ease was in his own house. The size of the President's staff and the privileges they enjoyed had been hallmarks of the Imperial Presidency, and during the campaign Carter had made plain his intention to cut back on both. He promptly announced that he proposed to reduce the staff by one-third from the level under Gerald Ford.* He also decreed that his top assistants would not have the chauffeured limousines their

*After a few weeks the White House acknowledged that the staff had actually increased in size. The increase was said to be temporary and due to the flood of mail that greeted the new President and the need to draft the energy program. Permanent cutbacks were promised eventually. But some aides doubted that the President's goal of a 30 percent reduction could ever be met.

predecessors enjoyed. This move was of no great practical consequence, since it involved only a dozen or so cars. But the President
intended, as Jody Powell explained, to set an example for the rest
of the executive branch. Another example was the removal of
television sets from a good many White House offices.

Carter made the point directly to the members of his cabinet
at their regular Monday meeting on January 31, urging them to
surrender some of the privileges that traditionally accompanied
their rank. "There's a natural instinct to accept it," he said. "I
have a natural instinct to accept it, but I want to cut back on that
drastically."

This was a matter close to the President's heart, and essential
to his early approach to his office. As Stephen Hess pointed out
in a memorandum to Carter during the transition, the trappings
of office, whether or not they actually influence the behavior of
Presidents, "offend a good many Americans and are symbolically
counterproductive to restoring trust in the Presidency."

For the benefit of his cabinet the President recalled that in the
early days of his campaign, before he had a chartered plane at his
disposal, he had always flown coach class: "I feel very strongly
about that." He referred to the elaborate travel arrangements
made for past Presidents, and for Henry Kissinger, with evident
disfavor. "We're going to cut out the ostentatiousness of things."
Even security considerations would no longer be sacred. He noted
that the Secret Service had planned to fly several armored limousines to Europe for Mondale's use during his trip to the Continent.
But the President had decided his Vice President would be safe
enough driving with his distinguished hosts. "I don't want to
endanger anyone's life, but I think that's adequate."

Though the cabinet members had no choice but to accept the
President's new guidelines on the use of Air Force planes and
Secret Service limousines, they could and did disagree on some
innovations. They unanimously opposed his proposal that their
meetings with him be opened to coverage by the press. As the
President later explained, his appointees argued that the admission of reporters to cabinet meetings would only result in a "sub-

terfuge," because sensitive quesions would be set aside to be settled in private. In addition, cabinet members were concerned about "looking silly and having their ideas shot down" in the presence of reporters.

The members of the cabinet might balk at some Presidential directives and drag their feet on others. Essentially, though, they are the President's men and women, serving at his pleasure. They would ultimately have to follow his lead on most matters, and they could be counted on to keep to themselves whatever reservations or misgivings they harbored.

The President's relationship with Congress, of course, was bound to be very different. Here, he had to deal with men and women who had been elected to office in their own right, many of them by larger majorities than his. Their leaders had built their power largely on seniority and on a knack for accommodation. Sam Rayburn's old maxim "To get along, you have to go along," still rang true in the corridors of the Capitol. The new President's image as a political outsider, which his advisers believed had broad public appeal, grated on the sensibilities of the leaders, whips, and ranking committee chairmen. Nor could these legislative potentates, who jealously guarded their own perquisites, avoid feeling a measure of suspicion and resentment about the new atmosphere of austerity and informality which had become the style at the White House.

The leaders displayed their irritation by grumbling publicly even over trivial matters, such as the breakfast menu for their biweekly meeting with the White House. On their first visit the legislators dined in style, on poached eggs and sausage. But when they returned on February 7 they were ushered into the cabinet room and served nothing more than juice, coffee, and a roll. "We had our first real taste of the nonimperial White House and it wasn't very tasteful," Alan Cranston of California, the Senate majority whip, reported afterward. "I guess you'd call it a Continental breakfast," said Speaker O'Neill, who complained he needed more than that to sustain his 265-pound frame. "It must be that economy wave that's hit the White House."

Of more serious concern to the lawmakers was the laxity of the new White House team in consulting them on matters of joint interest. On January 26, before the President had completed his first week in office, Senate majority leader Robert Byrd of West Virginia noted that the White House had failed to ask him in advance which senators should be briefed on the President's emergency energy legislation. This omission had made it necessary to hold a second briefing for those not invited to the first. President Carter would be prudent, Byrd said, "to let the leadership know about these meetings so that we can suggest which senators should be involved."

O'Neill was even more nettled that the White House had made two nominations from his own state without so much as mentioning their names to him. It added considerably to his irritation that both appointees were Republicans, and that one of them, Elliot L. Richardson, selected to represent the President at the international Law of the Sea Conference, was believed to have an eye on the Massachusetts governorship—which happened to be the same position that also interested O'Neill's own son, Thomas P. O'Neill III, the state's present lieutenant governor. Taking note of Senator Byrd's complaint about Carter, O'Neill remarked to reporters: "I think it's also obvious that he better be in contact with the Speaker of the House." He was even blunter in private conversation with Hamilton Jordan, who called on him to make amends. "I don't think you understand, son," the white-haired Speaker told the President's young aide. "The next time you do this, I'm going to ream your ass."

The President sought to heal the initial rift with the Hill by publicly confessing error at his first press conference, on February 8. "We've given them cause" for dissatisfaction, he said of Congress. "We've made some mistakes." Now he was keeping in touch with individual legislators almost daily, and with their leaders every two weeks. "And I believe that we've made a great deal of progress in correcting those early mistakes." But even if minor personal strains could be healed, a basic institutional tension remained between the Chief Executive and the legislature. The President would have to reckon on some delays before Congress disposed of what he proposed. "I don't know if he understands this now," said Senator Byrd. "But it will be a fact of life before it's over."

Most of what the President would ask from Congress could only be guessed at during his first month in the White House. The thrust of his proposals for welfare reform, tax reform, health insurance, energy and government reorganization, the heart of his domestic program, was still unknown, certainly to anyone outside Carter's inner circle.

By contrast, the President moved vigorously to put his personal stamp on policy in the field where he had come to the White House with the least claim to expertise, foreign affairs. And in this he seemed to be following a familiar Presidential pattern. Lyndon Johnson, dedicated to creating a Great Society at home, diverted his energies to the struggle against what he regarded as the menace of communism in Indochina. Richard Nixon, though committed to heal the domestic divisions left by Johnson, was far more interested in achieving "peace with honor" in Indochina and establishing a new relationship with Communist China.

The reasons for this behavior are as old as the Constitution and as modern as an ICBM. As the Mondale agenda noted, on inauguration day Carter became commander-in-chief, in charge of the nation's security, and "chief negotiator, responsible for the nation's foreign policy." A President is freer to act on his own in these areas than in the domestic arena. Moreover, no matter how pressing domestic issues might seem, foreign affairs in the nuclear age are quite literally a matter of national life or death.

Early in the transition Carter's aides said he had no plans to travel overseas during his first year as President. But he could not long resist the magnetism of global diplomacy. Two weeks before his inauguration, the President-elect announced his intention to attend an economic summit conference in London in the spring, a venture to which he attached progressively greater importance as time went on.

More dramatically, immediately after becoming President, he broke the previous pattern of United States diplomacy by pressing the Soviet Union for new strategic arms limitations agreements and, at the same time, offering his support to Soviet dissidents in the cause of human rights. These tactics were consistent with Carter's own campaign pledges to curb the arms race and demonstrate United States moral leadership to the world. But in the past, under Henry Kissinger's policy of linkage, the United States had tied its dealings with the Russians together, trading off concessions in one area for an advantage in another.

Carter privately signaled to the Soviets the end of linkage on February 2, at his first meeting as President with Soviet ambassador Anatoly F. Dobrynin. He was determined to negotiate a new SALT pact quickly, the President told the ambassador, and he offered some new ideas to expedite negotiations. But he also stressed to Dobrynin his deep concern with human rights.

Even so, Dobrynin and the Kremlin could not have been prepared for Carter's next move. Right after the meeting with Dobrynin, the State Department forwarded to the White House a letter to Carter from the most prominent Soviet dissenter, Nobel Prize winner Andrei Sakharov. The department suggested that the President reply through some lower-level American official in Moscow. Instead, the President wrote to Sakharov himself, promising that "the American people and our government will continue our firm commitment to promote respect for human rights not only in our own country but also abroad. We shall use our good offices to seek the release of prisoners of conscience and we will continue our efforts to shape a world responsive to human aspirations . . ."

While the letter was still on its way to Sakharov, Carter held his first Presidential press conference and stressed his eagerness to reach agreement on arms with the Russians. He would be willing, the President said, to table discussion on certain weapons—the Soviet backfire bomber and the United States cruise missile—to hasten some form of pact. But, he stressed, he was not prepared to back away from his commitment to human rights. "I think we come out better in dealing with the Soviet Union if I am consistently and completely dedicated to the enhancement of human rights," he said. The previous administration, he noted, felt that support for human rights might endanger the progress of arms talks. "I don't feel that way," he said. "I think it ought to be clear."

It was by no means clear, though, that the Soviets felt that way. To the contrary, the Russians responded by complaining that the new President was interfering in their internal affairs and by warning of possible damage to Soviet-American relations in general. Moreover, Carter's human rights offensive against the Russians raised questions about how he would deal with authoritarian regimes in Latin America and Asia, including some traditional United States allies.

No one at home quarreled in principle with the President's support for "prisoners of conscience" in the Soviet Union and elsewhere. But it remained to be seen how far Carter could carry his crusade without disrupting other United States interests abroad, and what, if anything he could accomplish to actually enhance the rights of dissidents. For the time being, the human rights campaign seemed mainly an exercise in symbolism, like many of the administration's actions and utterances on the domestic front.

And this was at the heart of the most widely voiced criticism of Carter's Presidency during his first month in office. The fault finders in the Washington press corps contended that he relied too much on gestures and offered too little in substance. It was not a brand-new complaint to make against a President, but it had not been heard much since John Kennedy's days in the White House. The Presidents between Kennedy and Carter—Johnson, Nixon, and Ford—lacked the theatrical imagination and personality necessary for the effective use of symbolism, a handicap which in fact limited their ability to lead the country. "The old cliché about mistaking style for substance usually works in reverse in politics," Pat Caddell said. "Too many politicians mistake substance for style. They forget to give people the kind of visible signals that are needed to understand what is happening."

This axiom was certainly understood by Franklin Roosevelt. He launched his campaign against Herbert Hoover in 1932 by flying through a raging summer storm to the Democratic Convention in Chicago to accept his party's nomination, defying what he called the "absurd tradition" that a candidate should pretend to remain unaware of his nomination until weeks after the event. "You have nominated me and I know it, and I am here to thank you for the honor," he told the cheering delegates. "Let it . . . be symbolic that in so doing I broke traditions. Let it be from now on the task of our party to break foolish traditions."

In May 1933, in the midst of Roosevelt's celebrated first hundred days, a Bonus Expeditionary Force arrived in Washington similar to the army of unemployed veterans who had marched on the capital the previous summer, seeking early payment of the promised bonus. Herbert Hoover had had the Army banish the veterans with tear gas and bayonets. FDR dispatched Eleanor Roosevelt to greet the veterans and lead them in singing "There's a Long, Long Trail Awinding." "In two weeks," Arthur Schlesinger, Jr., wrote, "most of the veterans had vanished into the Civil Conservation Corps and the second BEF had met a painless Waterloo."

But Presidential symbolism is effective only if it seems natural to the President. Stephen Hess wrote in a memo to Carter that the Sunday worship services Richard Nixon held at the White House appeared "forced and unnatural" because Nixon had never had the reputation of being a particularly religious person. Carter's inaugural walk seemed in keeping with his personality and so, most people thought, did his fireside chat. But the latter came close to being overdone. After watching the sweatered President's performance on television, Sander Vanocur wrote in the *Washington Post* that he was reminded of Oscar Levant's description of Hollywood: "You have to sweep away the surface tinsel to get to the real tinsel underneath." Vanocur's criticism was not aimed at the speech itself but rather at the various props—the fireplace, the sweater, the Washington portrait—"which kept getting in the way of what I thought he was trying to tell us."

The ultimate test for political symbolism is whether it is intended, as Caddell said, as a signal for action, or, as Vanocur worried, "as a mind-gratifying substitute for decision and action." Roosevelt's symbolism strengthened his Presidency because it was a prelude to action. After being cheered by Mrs. Roosevelt's presence, the members of the BEF were able to join the CCC, which Roosevelt had pushed through Congress. The months ahead would tell whether Carter's symbolism could meet this standard.

For the time being, though, the country was apparently willing to take him at face value. After he had been in office for two weeks, 66 percent of those surveyed by the Gallup poll approved of Carter's performance in the White House; and by the time his first month as President was ending his Gallup job rating had climbed to 71 percent. The fact remained, though, that he had yet to be seriously tested by a major public controversy. Other Presidents who had scored well in the polls during their initial honeymoon periods had seen their popularity plunge under the pressure of events.

Mindful of that danger, the President seemed determined during his first month to build a reservoir of goodwill against the future by the force of his personality. He had cast himself as the central figure in his symbolic strategy and played his role with aplomb, most of the time. To display his openness and mastery of the Presidency, he made himself accessible to interrogation at every opportunity, responding freely to queries on even the most complicated and sensitive matters. The colloquy over disarmament he conducted at his first press conference was a stunning piece of showmanship. Here was the President of the United States striding confidently across the tightrope of nuclear weaponry, pairing the backfire bomber with the cruise missile, contrasting the SS-20 missile to the SS-16, in effect carrying on complex negotiations traditionally confined to confidential meetings and diplomatic nuances in the most public of circumstances and in the plainest of language.

But his eagerness and his occasional lapses into imprecision sometimes tripped him up. During one of a series of visits to federal agencies in Washington, he was asked whether he would favor eliminating the deduction for home mortgage interest as part of his tax reform package. The question was inaudible to many people in the noisy meeting room, including, as it turned out, the President himself. But he answered it anyway.

He said that he favored substituting a tax credit for the existing "standard deduction," which, he contended, "helps much more the very high-income families. . . . We are going to shift away from the regressive tax structure to a much more fair one for the low- and middle-income taxpayers in this country."

Later, Jody Powell explained to puzzled reporters that Carter had not heard the question. And that when he referred to standard deduction, which few high-income taxpayers use anyway, since they generally itemize their deductions, he really meant the $750 personal exemption. Moreover, the specialists working on the President's tax proposals told the *Los Angeles Times* that, despite the President's implication to the contrary, the overall effect of his reforms would not be to soak the rich for the benefit of the poor.

But this experience did not faze the President at all. That next weekend, he returned to Plains for the first time after three weeks in the White House, and took a walk through his hometown in blue jeans and a sweater, answering any question reporters could think of as he went. During the course of his ninety-minute strolling press conference, he disclosed, among other things, that he favored mandatory automobile efficiency standards, that he hoped for improved relations with Cuba, and that his new defense budget would be less than what President Ford had asked for but more than last year's, despite his campaign promise to cut Pentagon spending by $5 billion.

During the campaign Carter's tendency to think out loud, or to speak without thinking, had sometimes caused him trouble. But he was intent on showing that as President he had conquered that difficulty.

"I just study all the time," he told his cousin Hugh during his visit to Plains. "I don't go in there for two hours and let people tell me about what's to be asked at the press conference. You know, I'm studying all the time. So I don't need any briefing much, except just on things that have been in the newspaper that morning."

Hugh Carter wondered if the President did not worry about the impact of his words. "With all the power you have, doesn't it sort of frighten you?"

Leaning on the counter of Hugh's antique shop, while reporters listened with fascination, the President told his cousin that a sense of security went with the White House. "I learned how to be cautious during the campaign because then you didn't have any substance, you were just kind of a floating candidate. If you made a mistake, that was all there was. Now, if you make a mistake, you've made a mistake, but you're still President."

"Yeah, that's right," said Hugh Carter, and the two cousins laughed.

The additional confidence he had acquired with his office had also helped to sharpen his sense of humor, or at least to make it more evident. Wit and laughter had been conspicuously absent from his candidacy. "A little, he seems to believe, goes a long way," Charles Mohr of *The New York Times* wrote about Carter's humor during the campaign. Carter was certainly quick enough but also terribly solemn, reluctant ever to laugh at himself, perhaps because he was trying so hard to get other people to take him seriously.

But at the first major social outing of his Presidency, the Washington Press Club dinner a week after his inauguration, he proved that he could be funny if he tried. "I had been anticipating the inaugural ceremonies and parade for a long time," the President told the gathering of journalists and congressmen. "I started walking down the highway and streets and could hear the vast crowd saying: 'Look, look, look!' And I was feeling very good until they said, 'There goes Billy's brother.'" On the day after the inaugural, Carter said, the mayor of Washington had called "to thank me for restoring faith in the city by walking on the street unprotected and by getting my brother back to Plains."

Though these jokes were at least as much at his brother's expense as his own, Carter ribbed himself a bit, too. He had told his staff, he said, that he wanted "to put on the image of a common man, someone who didn't have the accolades of the crowd and the homage paid to a strong and able leader. They said so far I have succeeded very well."

He claimed to have heard from his Vice President, then traveling in Europe, who on finding himself in Paris without his wife "wanted to be very careful not to violate my own high standards of ethics and morality. He gave the State Department an urgent call for a copy of my *Playboy* interview."

The joke about the *Playboy* interview reflected Carter's relaxed mood during his first month in office. But religion and morality remained serious matters to him. Only twelve hours before his appearance at the Press Club dinner, he had talked, with characteristic intensity, about sin and humility at a prayer breakfast. As he maneuvered through his early days in the White House, he kept his Bible close at hand, on his desk in the Oval Office, next to a plaque from his days as a submariner, bearing the inscription: "Oh God, thy sea is so great and my boat is so small." Carter's relationship to God had been a major influence all his life and, the initial evidence suggested, it would help to shape his Presidency.

The Eye of a Needle

February 20, 1977—The five-car motorcade forms outside the south portico of the White House about 9:30 Sunday morning. At 9:48 the President, who is not wearing a topcoat, the First Lady, and Amy come out the door and get into a tan Lincoln. The motorcade starts up, leaves the White House grounds through the southwest gate, and swings north. It is a bleak, cold morning, but a cluster of tourists are waiting on West Executive Avenue. They wave and snap photos as the First Family drives by. The motorcade heads up Connecticut Avenue and makes a series of right-hand turns. Just before 10:00 A.M. the Carters arrive at the First Baptist Church, which they joined on the first Sunday of his Presidency, where Amy has been baptized and where Carter today will teach Sunday school.

With the exception of Richard Nixon, who had services conducted at the White House, most Presidents have gone to church on Sunday mornings on a fairly regular basis. Truman used to worship here at First Baptist when he was President. This practice has been so routine that it has drawn little attention in the past, except for an occasional photo in the Monday morning papers. But Jimmy Carter's presence in the White House has given extra meaning to the Sunday ritual. No other President in recent memory taught Sunday school. More fundamentally, no other modern President has so personally and publicly stamped himself as a man of God.

"His identity is so bound up with his religion that it would do considerable damage to him as a person to be separated from that," the Reverend Charles Trentham, pastor of Carter's new church, told me.

Carter's faith has been so well advertised that he has taken pains to assure the country that he will not let his religion dominate his Presidency. "One thing the Baptists believe in is complete autonomy," he said in his *Playboy* interview during the campaign. "I don't accept any domination of my life by the Baptist Church, none. Every Baptist church is individual and autonomous. . . . The reason the Baptist Church was formed in this country was because of our belief in absolute and total separation of church and state."

In *Why Not the Best?* Carter relates a conversation with a visiting pastor about his decision years ago to run for the state senate. When the clergyman asked why he did not seek a more honorable line of work, Carter replied: "How would you like to be the pastor of a church with 80,000 members?" But in recalling that story last spring, in a televised interview with Bill Moyers, Carter said: "I don't look on the Presidency as a pastorate. . . . I don't look on it with religious connotations. But it gives me a chance to serve, and it also gives me a chance to magnify whatever influence I have, for either good or bad, and I hope it will be for good."

Still, it is impossible to separate Carter's faith from his Presidency. As he acknowledged in a later interview: "My life has been shaped in the church. My deep commitment as a Christian, and my knowledge of the example of the life of Christ, and the observations of my own religious learning of the attitude of Christ toward other human beings has been obviously an example that I followed." His religion has made him the kind of person he is, and during his first month in the White House there have been indications of its continued influence on his values.

One example is the fervor with which he has pursued his campaign for human rights in the Soviet Union and other countries. This is of course also a legal, social, and political issue. But arguments made on those grounds are often subject to qualification and compromise. Carter's position appears to be categorical and unyielding because it is based at least in part on his own perception of morality.

Ten days ago, the President felt called upon to advise Housing and Urban Development employees on their personal behavior. "Those of you who are living in sin, I hope you'll get married."

Some in the audience laughed, but Carter added: "I think it's very important that we have stable family lives. And I am serious about that." His counsel against premarital relationships struck some people as sanctimonious. "He sounds like a very good evangelist," Betty Ford remarked. "I don't think that's his business."

This President, though, is evidently very concerned with sin. Last month, addressing the annual national prayer breakfast, he disclosed that the biblical reference he originally intended to use in his inaugural address was God's admonition to Solomon from the Second Book of Chronicles: "If my people, which are called by name shall humble themselves and pray, and seek my face and turn away from their wicked ways, then will I hear from heaven, and will forgive their sin, and will heal their land."

But his staff members had objected. They argued, Carter recalled, that "the people will not understand that verse. It is as though you, being elected President, are condemning the other people in our country, putting yourself in the position of Solomon and saying that all Americans are wicked." Reluctantly Carter substituted Micah's gentler urging "to do justly and to love mercy and to walk humbly with thy God."

Carter told the prayer breakfast guests: "Sometimes we take for granted that an acknowledgment of sin, an acknowledgment of the need for humility permeates the consciousness of our people. But it doesn't." The lack of humility seems to be the sin that troubles Carter most of all. "As those of us who are Christians know," he said at the breakfast, "the most constantly repeated admonition from Christ was against pride." Most likely this is the cause of some personal difficulty for Carter, because, outwardly at least, he appears to be one of the least humble of public men. Politicians are not noted for self-effacement, yet most would shrink from the idea of titling a campaign autobiography *Why Not the Best?*

My understanding of the President's religion is colored and perhaps limited by my own Jewish-Unitarian-agnostic point of view. At any rate, it seems to me that Carter's religion serves the purpose of helping him to live with his own pride. Believing in a forgiving God, he can confess his pride to himself and to the Almighty. "If we know that we can have God's forgiveness as a person, I think as a nation, it makes it much easier for us to say, 'God, have mercy on me,' " Carter told the prayer breakfast. If Carter cannot conquer his pride, at least with God's help he can keep it under control. But it is a never-ending struggle which provides one of the underlying themes for today's Sunday school lesson.

The class meets in the east balcony of the church. Its regular membership, like the congregation as a whole, is made up mostly of middle-aged couples, moderately well off, who commute to their church and their jobs from the suburbs. The church does not exclude members on racial grounds but only about 50 of its 950 members are black. Among the seventy people gathered in the balcony for Sunday school are a few black faces, some of them evidently visitors. Carter and Rosalynn take seats in the second row. I sit well up in the back, with three other reporters who make up the press pool permitted to accompany the President.

Fred Gregg, an insurance company official and the regular teacher, opens the class by recalling that last week the President did not attend because he had gone home to Plains for the weekend. "I was embarrassed," Gregg says, "because I told people the President wanted to see his mother and get some of her cooking." But Miss Lillian went off to India, where she had been a Peace Corps volunteer, to attend a state funeral. "So some wiseacres said," Gregg goes on, addressing the President directly, "that you wanted to hear a good Sunday-school teacher." The Carters join in the general laughter and then Gregg proudly calls upon Carter to give the lesson.

First Baptist Church, with its vaulted ceilings, intricate stained-glass windows, and pews for 1,400, is far more imposing than the modest building back in Plains where Carter used to regularly teach the men's bible class. But the President seems very much at home at the lectern here. He is wearing a grayish-blue

Glen plaid suit and holding his black-bound copy of the King James Bible. He tells the class that Gregg called him during the week and complained that "his reputation was damaged a little bit" because Carter had gone to church in Plains last Sunday. "So he wanted a demonstration of inferiority to make him look good."

Again laughter, after which the President says seriously: "In the daily life of a President there is some disharmony. But certain things in our lives never change—our love for Christ and our ability to find Christian fellowship wherever we go. I want to thank all of you for making us feel welcome."

He begins the lesson by asking the class to define the Bible. Hands shoot up all over the balcony, and one by one, as Carter calls on them, the members of the class offer their answers—a law, a road map, a love letter from God, an almanac, a description of what God is like. Finally, Carter provides his own definition: "A debate between God and man, God and woman over the laws of God, a constant interchange between God and human beings in which we struggle to justify ourselves."

The lesson is based on the chapters of St. Mark which describe the beginning of Jesus' final journey to Jerusalem. Carter reads aloud the verse in which Jesus asks his disciples: "For what shall it profit a man, if he shall gain the whole world, and lose his own soul." Everyone has worldly aspirations of one sort or another, Carter says. "If you are social it might be to have the most elaborate parties, if you're a young man it might be a beautiful woman, and if you're a politician, it might be being President. But if you gain these things and lose your relationship with God," he asks, "what good does it do?"

I wonder if Carter feels he has jeopardized his relationship with God by winning the Presidency. He does not really say, one way or another. Instead he suggests that such questions must be constantly examined. "Judge not that ye not be judged," Carter says. Instead of judging others, he tells the class, judge yourselves. "We all have a responsibility for self-analysis. What is it in our lives that separates us from God? How many of us have been on our knees in the last twenty-four hours, in the last ten hours?" he asks. No one answers. "I have," he says quietly.

In his *Playboy* interview Carter guessed that on "an eventful day" he might pray as often as twenty-five times. "If something happens to me that is a little disconcerting, if I feel a trepidation, if a thought comes into my head of animosity or hatred toward someone, then I just kind of say a brief silent prayer," he said. "I don't ask for myself, just to let me understand others."

But the sort of prayer he is talking about now is more disciplined and rigorous, a spiritual stock-taking. "There has to be some realization whether what we do is acceptable in the eyes of God," he says. "Jesus said, 'Stop every now and then and think about your life.' "

It occurs to me as I listen to him here in the church that a year ago this month he was speaking to groups not any larger than this in New Hampshire before the first Presidential primary. They were not Sunday school classes, but Carter's manner, informal yet serious, his irregular speech patterns, and his short, choppy gestures were much the same then as now.

Carter reads on to the passage which is the crux of his lesson, the story of the rich young ruler who asks Jesus for the gift of eternal life. Reminded of the Commandments, the young man says: "All these have I observed from my youth."

Jesus tells him: "Sell whatsoever thou hast and give to the poor, and thou shalt have treasure in heaven: and come, take up the cross and follow me." This was more than the young man was prepared to do. "Jesus knew from looking at people what their attitudes were," Carter says. "He knew that the young man clung to his wealth." Everyone has something he does not want to give up, Carter says. "It doesn't have to be wealth. It could be anything precious to you—reputation, money, jewels.

"This is the turning point in the young man's life, a watershed, a direct confrontation with God. God told him: 'Give up your money and come live with me.' But the young man couldn't do it; he walked away from God."

Carter pauses briefly, then adds: "I can see some very close parallels between this young man's attitude and my attitude."

Once again he has brought us to the edge of his personal dilemma and left us dangling. He does not say whether he would walk away from God. He does say that of all the episodes in Jesus' life recounted in the New Testament, he considers this among the most significant. "It touches us so deeply because it epitomizes the struggle of human beings against God."

Carter reads on: "It is easier for a camel to go through the eye of a needle than for a rich man to enter into the kingdom of God." The disciples ask who, then, can be saved and Jesus answers, in Carter's words: "Anything is possible with God.

"Can we save ourselves?" Carter asks. "No," he answers. "But God loves us so much that in spite of our obsession with riches he gives us eternal life."

Nearing the end of the lesson, the President discusses the various meanings of Jesus. "He is a kind judge, but strict. He is also a teacher of laws, of the way you're supposed to act, a very gentle way, a clear way, based on simplicity and truth."

He digresses to make two secular remarks, which I would guess are directed mainly to the reporters who, the President fully realizes, are listening intently.

"God's laws are the same in Washington, D.C., and in Plains, Georgia, and in Russia, China, and Pakistan," says the President, who has been promoting the extension of God's laws to Soviet dissidents.

He also has a word for members of the other branch of government on Capitol Hill, who, like the Russians, represent a separate and adversary force in his world. "Congress meets and Congress goes home," Carter says with a smile. "But God's laws do not change."

He turns his attention back to Jesus, who he says is also "a redeemer," "a reconciler," and "an example." Taking note of the presence of the Reverend Trentham, Carter says he does not mean to be sacrilegious, but he thinks that "Jesus is a picture of what we could be if we were perfect."

Transfer of power: Carter takes the oath.

Walking home to the White House.

Drafting the February fireside chat in the Oval Office.

The President and his men:
(top) Mondale and Brzezinski; (center) Press Secretary
Powell; (bottom) Secretary
of State Vance.

Questions and answers in Clinton's Town Hall.

Carter and Vance meet the press in the Rose Garden
after the return from Moscow.

A word to the wise from Speaker O'Neill.

Defense Secretary Brown briefs the cabinet, March 21
(author is seated second from right).

Jordan takes an after-tennis phone call.

Meeting of minds: (from left) Eizenstat, Strauss, Moore, and Lance.

Mapping energy strategy: (from left) Schlesinger, the President, Lipshutz, and Moore.

Powell and speech writer James Fallows polish the energy message to Congress.

Dress rehearsal: Rafshoon (left) and Jagoda prep Carter for
energy address to the nation.

Sacrilegious or not, it seems to me Carter has sketched an outline of how he would like to be regarded as President. The qualities he has ascribed to Jesus are similar, after all, to the themes suggested by his advisers for his Presidency. The overall image may be as impossible to achieve as perfection, but it is a goal for him to keep in mind.

After forty minutes he finishes, shakes hands with Fred Gregg and some of the others in the class, and then takes Rosalynn downstairs for the regular worship service. On the way out I stop to talk to Gregg. "It was good to be in the house of the Lord today," he says. "Here is a man who knows the scriptures. Here is a man who knows Jesus."

From what I can tell, Carter's talk was characteristic of the Protestant evangelical movement in general and of Southern Baptism in particular. Broadly speaking, evangelicals are conservative Christians who take the Bible quite seriously, sometimes literally, and consider it mainly a guide to personal morality rather than a touchstone for social reform. One of the most puzzling aspects of their faith to outsiders is the apparent contradiction between the sense of self-righteousness that comes with being born again in Christ and the sense of humility that comes from the awareness of human susceptibility to sin and temptation. Those who, like Carter, have been born again have achieved a measure of salvation, but they must constantly be on guard to avoid slipping from grace.

Thus, Carter's faith is surrounded by tension. One type of tension is internal and personal, produced by his continuous self-examination, when he is on knees sorting out his conduct, measuring it against the expectations of God. But another tension is public, reflecting Carter's frustration with the unwed couples at HUD and with a country, most of whose citizens are not prepared to accept the Lord's advice to turn from their wicked ways.

The tension and the faith are a source of strength and also a potential weakness. His private contemplation is a reminder of his own human frailty. It is hard for anyone, even a President, to be arrogant when he is down on his knees, pondering the camel and the needle. The public dimension of Carter's religion helps to inform his Presidency with a sense of compassion. His religion, he has said, has contributed to his conviction "that those who are poor, deprived, despised, unfortunate, illiterate, afflicted, who belong to a group against which there is discrimination ought to be the prime responsibility of me as a powerful, influential public servant."

There is always the danger, of course, of excessive zeal. As history has amply demonstrated, this can lead to rigidity and various forms of intolerance. Whether he can resist these tendencies, along with the world's other temptations of the spirit and flesh, will be a test of Carter's Christianity, and also of his political skill.

6

Road Show

Hanscom Air Force Base, Massachusetts, March 16, 1977—About two thousand people are waiting here this afternoon near the main runway for Jimmy Carter to arrive at the first stop on his first full-scale trip as President. Many in the crowd work at the base for the air force; others live in the surrounding towns. I have always had doubts about whether it is meaningful to interview people picked at random from a crowd. But the same logic that underlies Carter's visit—that the President can take the nation's pulse by answering a few questions from his fellow citizens—leads me to strike up a conversation with Mrs. Judy Gaber, a Bedford housewife.

Mrs. Gaber is a great admirer of the President. "He doesn't go for all the frills," she says. "He's just an ordinary person."

I ask her how an ordinary person managed to get elected President. She says: "What I mean is that he understands ordinary people."

However representative she may be, Mrs. Gaber is at least one American who feels about Jimmy Carter exactly the way he and his advisers want her to feel. Carter has been President now for a few more than half a hundred days, and much of his effort during this period has gone into persuading the electorate that if he is not exactly ordinary himself, he is keenly aware of the needs and aspirations of plain folks. One of the "stylistic points" which Pat Caddell has urged the President to stress is that "he has an intimate relationship with people; he is anxious to relate to them and to restore power to them." This trip is aimed in part at strengthening that impression.

But the overall purpose of this thirty-hour journey is much broader than that. It is intended to carry forward, and out of Washington, the strategy for building support that has molded the early weeks of Carter's Presidency. The trip seeks to exploit the Carter administration's greatest asset, Carter himself, by turning him loose in the country where people can see him being President. The timing makes this effort particularly important; the President is taking to the road just as his major policies are being developed and emerging into the public arena.

The schedule carefully combines the symbolism of his Presidency, which has been so evident since January 20, with some substance. Tonight Carter will answer questions at an open meeting in nearby Clinton and sleep in a local citizen's home. Tomorrow he will go to Charleston, West Virginia, to lead a panel discussion on energy and then to the United Nations to make a major speech on foreign policy. The meeting tonight and the UN speech tomorrow night both will be televised nationally. A huge press corps, which almost fills a chartered 707, will accompany him every step of the way. He will be highly visible as he meets people face to face in Clinton, grapples with the most pressing domestic problem in Charleston, and speaks for his country to the rest of the world at the UN.

He arrives right on schedule. At 4:50 P.M. *Air Force One* sweeps down from the sky and taxis to a stop. The door opens, the President peers into the bright sunshine and waves at the

cheering throng. Ted Kennedy and several local congressmen
have come up on the plane with him. But all eyes are on Carter
as he shakes hands with the welcoming committee and then walks
over to shake more hands in the crowd.

Someone asks him how it feels to be back in New England.
"Great," he says. He gets into his Lincoln and the motorcade
starts the twenty-minute trip to the Sheraton Motel in Boxboro,
where the President will have a chance to eat and rest before the
main event in Clinton.

Weeks of planning by the Carter White House have gone into
this journey. It was conceived even before there was a Carter
White House, during the transition, as a natural outgrowth of
Carter's candidacy. Carter had presented himself to the country
as an outsider who, once he got to Washington, would remember
where he came from, and who would strive for what he liked to
call an "intimate" relationship with his constituents.

Just before the New Year Jody Powell disclosed that the
President had created a special staff group "to study ways to make
the President more accessible to the people of the country and the
people more accessible to the President." This enterprise inevitably came to be called the "people program," one result of which,
earlier this month, was a two-hour Presidential radio phone-in
show. With Walter Cronkite at his side, Carter answered forty-
two questions flawlessly while about 24 million people listened;
some nine million had tried to reach him on the phone, and the
entire performance was judged a huge success.

This trip, a much more elaborate enterprise, was originally
envisaged in the Mondale agenda last December as a cross-country tour "to demonstrate concern for the impact of government
across the country and gain support for the Presidentially announced budget and economic programs." The suggested itinerary included conferences with governors and mayors, meetings
with "lower-level federal field personnel," and "confidential talks
with ordinary citizens on how to improve the quality and efficiency of services."

Frances Voorde, head of the White House scheduling office,

took over the planning late in January. The cross-country journey along with some of the other agenda suggestions were discarded as too time-consuming and complicated. Instead, the scheduling staff, working with the press office and political aides, seized upon an alternative mentioned in the agenda, and enthusiastically advocated in Caddell's political memo for a sort of town meeting. The President, Caddell proposed, "should allow 400 to 500 people to gather in an auditorium to hear him, to question him, to raise questions, to have an interchange in a way that has never been attempted by a President of the United States. I think it could have a dramatic impact on the public."

Actually the idea was not entirely new. President Ford had done something of the sort, meeting with local officials in communities around the country, and had achieved moderate success. But that was certainly no reason to prevent Carter from trying another and, his aides believed, more colorful version of the grassroots formula.

The scheduling office began mapping a three-day, three-state journey that would take the President to a town meeting in New England, the home of that venerable institution, to New York for the St. Patrick's Day parade, and to Bethlehem, Pennsylvania, for a potluck supper and visit to a factory gate. But before the planning had gone very far the tentative proposal bounced back from the Oval Office with a disapproving notation: "Too cute," the President wrote. "Sounds too much like a campaign trip."

The Voorde team went back to the drafting boards. They had decided meanwhile to scratch Bethlehem because the President had already been to Pennsylvania, on his helicopter trip to Pittsburgh during the January cold wave. Hamilton Jordan suggested Ohio, the state that had been so vital to Carter's political success, as a substitute. But Ohio's Republican governor John Rhodes was no great friend of Carter's and his cooperation could not be relied on. West Virginia presented itself as a suitable alternative. It was a major coal-producing state, providing an ideal setting for a discussion of the energy crisis. Moreover it had a friendly Democratic governor, Jay Rockefeller, and was the home state of Robert Byrd, the Senate majority leader.

In New England, the schedulers had settled on the equally friendly terrain of Massachusetts, the most Democratic state in the union, one of whose favorite sons, Tip O'Neill, happened to be Speaker of the House. To add weight to the New York visit, balancing off the St. Patrick's Day parade, the planners proposed a panel discussion on government reorganization with local and Washington officials.

But in the first week of March, Carter added an extra complication. He wanted to use the New York trip to address the United Nations and deliver the first major foreign policy speech of his Presidency. A United Nations talk had long been contemplated; it was down on the Mondale agenda for March 27. But the President, who was being accused of making up his foreign policy as he went along, did not want to wait that long. The speech was promptly shoehorned into the schedule and the St. Patrick's Day parade, which had been the original reason for visiting New York, was scrapped. It was too fluffy, in any event, and too difficult to fit into the New York schedule along with the panel discussion and the UN speech.

The starting date was moved up to March 15, one day earlier than originally planned, thus bringing the President to New York on March 16. Since Carter would not march in the parade, his staff decided that he would be better off not to appear in New York at all on St. Patrick's Day. As Jody Powell had explained last week at a planning meeting in his office that I attended: "If you're going to New York on St. Patrick's Day you have to be in the parade."

Even without the parade, though, the New York schedule was still unwieldy, as Powell pointed out to the assembled schedulers and advance men. The President was supposed to arrive at Kennedy Airport early in the afternoon, hurry to the Federal Building in lower Manhattan to lead the panel discussion, and then head uptown to the United Nations. That would be easy enough for him to do by helicopter. But the distances between stops, New York's maddening traffic, and its obdurate police force all would make it next to impossible for the press buses to keep up with his schedule.

Powell still remembered trying to cope with the police, the national press, and the huge contingent of local reporters on Carter's climactic campaign stop in New York last October. The general frustration and wrangling undermined an otherwise successful rally. "It looks like this is going to be another one of our typical New York visits," he said sourly.

Someone suggested changing the subject of the New York issues panel to something besides reorganization. But Powell shook his head. "It's not the substance, it's the logistics that are terrifying."

The consensus at the meeting was that Powell should send Carter a memo explaining the problem. He picked up a pen and half-seriously began to write: "Dear Jimmy: In re New York trip. Aw shit."

He laughed and started over: "Dear Jimmy: In re New York trip. Sweet Jesus, please let this cup pass from me."

Finally, he abandoned the idea of the memo and decided to talk to the President personally.

In the next twenty-four hours two developments produced changes in the schedule. The President agreed to drop the issues panel in lower Manhattan. And Barry Jagoda, the President's media adviser, suddenly remembered that the public television network, which he was relying on to provide the only live TV coverage of the President's scheduled Tuesday night appearance in Clinton, was committed to televise the Metropolitan Opera's performance of *La Boheme* on the same Tuesday night. The Met would not reschedule, so the White House did, going back to the original timetable. Carter was to depart Washington on March 16 for Clinton, and visit Charleston and New York the next day. The arrival in New York was scheduled for late afternoon, long enough after the St. Patrick's Day parade ended so that, the White House hoped, no one would be offended.

But the trip has managed to capture some of the flavor of St. Patrick's Day in Clinton, which is so heavily Irish—about 80 percent—that it starts celebrating the holiday the night before. Clinton commended itself to the White House advance teams because of size, demography, and location. Not an upper-middle-class suburb, it is a small industrial city of about 13,000 people, and off the beaten track, about 50 miles west of Boston. Like other New England factory towns, Clinton would ordinarily be considered dreary. But the combination of St. Patrick's Day and the President's visit has given Clinton a festive air and a touch of color.

As might be expected, the President's visit has caused great excitement in town. A lottery was held among Clinton's 7,500 registered voters to determine who among them would be entitled to the 850 seats in the Town Hall and a chance to question the President. Most of the winners, who begin filing into the hall about half an hour before the President is due, are wearing something green. I find a place in the press section in the balcony, not far from where Senator Kennedy, Massachusetts governor Michael Dukakis, and some congressmen are seated. About two thousand people wait outside the hall, hoping for a look at Carter.

Clinton's regular town meeting, when the municipal budget and other such matters are discussed, won't take place until later in the year.* The first order of business tonight is consideration of a special motion to suspend the rules "and refer this meeting to the pleasure of the President of the United States of America." The motion is offered by the chairman of the board of selectmen, Alan D. Jewett—who, a longtime Clinton resident informs me, is known locally as "Rocky"—and it passes without dissent.

Carter is supposed to arrive at 7:30, but he takes some extra time to greet the crowd outside. When he marches in, nearly ten minutes late, wearing a gray suit and a green carnation, he gets

*The President proved to be a much bigger attraction than the budget. When the actual town meeting was supposed to be held, on April 25, only 268 citizens appeared, not enough for a quorum.

a standing ovation. He gets another one the first time Rocky Jewett mentions his name. Jewett says he is confident "that this meeting will be the forerunner of a successful nationwide visit with the common, ordinary American citizens such as we have here." I recall my conversation with Mrs. Gaber at the airport and I wonder why Americans are so fond of describing themselves as "ordinary." Jewett wishes Carter a happy St. Patrick's Day, producing a third standing ovation, and finally introduces him, which brings the crowd to its feet again.

Now the President is alone on the stage, behind the podium and in front of a huge pastoral mural, which was retouched after it was discovered that patches of peeling paint showed up under the television lights. Carter says he had asked his staff to pick "an average American city" for him to visit. "They made a terrible mistake, because this is no average city. This is an extraordinary city."

The Clintonians, despite their pride in being ordinary, love that, and there is another burst of cheering.

"I am not going to take any time making a speech," the President says, and then proceeds to do just that. He begins quietly and modestly. "I haven't been in politics very long. I have got a lot to learn. I am eager to learn. I don't claim to know all the answers, and the day I leave the White House and another President takes over, I still won't know all the answers."

As he goes on, describing his economic program and mentioning his forthcoming proposals for energy, welfare, and tax reform, his intensity builds. He begins to sound like a candidate at an election eve rally. "Those are our goals," he says, and adds, as he always did during the campaign, "and I don't intend to lose." He catches himself quickly and amends his statement. "I don't intend to lose that struggle." It is clear he sees himself as embattled, and wants to be seen that way.

The first man up wants to know the President's ideas for peace in the Middle East. Carter says that, among other prerequisites, "There has to be a homeland provided for the Palestinian refugees who have suffered for many, many years." He has said this often before as a candidate, but this is the first time he or any other President has made the point in public. Consequently, his words are bound to create a stir outside this hall, just as his other remarks about sensitive foreign policy issues at press conferences have caused tongue clucking in the press and in diplomatic circles. Carter realizes this and evidently welcomes it, because it helps to establish him as a politician who confides in the people and also as a President assured enough of himself so he can speak off the cuff on complicated matters.

Nearly all the questions that follow are focused at home, not abroad, and some very close to home. The President seems well prepared. He gets one query, on oil spills off the East Coast, that fits into the I'm-glad-you-asked-me-that category. This very morning, either by good fortune or foresight, the President has sent a message on oil spills to Congress, proposing a wide range of solutions which he is glad to recite.

A soldier who wants to know about plans to shut down part of nearby Fort Devens is let down easy. "I can't give you an answer on whether it will be shut down or not," Carter says. "But it won't be done lightly."

One questioner says, "I am a little bit nervous."

"Well, so am I," Carter tells him. But if he is, it is impossible to tell. He seems to be enjoying himself thoroughly, smiling often, gesturing easily, answering patiently. This is his show and he is the only star. Everyone else—the audience, the press, the other politicians, who are seated in the balcony—are props for his performance.

The evening is more than halfway over before he acknowledges the presence of Edward Kennedy, a politician of fairly good standing in Massachusetts. As an afterthought, following his answer to a question on health insurance, a cause for which Kennedy has been probably the Senate's foremost advocate, Carter adds: "I might say, since he is here, that Senator Kennedy has been the leading member of Congress in many of the items that I have discussed tonight." The audience applauds, Kennedy rises briefly, bows slightly, and sits down. Not until later does Carter mention Clinton's own congressman, Joseph Early, and Governor Dukakis, who are sitting next to Kennedy in the balcony.

Perhaps the most interesting dynamic observable here this evening is the personal rapport between Carter and the people of Clinton. Carter carried Clinton by two-to-one against Gerald Ford last November, but that was no great accomplishment. No one can remember the last time Clinton voted Republican. Last March, in the Presidential primary, when Clinton's voters had other Democrats to choose among, Carter ran third here, behind Henry Jackson and Sargent Shriver. And across the country last November Carter did not do as well with Catholic voters and with what Pat Caddell calls "urban ethnics" as Democratic candidates are expected to do. The reasons for this are not entirely clear, though Carter's aides believe they have something to do with his Baptist faith and his Southern rural origins.

But his answers tonight seem to bridge the gap between him and this constituency and find the common ground.

Eleanor Filman of 156 Main Street tells the President: "We are very, very happy that you came out and spoke against the federal funding for abortions." But a federal court has ruled that needy women seeking abortions cannot be denied Medicaid payments of federal funds. "What more can you do for us?" Mrs. Filman says.

"As you know, I have to abide by the laws of the land as interpreted by the courts," the President says. "There is a great deal, as you know, that we cannot do to prevent abortions completely. But what we can do under the law we are doing and will continue to do it."

The audience applauds and Carter says: "I think this is the first time I have ever given an answer on abortion and got applauded. I always give the same answer . . ." That is approximately true, though he did not mention tonight that he has pledged not to support a constitutional amendment banning abortions.

The federal judiciary, which ties Carter's hands on abortions, is a highly unpopular institution in Clinton. In addition to its resentment of the rulings on abortion, Clinton is close enough to Boston to share in the resentment against the federal court orders there in favor of school busing.

"Sometimes under the guise of constitutional interpretation, some federal judges impose their biases and their ideologies on the average American citizen," says Bill Constantino. "Is this situation going to continue in your administration?"

"First of all," the President says, "I agree with you. And second, I hope to cut it down as much as I can."

One reason for the problem, Carter says, is that "Congress has passed legislation without consulting with the local and state officials and the President and vice versa," a practice he hopes to curb. "Another thing we need to do is to move toward appointing federal judges on the basis of merit and ability instead of a cheap political payoff."

Richard Nixon always liked to remind us that he was a lawyer, and Carter likes to point out that he is not. But the two men's views on the federal courts do not sound greatly different. Like Nixon, Carter talks about this other branch of government as if it were a nuisance. I wonder if Carter considers John Kennedy's appointment to the federal bench of Griffin Bell, who had served as co-chairman of Kennedy's Presidential campaign in Georgia, as a political payoff. At any rate, the selection of judges on the basis of merit is not likely to make them any more reflective of the attitudes of the people of Clinton, or of the President. Moreover, as Carter must know, many of the people who helped elect him President consider the independence of the federal courts their best protection against injustice.

But the people in the Town Hall are pleased with his answer, and seemingly with everything he says. Only once does Carter get anything resembling a hostile question, and this comes from a high school freshman named Mary Correia, who picks up on an earlier statement by the President that he would consider reinstituting the draft if he felt the nation's security required it.

"If you believe in the draft," she says, "why, may I ask, did you pardon the draft evaders?"

Carter says he issued the pardon because "it is time for us to get over the horrible consequences of the Vietnam War and I feel that those young people have been punished enough. . . . I let the people of the country know I was going to do it before I was elected. Nobody voted for me through false pretenses, and so I don't have any apology to make. I hope I have answered your question as well."

Mary Correia is persistent. "It is not that I don't believe in the draft," she says. "I was just wondering why you did say something about the draft if you did pardon them."

Carter tries a different tack. The draft is not needed now, and he hopes it will not be needed in the future. "I think the restoration of patriotism and an eagerness to serve our country will stimulate recruitment in the armed forces. If we can restore that sense of patriotism and pride in serving our country, we won't need a draft. I believe that is the best way to avoid the draft in the future."

This has to be considered one of the evening's better moments. Carter has given a reasonably straight answer to a question for which there is no easy answer. Moreover, the spectacle of the President of the United States challenged by a high school freshman, and responding civilly, is, I think, an encouraging and reassuring sign about his Presidency.

Some of Carter's other responses are less edifying. Bill Clinley tells the President "that we consider you one of us, a man of the people whose energies are directed toward the welfare of the average citizen." Clinley presents Carter with a list of grievances: a dime loaf of bread in 1939 now costs almost a dollar; the minimum wage is only $2.30 an hour; welfare has become a way of life for many people; taxes eat up one-third of his salary.

"Bill, do you have a question?" Carter asks.

But Clinley only wants to say that "we trust you, we pray for you, and we will follow you in your efforts to make the country a better place than it was when you were elected."

"That was kind of a long statement, but I liked it," Carter says. "I found out at firsthand when I got to the White House how much food costs were. We have to pay, of course, all of our food bills in the White House ourselves, and they keep a separate accounting for everything that is done for me and my family and all our guests, even when we have a head of state come and stay with us in the White House. We pay for the food." For the last ten days of January, he says the food bill was $600. "We have been really watching the food bill since then. So I am in the same boat with you."

These remarks seem intended to help allay any public resentment about the President's providing bed and board in the White House for two of his sons and their wives and one of his grandchildren. During the radio phone-in one caller had grumbled, inaccurately, that they were "living off the taxpayers." But Carter, as he sometimes does, has overstated the case for the defense. Foreign dignitaries usually stay at Blair House, not the Executive Mansion, and state dinners held in their honor at the White House are billed to the State Department. The size of the President's grocery bill, which he does pay for, is an index to the size of the Carter family and the flock of friends and relatives they entertained in the postinaugural period.

Presumably Carter does incur extra expenses because of his official duties. But he is paid $200,000 a year in salary, $50,000 for expenses, and another $100,000 in nontaxable funds to cover travel and official entertainment—which puts him in a far different economic boat from Bill Clinley and most other Americans.

But the image of himself as Mr. Average is one that the President is determined to establish tonight. "I am a small businessman myself," he says at one point, in an exceedingly modest reference to his million-dollar enterprises in Plains.

"I would like to leave tonight by reminding you that we are partners," he says in his closing remarks to the people of Clinton.

"I don't have any more intelligence or ability than you do. . . . I need your help, I need your prayers, I need your advice, and I also need and welcome your tough criticism when I make a mistake. . . . It is not an easy thing for a President to stay close to the people. But I am going to do my best."

Another ovation, and the President jumps down from the stage to shake hands with members of the audience. His performance has been a smash hit and, generally speaking, in a good cause. It is healthy for the country for the President to show concern, and to give an account of himself, even if the accounting is not very rigorous. It is hard to think of another President who could have carried this evening off so well. Gerald Ford would have been too dull, Richard Nixon too stiff, Lyndon Johnson too contrived. What distinguishes Carter's style is that the same words, which coming from him sound warm and convincing, would sound banal and embarrassing if others said them.

But he does have an unfortunate tendency toward excess. It is hard to believe that this President genuinely feels he has no more intelligence or ability than the average citizen. Certainly that is not the basis on which he was elected. This hyperbole is so evident that it may be harmless in itself. But the cumulative effect of such exaggerations is bound to diminish credibility.

More important, staying close to the people demands not just the President's physical presence in a town hall but also his candor and frankness. At no point tonight did he focus on the dislocations and sacrifices that will be required to carry out his promised programs of reform and reorganization. In discussing national health insurance, he left his audience with the questionable proposition that "we can have good health care without spending much more money on it." If his reception in Clinton is any guide to the feeling about him in the rest of the country, and the polls suggest that it is, he can get away with answers like that for a while. But sooner or later he is going to have to confront the country with the hard, complicated truth about its problems and how they can be dealt with.

From the Town Hall, the President goes to the white frame home of Edward "Gunner" Thompson to spend the night. Thompson is a beer distributor, one of Clinton's more prosperous citizens, and the father of eight children, six of whom are grown and living away from home. The spare bedrooms in the house were the main reason Thompson was chosen as Carter's host. Carter has never met the Thompsons before, but he is used to staying with strangers, having made a practice of it during the campaign. He takes off his coat and tie, chats with the family for about an hour, and retires to an upstairs bedroom about 10:30 P.M. The bathroom is down the hall. Carter's appointments secretary, Tim Kraft, sleeps in another bedroom, and the Secret Service sets up a small command post on the back porch.

Next morning Carter is up at 7:00, makes his bed, and goes outside to greet about 150 townspeople who have gathered on the street. After breakfast with the Thompsons he leaves for Hanscom field at about 8:45. *Air Force One* is off the ground at 9:30, and at 11:10 it lands in Charleston, West Virginia, for the second stop of the trip.

The President arrives at the state capitol to the cheers of several thousand people, among them members of a conservationist group called Save Our Mountains who carry posters, one of which says: "Topless Mountains Are Obscene."

Governor Rockefeller and his wife, Sharon, lead Carter downstairs to the cafeteria where Carter gets a cheeseburger, french fries, and a carton of milk. He sits down at a table with some state employees, asks for a bottle of ketchup, and eats his french fries with his fingers. In twenty minutes he is finished and on his way to the nearby state conference center for the main event of his visit here, a roundtable discussion of the energy problem.

The stated purpose of this conference, according to a White House press release, "is to allow the President to hear firsthand the energy and environmental concerns of various constituencies prior to formulation of a comprehensive national energy policy." Presumably the President could have learned about these concerns in Washington. But by coming out here, one of his aides contends, he also gets "the tone and texture" of the problem.

More to the point, he gets a lot of attention this way. He is being seen, by the national reporters covering the trip, and on statewide television here in West Virginia, actively working on an important problem. This, the White House hopes, will help to counteract the stress placed by the press on his reliance on imagery and symbolism. The conference also dramatizes the President's efforts to draw on all sectors of opinion in shaping his energy proposals. Much human energy and a fair amount of money is being expended for this purpose. The White House has mailed letters to 450,000 people, soliciting their views, the Federal Energy Agency is sponsoring a series of citizens' meetings in ten cities, and twenty miniconferences, similar to today's meeting, are being conducted in Washington.

The President has spared no effort to lend importance to this conference, bringing down from Washington his chief energy adviser, James Schlesinger, his Interior Secretary, Cecil Andrus, and the head of the Environmental Protection Agency, Doug Costle. They assemble in an auditorium with bright yellow walls and room for about two hundred spectators and take seats next to the President at the head of a long table. Flanking them are Rockefeller, Mayor John Hutchinson of Charleston, Democratic senator Jennings Randolph of West Virginia, and fifteen people who represent the coal industry, power companies, miners, environmentalists, consumer organizations, and other groups concerned with the energy problem.

In a way, the energy shortage promises to be a boon for the West Virginia economy, which has been suffering for years because of the decline in coal consumption. Now, as Carter notes in his opening remarks, West Virginians can look forward to a shift away from oil and natural gas, toward the use of coal, which their state still has in great quantities. But the decisions about how this coal will be developed and how it will be used have yet to be made. And those decisions will affect the various groups at this table in different ways.

Carter, who serves as keynoter and moderator for the discussion, reminds the panel that he will present his energy proposals to a joint session of Congress on April 20, little more than a month from now. "It is one of the most important considerations I will ever face as President of the United States," he says. It takes on particular significance because this will be the first major test of his ability to reconcile divergent interests on a critical issue—in other words, of his capacity to lead the country.

Recently, Carter says, he warned his cabinet "that we now have about a 70 percent favorable rating in the polls for our job so far, but when we come out with an energy policy on April 20 we will probably lose about 10 or 15 percent of that." He adds: "I am willing to give up some of my own personal popularity among the people of this nation to require them to face the brutal facts that we all are going to have to work together to deal with the impending crisis."

This is a classic Presidential stance, that of a statesman willing to sacrifice his own political welfare for the good of the country. But politics and government do not necessarily work that way. If the President can persuade the country that his energy proposals are fair and effective, he can probably retain his popularity and also get some of his ideas through Congress. He is trying to lay the groundwork for that now by participating in this panel, giving the groups with conflicting interests a chance to be heard.

A rough outline of some points of conflict and of Carter's own attitude emerges during the discussion. Carole Ferrell, a black woman who is an official of the West Virginia Human Rights Commission and the consumer representative on the panel, complains about the policy in most states permitting power companies to pass on increased fuel costs to the consumer. "That almost straightens my hair," she says. "When I think about people whose welfare checks only come to $200 a month and their utility bills come to $150 and they have to buy food stamps with that money, the cost cannot be passed on to the consumers. There is not much more we can stand."

Carter suggests that consumers can cut their fuel bills by

upgrading the insulation of their homes. And Jack Lloyd, who is vice president of the Appalachian Power Company, reports that his firm has an experimental program to finance home insulation costs.

Mrs. Ferrell is suspicious. "I don't think the power company has any business in the insulation business." Her idea is for the government to provide low-interest loans for insulation.

But the President's free enterprise instincts are aroused. "In most cases, I agree with the consumer," he says, smiling. But not in this case. A government loan program would require "an enormous bureaucracy." Better to have the power companies handle it, "with maybe the government guaranteeing part of the loan cost."

Eric Reichel, the coal company representative, warns the President against expecting that the energy programs will produce rapid changes in the coal industry. "The energy system is enormously complex and massive and any change that a new policy brings about will take significant time to show effect."

The President fastens what his staff calls his "steely blues" on Reichel. "It is very important that Dr. Schlesinger have that kind of advice," he says sternly. "Because when we spell out an energy policy and a time schedule for putting it into effect, I am going to be very determined as President to make sure we get our time schedule."

It becomes evident during the discussion that the President wants conservation to be the dominant element in his program, and this idea begins to trouble Jack Lloyd, the power company man. "I know we have to conserve," he says. "At the same time I do not think we can let up on the supply. If we are going to enjoy the economy we enjoy today, if we enjoy sitting in a room that is air-conditioned, ample lighting, ample energy supply, there is no other way we can do it."

The President is unrelenting. "I have a hard time seeing that waste contributes to economy. I think we have a long way to go before we damage the quality of our lives, if we just eliminate obvious waste."

He is rather different here this afternoon from the way he was in Clinton last night. The friendly neighborhood President has been replaced by the hard-headed executive. He is courteous but brisk and businesslike.

At times he gets a bit confused by the complications of the bureaucracy he is trying to reorganize. One panelist makes an urgent plea for a change in government policy which otherwise would turn a wilderness area over to mining. "You have to act in a matter of a few weeks to stop the Forest Service from carrying out the previous administration policy or that area is gone."

"The Secretary of Interior said he is familiar with that problem," Carter replies.

Slightly embarrassed, Andrus says mildly: "Except Agriculture has the Forest Service."

But as the discussion grinds on for more than two hours, covering "second-generation coal scrubbers," "toxic sludge," "magneto hydrodynamics" and other esoterica, Carter's attention never strays. His engineering background stands him in good stead here, and he seems intrigued by gadgets and technology. He speaks favorably of "a little red light" some utility companies are installing in kitchens to signal when the demand for, and the price of, power is at a peak. He talks knowledgeably of "tall stacks," 1,100 feet high, which he claims permit electric power plants to burn coal with minimal air pollution.

In one passing comment he discards the concept of energy independence for the United States, which had been the cherished goal of the Nixon and Ford administrations. "I do not see any prospect nor need for our own country to be energy self-sufficient, anytime in the future. It might very well be that the oil that we purchase now at, say, $4 a barrel is a very good bargain and the oil and gas that we leave in our own ground for use later on might be one of the most precious deposits that we have."

Carter says the country must be prepared to readjust its priorities and goals on all its natural resources. "I believe that we have got, and the whole country has got, to go into the process of reexamining past considerations that were accepted just as a routine matter and say, 'Have we made a mistake? Have we started down the wrong road?' "

A few minutes after 3:00 P.M. Carter concludes the session by reminding the panelists that energy is a worldwide problem, and one of the issues he will discuss in his speech this evening at the United Nations. He speaks approvingly of the "great concern" about protecting the environment he has noticed in the state. "I hope that as Jennings Randolph reminded me when I got off the plane by giving me this beautiful West Virginia tie that the phrase 'almost heaven' will always apply to West Virginia."

Air Force One gets him to Kennedy at 5:45 and *Marine One* to the Wall Street helipad twenty minutes later. His staff's desire to avoid logistical problems has turned his arrival in the nation's largest city into a nonpublic, semiprivate affair. Only some city officials and reporters are there when the helicopter lands. A few minutes for handshaking, then his limousine speeds along Franklin Roosevelt Drive to the U.S. Mission to the United Nations.

After a quick dinner with Secretary of State Vance and United Nations ambassador Young, he heads for the United Nations, where he is welcomed by an honor guard and Secretary General Kurt Waldheim. The General Assembly is not in session, but a meeting of the representatives of the United Nations delegations has, like the town meeting in Clinton, been arranged for the President's convenience. The U.S. mission, as host, will pay the extra expenses involved, amounting to about $2,000. The interpreters who will translate his remarks into four languages—French, Spanish, Chinese, and Russian—have prepared themselves for his Georgia drawl by listening to recordings of his inaugural address.

The two thousand delegates and guests in the General Assembly Hall stand and applaud when Waldheim introduces the President. Jimmy Carter begins with an addition to his prepared text, a graceful bridge between this occasion and the start of his trip last night, between the American tradition and this international assembly.

"Last night I was in Clinton, Massachusetts, at a town hall meeting where people of that small town decide their political and economic future. Tonight I speak to a similar meeting, where people representing nations all over the world come here to decide their political and economic future."

But this audience of diplomats is quite different from the enthusiastic throng in Clinton. They listen to the President politely and attentively, but with professional detachment. They have, after all, been hearing speeches from American Presidents for years. Carter himself is poised and direct. There are few flourishes in the text and none in his manner.

The main reason for this speech, according to the President's advisers, is to formalize for the benefit of the rest of the world the broad outlines of the new President's approach to foreign policy. He acknowledges what one adviser calls "the essential intractibility and complexity" of international problems. "We can only improve this world if we are realistic about its complexities. The disagreements we face are deeply rooted and they often raise difficult philosophical as well as practical issues."

In a refreshing note, he also concedes the limitations of United States power. "I recognize that the United States cannot solve the problems of the world. We can sometimes help others resolve their differences, but we cannot do so by imposing our own particular solutions."

He goes on to elaborate on his three major foreign policy goals—slowing the arms race, fostering economic cooperation, and last, but certainly not least, protecting human rights. About halfway through the speech he gets his first applause with a call for strict controls on new weapons and sharp reductions in strategic arms. "Such a major step toward not only arms limitations but arms reductions would be welcomed by mankind as a giant step toward peace."

His most provocative paragraph is tucked away near the end of the text and bears on human rights. "No member of the United Nations can claim that mistreatment of its citizens is solely its own business. Equally, no member can avoid its responsibilities to review and to speak when torture or unwarranted deprivation of freedom occurs in any part of the world."

Carter seems to be going out of his way to make certain that everyone, at home and abroad, realizes he is determined not to back away from his position on human rights. In a speech that seems meant mainly to affirm and explain what the President has already said, rather than to reveal anything new, this is the newsiest part, the point that many reporters will use to lead their stories. But it is received here in silence. The UN delegates have obviously not been swept away by the spirit of Carter's crusade. They do applaud vigorously, though, when he promises to press the Senate to ratify the UN genocide convention and the treaty for elimination of racial discrimination. At the finish the delegates stand and clap politely, as they did at the beginning.

Now there is one more hurdle to clear, a reception for all the member countries, which the representative of the Palestinian Liberation Organization also will attend. A sensitive point of international protocol has been raised. Will the President risk irritating the Israelis and their supporters by greeting the PLO representative? As it turns out, the two men are introduced and do shake hands. But Carter later softens the impact of that gesture by insisting that the United States will not change its attitude toward the PLO "until the PLO changes its attitude toward Israel."

At 9:15 P.M. the President leaves the reception and heads back to the White House via the Wall Street helipad, JFK airport, and Andrews Air Force Base. He has accomplished everything he set out to do on the road. He has been on television two nights running and has successfully played three different Presidential roles—politician, policy-maker, and diplomat. His performance has gone over very well in the outside world. But he will need more than showmanship to deal with the inside world of Washington.

7

The Cabinet:
Morning Report

—————— ★ ——————

March 21, 1977—Franklin Roosevelt looks out from above the fireplace at the portraits of Jefferson and Lincoln on the opposite wall. A huge mahogany table dominates the room. Around it, in chairs with brass nameplates giving their titles and dates of swearing-in are the senior officials of the Carter administration, the members of the cabinet and the cabinet-level advisers to the President. Carter, wearing a blue suit, is seated in the center, a stack of papers in front of him. Behind him are the American flag and the Presidential flag and windows opening on the Rose Garden. White House staff members are clustered next to the wall on each side of the room.

One of the changes Jimmy Carter promised to make in the government was to turn his cabinet into an effective instrument for helping him shape and implement government policy. This morning, here in the cabinet room, I am getting a chance to see firsthand how the new President and his cabinet work together.

Carter's ambitious plans for his cabinet, like a number of his other goals, have been viewed with skepticism in Washington. That sort of talk has been heard before from other new Presidents. But only Eisenhower, among modern Presidents, depended heavily on his cabinet. Presidents who have been strong, activist executives, the kind of President Carter evidently wants to be, have paid little attention to their cabinets. Kennedy, according to Arthur Schlesinger, declared cabinet meetings to be "simply useless." Richard Nixon, who initially conceived of a major role for his cabinet in his administration, abandoned the idea because he was bored by the tedium of cabinet meetings and frustrated by the mediocrity of his own appointees.

Other Presidents have felt the same way. The cabinet is an unwieldy group for decision-making. Besides the heads of the eleven major federal departments, the modern cabinet includes several special White House advisers, whose number keeps growing. (Carter has added one to the list by making James Schlesinger his energy adviser.) Cabinet members obviously vary greatly in their experience and personality, and some Presidents have tended to lean on one or two for advice while all but ignoring the rest. In the early years of the Nixon administration, Attorney General John Mitchell probably exercised more influence on more issues of direct concern to the President than the rest of Nixon's cabinet put together. Many cabinet members, however broad their background and interests, tend to become absorbed by the problems of their own departments. "Why should the Postmaster General sit there and listen to the problems of Laos?" Kennedy demanded to know. No one could give him a good answer, so he dispensed with regular cabinet meetings and instead asked his department heads to give him weekly reports on their activities.

But someone has to coordinate the far-flung bureaucracy, prevent the agencies from operating at cross purposes to each other, prod them into carrying out the President's will. In the recent past, that task has generally fallen to the White House staff, which steadily increased in size and authority, reaching the absolute corruptibility of power under Nixon and becoming the mechanism of his destruction. Ford, because of Nixon's example and his own temperament, moderated the authority of the White House staff, but it was still the dominant influence in his administration.

But Carter and his aides insisted, even before the election, that his Presidency would be different. "If Jimmy is elected, you'll see a strong cabinet," Hamilton Jordan told me last October. "If I were Jimmy Carter I'd tell my cabinet members this," added Jordan, who is now the dominant figure on the White House staff: "If any of my staff people, any of them, start jerking you around or calling you to tell you what to do, you come and tell me, because you work for me, you don't work for them." That, said Jordan, was how Carter operated in the governor's office in Georgia.

Carter himself has been less graphic but just as emphatic on this point. "I believe in giving cabinet members authority," he said during the transition. "I don't intend to run the individual departments of government out of the White House or through staff members." Moreover, he indicated that he expected his cabinet meetings to serve as forums for vigorous debate. "I don't want a group of yes men or yes women in my cabinet," he said. "I need to have strong advocates for their positions, particularly when we meet as a group."

This morning's cabinet meeting is the ninth of the Carter Presidency, which is now sixty days old. If any of the eight previous meetings have been marked by serious disagreements, they remain a well-kept secret. The only public information about cabinet meetings comes from Rex Granum, the deputy press secretary, who attends every session, takes notes, and briefs reporters later. Granum's briefings have concentrated on the President's remarks to the cabinet, which seem to have dwelled on the need to curb waste, frills, paperwork, and other bureaucratic excesses.

The one reported instance of the cabinet members asserting their collective will was their rejection last month of Carter's proposal to open their meetings to press coverage. That policy still stands. My presence here this morning is in the nature of a dispensation granted by Jody Powell and the President on the grounds that I am writing a book. Since its publication is several months off, it is presumably less threatening to the confidentiality of these discussions than a daily newspaper story.

Shortly before the meeting opened, I am told, the President informed the cabinet that I would be present to gather material for my book. Then the door opened and Charles Kirbo walked in. "I didn't know you were writing a book, Charlie," Robert Lipshutz, the President's counsel, said, amid general laughter. This is not the way Charles Kirbo is accustomed to being received when he enters a room. He stares at me bleakly when I come in and nod hello to him.

The session starts at 8:00 A.M., an hour earlier than usual, because the President must leave at 10:00 to welcome Prime Minister Fukuda of Japan. To add focus to the cabinet sessions the President has just begun the practice of asking one member each week to make a special report on some aspect of his or her responsibilities. The inaugural presentation is to be given today by Harold Brown, the Secretary of Defense, and it has to do with the domestic impact of the Pentagon budget.

Brown sets some colored charts on an easel off to the side of the table, near the fireplace, and ticks off some imposing statistics about the huge agency he runs: one million civilian employees, two million in uniform, a combined total which is more than half the number of all federal employees. The total budget for fiscal 1978 is $110 billion; the annual payroll, $40 billion. Some $7 billion yearly goes for military retirement pay; another $3 billion for civilians.

The President is struck by the retirement pay figures.

CARTER: That's tripled in the last ten years.
BROWN: Actually more than that. Since the early 1960s it's gone up from $1 billion . . .

CARTER: By the year 2000 it [the defense budget] will all be in retirement and no defense. [*laughter*]

BROWN: That's true. But it's not true just in defense, Mr. President. It's happening everywhere in the government and in the private economy, too.

Griffin Bell, the Attorney General, asks about the number of "double dippers," civilian employees who are on military pensions, a practice Carter wants to eliminate. Brown has no figures available, and turns back to his charts. The next one shows military and civilian personnel in each state. It reflects a heavy concentration in the South, including Georgia, a point that does not escape the President.

BROWN: This chart is too busy and complicated to go through in any detail . . .

CARTER: I see nothing wrong with that chart. [*laughter*]

BROWN: It gets better.

Indeed it does. The next chart, which breaks down defense salaries on a per capita basis, even more dramatically illustrates the clustering of military installations in the South, as well as the Southwest and California.

BROWN: Why is this? There are lots of objective reasons. Navy ports have to be on the ocean. Flight training is done best in places where there is clear weather. There have been in the past economic advantages to mild climates. In the Southeast the advent of air-conditioning has made more comfortable areas that weren't always considered to be comfortable. One also hears quite a lot about these bases being monuments to past political leadership, both in Congress and also the executive branch. And it's true that you can point to past Armed Service Committee chairmen and notice that in their states there's quite a lot. I think there's something to that

and also something to the so-called objective factors which I mentioned.

CARTER: These things work in reverse, too. For instance, in
Georgia, when [Senator] Sam Nunn was elected,
his only desire was to get on the Armed Services
Committee. And because the state does have a considerable commitment to national defense, he campaigned on the proposition that if he was elected,
he would get on the committee. That would
scarcely happen in many other states.

Brown displays more charts which show that the geographi-
cal pattern for defense contracting is much the same as for military installations.

BROWN: There was an article recently in the *National Journal* to the effect that the whole country's economy
is shifting into the Sun Belt. . . . The thesis some
people have is that federal activity, and particularly
defense contracting, is driving this. I don't think
that thesis is proven. I think the same factors are
operating on defense contracting that are operating
on the private economy as a whole. To the degree
that people are able to move, they tend to move into
these areas.

When Harold Brown graduated from the Bronx High School
of Science at the age of fifteen, it must have been apparent that he
was a young man with a future. Now he is forty-nine, still com-
paratively young, and he has a record of impressive achievements.
He made his early reputation as a physicist, receiving his doctorate
when he was only twenty-three, and became a protégé of Edward
Teller, the developer of the H-bomb. At thirty-three, he was
named Pentagon director of research by Robert McNamara; and
he moved from that post to secretary of the Air Force and then
to president of Caltech.

He was known as an efficient administrator at Caltech who had little contact with students. But his manner seems cut out for the classroom. He is glib and easy as he glances at his note pad to answer questions from the President and from his cabinet colleagues. McNamara, Brown's former boss, used a pointer when he delivered his celebrated TV lectures on Vietnam. Brown has no pointer, is much more relaxed than McNamara, and seems affable and eager to please.

> BROWN: The natural question is why we don't use this social engine for social and political change. I think that we do as an adjunct. But there is a real danger if one tries to direct it entirely to nondefense and non-foreign policy purposes.

He recalls two Pentagon social experiments in the 1960s. One was "project 100,000," an attempt to improve the intellectual skills of 100,000 low-IQ servicemen which, Brown says, had "mixed results." The other, more successful he says, was an effort to break down racial segregation in housing patterns near military bases. Now the Pentagon is focusing its social conscience on setting up base deposit centers for bottles and cans and introducing solar heating in new housing. This helps to illustrate the difference between America in the 1960s and in the 1970s. Lyndon Johnson's administration sought social change through education and desegregated housing. Under Jimmy Carter the focus is on making the most our of soda cans and sunshine.

The Secretary moves on to another chart and another problem, the sticky business of shutting down military installations to hold down defense spending.

> BROWN: We've closed since 1969 about 20 percent of all the bases, but there are quite a few more that remain to be closed. Estimates are that we've reduced annual expenditures by about $4.5 billion by these base closures and that there's another billion to be

squeezed out of it. . . . What we're doing now is
going ahead with a number of additional proposals
for forty bases in twenty-six states and Puerto Rico
with a potential annual savings of $300 million. We
find that it takes an unusual and, from the Defense
Department's standpoint, unnecessary length of
time to get it done. One of the problems is that
Congress now requires notification . . . and that
gives them a fair amount of time to overturn or try
to overturn the decision.

CARTER: We're pretty well hanging tough on these projects.
I have, as you probably know, a constant stream of
telephone calls and delegates coming to see me.
What I tell them in each instance is that we're not
going to keep bases open if they are not necessary
in my opinion for national security. And if we do
close down a base, we'll ask HEW and HUD and
everyone else to work within existing federal programs to minimize the adverse economic impact.
. . . The other night in Massachusetts I was asked
about Fort Devens. I went through the whole campaign without ever promising to keep a base open.
I told them that about Fort Devens and they accepted it pretty well.

Seated across from Carter is Walter Mondale, who, on the
day before the election last November, during a visit to Philadelphia, promised to keep that city's Frankford Arsenal open, despite
the announced decision to the contrary by the Ford administration. The President is well aware of this. On his radio call-in show
he remarked: "If there's one question that the Vice President has
talked to me more about than any other thing since I've been in
the White House it has been the Frankford Arsenal." But the
army announced last week that it was going ahead with plans to
shut the arsenal down. I wonder how Mondale feels, being re-

minded of the President's greater restraint during the campaign. He makes no comment.

Brown is finished with his presentation, and the regular part of the meeting commences. Every Friday each cabinet member submits a written resume of departmental activities. These are in the President's stack of papers. Now each has a chance to elaborate, briefly. Carter starts on his left and goes around the table clockwise. Juanita Kreps, the Secretary of Commerce, is first.

> KREPS: Mr. President, I made a deal with Harold Brown in which I agreed that he would have my time today in return for which everything I propose from now on he'll support. [*laughter*]
>
> BROWN: That's fair enough. But what am I going to give you for your next favor? [*more laughter*]

A good deal of this sort of banter and exaggerated laughter goes on through the meeting. Much of it seems strained, an effort by sophisticated people to break the tension of a situation in which many of them feel ill at ease. Carter, who sits most of the time with his arms folded across his chest, seems more comfortable than most people in the room. He joins in the laughter, but he is not willing to let his Commerce Secretary off so easily.

> CARTER: How's the porpoise question? I wouldn't feel at home in a cabinet meeting without discussing porpoises.
>
> KREPS: I have resolved not to discuss porpoises. I think it's coming along without any immediate problem.

But Attorney General Bell interjects his view of the porpoise controversy, which has pitted commercial tuna fishermen against environmentalists, with the Commerce Department in the middle. Bell has just returned from San Diego where, he says, the tuna fishermen are incensed about government regulations, which the Commerce Department interprets and enforces, forbidding the fishermen from using a netting procedure that kills porpoises.

KREPS: Well, if you want to go into this, Mr. President.
. . . I've been teased so much by my colleagues about
being concerned with this question . . .

She explains that the courts have permitted the tuna fleets to
resume fishing, provided they do not kill more than a certain
number of porpoises. Meanwhile, the tuna industry is battling to
ease the government restrictions still more. Carter indicates he is
opposed to any further weakening of the law protecting the porpoises.

Through all this Juanita Kreps, petite and pleasant-looking,
maintains the same cool dignity that characterized her behavior
last December when the President presented her to the nation as
his Commerce Secretary designate. She suggested he could have
done more to recruit women for his cabinet. Mrs. Kreps realizes
that Commerce is not considered among the most important posts
in this cabinet. She can put up with being teased by the President
and her colleagues. But she will not accept being patronized or
ignored.

Brock Adams, the Secretary of Transportation, presents a
flurry of reminders and notices. A memorandum on Atlantic airline route negotiations with England is on its way to the President's desk. Oil pollution regulations have been presented on Capitol Hill. A congressional request for the administration's position
on marine cargo preference rules has been bucked to the Commerce Department. Hearings on automobile airbags and fuel
economy have been scheduled.

Thomas Bertram Lance tilts back in his chair, literally and
figuratively a heavyweight. He is a tall, hulking man who runs the
Office of Management and Budget, a critical post in any administration. Its importance in the Carter administration is increased
because Lance is one of two men at the table—Bell is the other
—who has a special relationship with the President, one preceding
his campaign for the White House. Lance was Carter's transportation commissioner in Georgia and also his banker. When Carter

was elected President his peanut business had loans from Lance's bank totaling $4.7 million. Lance was also considered for Secretary of the Treasury, but he preferred OMB because, his friends believed, that would place him closer to the power center in the White House. If he has anything important to say to the President, he does not need to say it here, in front of twenty or so strangers.

Lance brings up a story on the front page of this morning's *Washington Post* about an inventor who has had trouble getting the government interested in a new type of carburetor which reputedly could save "millions of gallons of gasoline."

LANCE: That attitude is obviously a holdover from the previous administration.

CARTER: I'm not sure how good the guy's carburetor is. . . . He might just be the reporter's brother-in-law.

LANCE: I wasn't trying to make a judgment on the carburetor. I was just concerned that he ought to have access to somebody in government.

Next to Lance, tapping his teeth with his glasses, white-haired and stern, is James Schlesinger. Among all those present, only he has been in this room during the preceding eight years. Schlesinger served two Republican Presidents as head of the Budget Bureau, Director of the CIA, and Secretary of Defense. He is here now as an adviser, without an agency to boss. But when and if the President's energy reorganization bill wins congressional approval, he will become the first chief of the new Department of Energy. He is concerned with pushing that legislation through, while he oversees development of the President's energy program. Carter, his eyes on Schlesinger, listens intently.

SCHLESINGER: We continue to reach out for ideas. We have now received 13,000 letters with substantive suggestions. There is a great range of quality. . . . On reorganization . . . large numbers of people want the opportunity to testify. . . .

But in addition, it has occurred to some that wouldn't it be a good idea to wait until they can see the whites of our eyes on substantive issues. . . . Our attitude on that is damn the torpedoes, full speed ahead. . . . We'd like to maximize impact by not having too much public revelation and leakage. On the other hand, we are inclined to touch all the bases in advance. . . . D day is approximately four weeks from today.

CARTER: I think our posture now is to listen and not talk. We're giving people a chance to have input . . .

Next is Patricia Roberts Harris, the HUD Secretary, one of two blacks with cabinet-level jobs. She wears large, dark-framed glasses and looks younger than her age, which is fifty-two. Her appointment was criticized by some blacks, who complained that she was too close to the white establishment, and by some whites and blacks who felt she had too little experience in housing and urban development. She sounds determined to overwhelm her detractors by sheer energy as she pours out a torrent of words, beginning with an outline of her strategy for dealing with a troubled HUD project.

HARRIS: We're going to be alerting members of the congressional delegation from the state about our plans. In case the mayor or members of the city council should call the White House, we're very much on top of it and we've been cooperating with the city council. . . . As soon as we have briefed the congressional delegation we will work with the developers. Our problem is that the city council wants to participate in a discussion with the developers and we're convinced that would be a disaster, but it's politically sensitive and I wanted you to be aware of it.

... Another politically sensitive area is an audit that
we are doing with a selected group of area offices.
. . . I don't want it to be taken as political in any
way. But you ought to be aware of it.

She has yet another potential crisis with a federally chartered
financing agency whose private directors have been criticized for
not providing enough help to low- and middle-income home buyers.

HARRIS: I had suggested it would have been wise when they
made up their management slate if they chose a
more representative group of directors. . . . The
response to that was that the present directors, all
white males, renominated themselves and sent ru-
mors to the financial community that we were about
to conduct a political purge. . . . I think we have
taken care of that. However, Senator Cranston is
very interested in trying to persuade me that I
should recommend to you that you should dismiss
some of the directors. I think that would be a disaster. . . . We think we have a procedure for dealing
with the problem. . . . We will recommend a series
of people to be appointed by you. You have a right
to appoint five out of the fifteen people on the board.
We just want you to know that we're on top of it.
The industry may complain to you that we're interfering. We're not. Senator Cranston may complain
to you that we're not doing enough to interfere and
I disagree with him on that. It is politically sensitive.

Seemingly unperturbed by the storm signals from Mrs. Harris, Carter turns to his Secretary of Agriculture, Bob Bergland,
who mentions that he must soon appear before the Senate and
House Agriculture committees, both of whose chairmen are press-

ing him hard for the administration's position on farm price supports and food stamps. The cabinet's Economic Policy Group—consisting of Lance, Kreps, Blumenthal, Schultze, Harris, and Marshall—has made recommendations on farm prices, but "two or three unresolved questions" can be settled only by Carter. Bergland must testify tomorrow.

> BERGLAND: One area that I haven't even sought your opinion, that's in peanuts, Mr. President. We have a peanut section that I hate to say will not be universally applauded by all the producers in Georgia. We are proposing to reduce the price of peanuts for those that flow into export market so that they can join the economic mainstream. And will reduce costs to the Treasury. We think it's on the right track.

The President accepts this news without comment and with apparent equanimity. He asks Bergland about the progress of a subcabinet nomination on the Hill, and tells Frank Moore, his chief congressional liaison, to make a few phone calls to help. He inquires about the drought in the West and mentions that Governor Brown of California will be spending the night at the White House. Cabinet members with special problems in California might want to talk to him, Carter suggests. As for the farm price decision, he will let Bergland know by noon tomorrow, which, as he acknowledges, will be the last minute.

On Bergland's left, chewing on a cigar, sits Secretary of the Treasury Michael Blumenthal. Forceful and aggressive though he is, Blumenthal must reckon with the two other economic policymakers, Bert Lance and Charles Schultze, chairman of the Council of Economic Advisers. Each has an advantage over him—Lance, his friendship with Carter, Schultze, his years of Washington experience. But in time Blumenthal will make his influence felt. He reports on the current congressional attitude toward the President's economic stimulus proposal.

BLUMENTHAL: All the indications we have is that the tax
rebate is not going to pass easily. We are
trying to count noses, but it's going to be
very, very close. The Economic Policy
Group will take up three issues, all of which
will find their way to you. One is shoe imports . . . the second is the minimum wage,
and the third is unemployment compensa-
tion.

CARTER: There are two problems with the tax rebate.
One is that [Russell] Long feels and [Lloyd]
Bentsen feels that we don't need a stimulus
anymore. The latest indicators show an encouraging trend. But my own information
doesn't confirm that the need for a stimulus
is past. The other is the use of the word
"rebate." People don't understand . . . that
it means a substantial reduction in their 1976
return. I tried to show that in my fireside
chat by pointing out that it means a 30 percent reduction for a $10,000 family.

We come to Walter Mondale at the center of the table, opposite the President. He is preparing a new long-term schedule for
the President, an updated version of the agenda he submitted after
Christmas, and asks for suggestions from the cabinet by the end
of the week. The President wonders if Mondale does not have
something else he wants to bring up.

MONDALE: Well, since Shogan's here, I'll wait until next
week.

I am not sure, at first, whether Mondale is joking or not. He
has a better sense of humor than most Vice Presidents. Later, one
of his aides tells me that Mondale did have a point in mind, but
decided to postpone talking about it.

The President next calls on his Attorney General, who has already made his presence felt by questions and comments. In his folksy way Griffin Bell has carved out a role for himself as sort of a cabinet interlocutor. Some of his remarks are amusing, some are on point, and some are neither. Now, in his heavy Southern accent, he describes his recent visit to a modern federal detention center in San Diego where he interviewed sixteen illegal aliens.

BELL: They're in a luxurious jail called the Tijuana Hilton. It's only one story right in the middle of town. It costs $21 a day to maintain a person there, about like the Holiday Inn charges. They have their own doctors and dentists there. I found three aliens there from El Salvador. . . . They've been there forty days. We furnished them with lawyers and everything. They've got all the rights of American citizens once they get in. Seems to me it would have been better to send them back. . . . The unemployment rate in Tijuana is 75 percent. . . . The thing that struck me was that they were all able to get jobs. . . . One man had been making $7 an hour. Not a single one of them had a Social Security card. Not a single one had any kind of credentials that would get them a job. If we could stop employers from giving them jobs, that would be the easiest way to cut off one end of it. . . . I found out a number of them are on welfare in California and there's some indication that California is going to sue us to get their money back that they're spending. We probably ought to sue them for putting them on welfare.

Bell mentions the possibility of borrowing army helicopters to patrol the Mexican border to check the influx of immigrants. But given the way the government functions, he says, this is an example of an idea "that will work in practice, but will never work in theory"—a remark that gets a big laugh.

The Attorney General has no clearer idea of how to solve the illegal alien problem in California than anyone else. His remarks strike me as superficial and somewhat lacking in sensitivity. But the President gives him good marks for trying.

CARTER: I think that's a good report and indicates how important it is to get outside of Washington and talk to people who are directly involved in the more controversial questions. If we could just partially resolve the illegal alien or undocumented workers' question, that in itself would be enormously helpful.

The Secretary of the Treasury, mindful that the President must soon decide whether to impose a high protective tariff on imported shoes, sees a chance to put in a good word for free trade.

BLUMENTHAL: What comes to my mind, Mr. President, is how closely everything is related to everything else. This is related to our economic relations with Mexico. You're going to be deciding the shoe question and Mexico is one of our most important producers of shoes. We have a long, open border. . . . If on one side of the border is a country that's very poor and has a lot of excess labor, it's going to press across. . . . You can't stop it. We have to work with them on the economic problems in order to reduce the pressure.

F. Ray Marshall, the Secretary of Labor, is a Southerner and a Baptist. But he is not having an easy time in Jimmy Carter's cabinet. The President is Marshall's boss, but the labor movement is his constituency, and Carter has not gone out of his way to please organized labor. Early on, Marshall publicly said he was disappointed in the President's economic stimulus package, which the AFL-CIO also complained about. Then he backed off after a concerned phone call from Stuart Eizenstat at the White House.

Now Blumenthal and others are pressing Carter to rule against tariffs on imported shoes, which, as Marshall knows, labor leaders strongly believe are needed to protect jobs. Marshall is no ideologue. But he has an intellectual commitment to many of the goals of organized labor. "He's a trooper; he'll go up there and fight," the AFL-CIO's Lane Kirkland told me about Marshall. This makes him something of an outsider among the President's economic policy-makers.

Today he asks his colleagues for their cooperation with the Occupational Safety and Health Administration. This agency was established six years ago to protect workers from suffering disease or injury on their jobs. Since then it has come to be regarded by infuriated businessmen as the apotheosis of bureaucratic red tape and intrusion. Part of the Department of Labor, it is therefore Marshall's responsibility and his burden.

MARSHALL: If another department wants to take over this agency, I'll gladly export it to you. But until that happens I'm trying to make it as effective as I can. I think it's a good law. It has, I think, some unwise procedures and regulations. I found out that the Labor Department is responsible for enforcing safety and health regulations for federal employees in all the agencies. I was shocked to also find out that OSHA itself couldn't make a very good record when it inspected itself, to see if they could meet their own rules and regulations. So there's something wrong somewhere. . . . The fundamental problem is safety and health, and frequently a lot of these regulations get in the way of protecting safety and health. . . . We need to induce more self-regulation. . . . I asked our lawyer to bring me the law. He said, "You couldn't understand it if you read it."

BELL: When they first brought that law into court, I made the statement that no congressman who had read that law would have voted for it.

MONDALE: Three of us did [Mondale, Bergland, and Adams]. [*laughter*]

BELL: There's no other law that's ever been passed where a government agent can go into somebody's plant and fine them right on the spot. They can say: "You owe a $50 fine, I fine you right here, $50." You have ten days to appeal. If you don't appeal in ten days you've got to pay that fine. There's no other law ever been passed in this nation like that.

CARTER: There is no sense of cooperation with the OSHA program anywhere in the United States. I bet you can't find a single employer in the United States who would say, "This is a good law and I'd like to work with you and put it into effect." The sense of animosity, hatred, and vituperation probably hurts the federal government's image as much as anything I know. And what should be done about it I don't know. . . . If I were an employer, I'd like for all my employees to be safe. But with the mention of OSHA there kind of rises something up in me to resist it and not cooperate with it.

When the OSHA discussion concludes, the President mentions that he has neglected to approve the minutes of last week's meeting. He tells Jack Watson, the cabinet secretary, that he will do so after this meeting is over. That reminds Zbigniew Brzezinski, the President's National Security Adviser, that the minutes contain classified material, mostly from his own remarks, and leads to the first open disagreement of the meeting.

BRZEZINSKI: While Jack is in the room . . . I think the minutes ought to be stamped "secret."

CALIFANO: Let me just dissent from that. I'd take the classified material out of them. I think the President is in a position where if this kind of discussion is classified as secret it will just be counterproductive to everything else he is trying to do in opening up the government.

CARTER: [to Watson] Jack, on national security matters, go over it with Zbig before you put it in there.

The entire exchange is over in less than a minute. No great substantive matter is involved, but the incident says something about both Brzezinski and Califano. It is understandable that the National Security Adviser should be concerned about security. But, in this case, his concern seems excessive. No verbatim transcript is kept of the meeting; the minutes are a summary based on notes taken by one of Watson's deputies, Jane Frank. Direct quotations are not often used. Distribution is limited to those who participate in the meetings. If the minutes were stamped secret, as Brzezinski suggested, they would have to be locked in a safe, and cabinet members could not show them to aides unless they were cleared to read secret material. All in all, it would be a large nuisance.

Everyone knows this, but Califano was the only one to challenge Brzezinski. A man has to have confidence in himself to challenge the National Security Adviser on a question of security, even so minor a matter as the cabinet minutes. Califano can afford to be confident; he earned $500,000 practicing law last year. He has irritated White House aides by taking to heart the President's mandate to his cabinet members to run their own shops, selecting HEW staff before checking with the White House. But Califano has been around the White House before, under Lyndon Johnson, and knows how to operate there. He deftly picked the ground for his little disagreement with Brzezinski. Califano's criticism was that Brzezinski's suggestion was against the best interests of the President.

Brzezinski knows how the White House game is played, too. He realized that Califano held the high ground, and let the matter drop.

Now he makes his report. Noting that he and Secretary of State Vance are to meet later in the day with the Nigerian External Affairs minister to discuss the fighting in Zaire, he launches into a broad analysis of political trends in Africa. His Polish accent is as heavy as Griffin Bell's drawl. Nevertheless, he is probably the most articulate person in the room.

> BRZEZINSKI: We are dealing here with two essentially contradictory but very fundamental processes. The first is the fragmentation of the post–Colonial structure in Africa, a process that is likely to accelerate and become more intense, and one which, if we become engaged in it, will be very difficult to extricate ourselves from. . . . The second process . . . however, is that we are also seeing in Africa the increasing self-assertedness of left-wing, radical, Soviet-backed regimes. And it is in our interest that the more pro-Western regimes do not collapse under such pressure. . . . These two processes are in conflict. And if we can get the African community and the more important African countries like Nigeria to take a more active role in resolving issues, it clearly would be to our advantage.

Brzezinski concludes by mentioning that his staff worked closely with the State Department in coordinating Carter's speech to the United Nations, and has also been developing SALT proposals for Vance's forthcoming mission to Moscow.

The President goes back to Brzezinski's initial reference to Zaire.

> CARTER: We are continually assessing the situation in Zaire with CIA reports and with reports from our European friends who are quite interested in Zaire. ... The stability of the region is very important. We get about 65 to 70 percent of our cobalt from Zaire. ... I don't think we have any indication as yet that there are Cubans in Zaire, do we, Stan?

This question is directed to an unprepossessing figure who has been sitting quietly at the side of the room with White House staff members. Holding his clipboard, with his eyes darting around the room, he looks like someone who has been called in to provide an estimate on painting and repairs. Actually, he is Stansfield Turner, the President's former Annapolis classmate who now heads the Central Intelligence Agency.

> TURNER: No, sir. We don't even have indications that are convincing that there are Angolans in Zaire.

The President mentions the absence of Andrew Young, who is serving this month as President of the UN Security Council, and of Secretary Vance, who is busy preparing for Fukuda's visit and his own "extremely important" trip later in the week to the Soviet Union to discuss new SALT proposals.

> CARTER: It's an extremely complicated subject. I've been doing a great deal of study recently. ... And at the NSC meeting this week we'll be talking about various aspects of our SALT proposals. It's like being in the dark because we don't know what the Soviet response will be. ... When Cy goes to Moscow later on this week he will be thoroughly conversant with the combined opinion of our leaders on what we can and cannot accept. And I think to the extent that we can arrive at a reduction that is to our

mutual advantage, ours and the Soviet Union's
. . . I believe we can sell it to the American people
and to the Senate for ratification.

Charles Schultze, chairman of the Council of Economic Advisers, a craggy-featured veteran of the Johnson administration, changes the subject and offers the President some potentially helpful news. A University of Michigan opinion survey on consumer attitudes shows that 78 percent of those polled favor the President's proposal for a tax rebate, which, as Blumenthal said earlier, is in trouble in the Senate.

SCHULTZE: More importantly, among those who expected the passage of a tax reduction, 53 percent expect good times in the next twelve months, compared with only 35 percent expecting good times among those who didn't think it would pass.

CARTER: It might be a good thing to let the Congress know about this. . . . [to Rex Granum] It also would be a good thing to cover in the press briefing.

SCHULTZE: You'd also be happy to know, Mr. President, that people's opinions of government economic policy have reached the highest level since they took the survey. But there are two important qualifications. Number one, they only started taking this question in 1972, so you're doing better than Nixon and Ford. [*laughter*] Second, what this meant was that those who thought government was doing a good job of economic policy rose from 9 percent to 22 percent. [*more laughter*] To be fair, the big bulk of the improvement is in doing fair, not good.

When Schultze finishes, it is 9:30 and thirty minutes are left. Califano begins his report, but Carter interrupts. He is troubled by a story last Friday in *The New York Times* about an administration plan to require federal agencies to estimate the inflationary impact of new regulations before they are imposed.

CARTER: There's been a good bit of adverse reaction. ... And this is something in which I believe very deeply. It doesn't mean that when you have a safety regulation and you assess that it's going to cost $1 billion, it doesn't mean that you're necessarily going to go back and repeal the safety regulation. I think it's good to know, the best we can estimate . . . that some of the decisions we make do have a high trade-off.

The President now refers to the dams and other water projects he has sought to eliminate, amid a storm of protest from the Congress.

CARTER: I think one of the water resources projects cost $1.5 million per farmer who was benefited. And there were only sixty farmers that would have benefited. That's something taxpayers don't know about. So we're going to proceed with this with an unabated degree of enthusiasm. It struck me as one of the moves we can make in our government to control inflation. I think that's going to be an increasing matter for concern. And the trend of popular support for strong employment policies neglecting inflation has very rapidly changed to deep concern about inflation and less concern about unemployment.

Finally, Califano gets his turn. He reminds his colleagues that he has submitted to them for comment proposed regulations, which he expects to be controversial, for implementing a federal law prohibiting discrimination against the handicapped. The law affects colleges and universities, other recipients of federal funds, and federal agencies. Pat Harris asks if Califano intends to include alcoholics and drug addicts in the handicapped category, an idea she opposes.

CALIFANO: The vast majority of people interested in this area on the Hill want these two groups included. . . . I don't think they should be either.

CARTER: I'd like to add my support to what Pat said.

CALIFANO: That's all the support I need. [*laughter*]*

CARTER: I wish you'd talk to Jerry Brown about that. They've got an organized system in California to take advantage of some of your other regulations, not just on handicapped, by drug addicts and alcoholics. They just make a profession out of being a drug addict or an alcoholic so they can get welfare payments. . . . Whatever starts in California unfortunately has an inclination to spread. . . . The drug culture and the alcoholics find they can abuse the welfare laws just like other people abuse the bankruptcy laws and the food stamp laws.

BELL: Have you given any thought to putting left-handed people under the rules? . . . I'm left-handed and it seems to me I ought to get some kind of extra benefit out of that.

Cecil Andrus, the Secretary of the Interior, is a man in the midst of a controversy he did not start—the furore over the President's decision to eliminate water projects from the federal budget. He loyally tells Carter of a recent report in a professional journal which shows that dams built by the Army Corps of Engineers yield relatively low economic benefits. And he says he is going to Jamestown, N.D., to attend a hearing on one of the controversial projects.

*Despite these sentiments, in their final form the regulations did include alcoholics and drug addicts. The Justice Department concluded that Congress intended them to be covered when it passed the law.

CARTER: I really believe the more the public knows about these projects, the better the chances are that I'll win. I know it's difficult. Some people say I won't win. . . . We may not get them all eliminated this year. . . . But I think we're on the side of the angels on this.

The rotation has come all the way around to the last man, Undersecretary of State Warren Christopher, a Californian who served in the Justice Department as Ramsey Clark's deputy attorney general, and who today is pinch-hitting for Vance. He talks briefly about the mission to Hanoi led by Leonard Woodcock to get information about Americans still listed as missing in action in the Vietnam War.

CHRISTOPHER: It's been a good trip. On a scale of 100 it's running about 90. . . . The MIA information from North Vietnam is as good as we can get, I think. We didn't expect more than we really got from Laos.

Only a few minutes are left, and the President has the last word. He leans forward, arms on the table, glancing around the room as he talks. His voice is low, his tone matter-of-fact.

CARTER: I don't want anybody to forget that in the first week in May we will have an economic summit conference in London. And this will be a broad-ranging discussion. Most of the leaders who have come here to see me so far will be there and I think out of that conference—I have an aversion to conferences usually—will come a set of policies and general priorities that will guide our government for the next three or four years. So if you have something that you think is important, economically, or to a lesser degree politically, do an analysis as briefly as you can and submit it to Dr. Brzezinski.

Then he turns to his strategy for energy policy.

CARTER: If we put forward one part of the energy program, it's going to be shot down because on its face it would be unfair to some major groups in our country. . . . We need to put the whole thing together in a comprehensive ball of wax that I could understand and so could the American people. So that they could say, well, I lost something on this issue but I gained my compensatory advantage here.

Once again he asks for suggestions, on domestic as well as foreign affairs.

CARTER: I don't want any of you to sit back and wait to be invited. . . . It's very helpful if you make recommendations on your own initiative. . . . In general I believe that so far we've done a good job. Most of the relationship with Congress has been favorable and pleasant so far. The disharmonies have been highly publicized. If you watch the progress of the legislation through the Congress . . . you'll see that we've made good progress. . . . I'm very much assured because of my own feelings about many of these things to have all of you around the same table every week helping me judge what we ought to do. It prevents a lot of problems. Also, when I've made a mistake, it's helped me get out of it relatively unscathed.

At 10:04 he calls the meeting to a close and returns to the Oval Office to prepare for Fukuda.

Any judgment of the meeting has to be qualified by the fact that I was there. Mondale had something he did not want to discuss in front of an outsider, and it is possible others felt the same way. But as the meeting went on, most people seemed to have forgotten my presence. Afterward, staffers who attend these sessions regularly tell me this meeting was much like the others.

At any rate, I have formed some impressions.

Of the President: His businessman's ethic was much in evidence. His most spontaneous remarks dealt with the flaws of OSHA, welfare cheating by drug addicts and alcoholics, and the need to curb inflation. I was struck by his intense interest in foreign affairs. The subjects he spoke about with greatest enthusiasm were the new SALT proposals and the London summit conference.

Of the cabinet: They are a mixed bunch, without much in common by way of background or belief to tie them together. They are still sorting out their relationships to the President and to each other. They can be grouped roughly into three categories: the special friends of the President, Lance, and Bell; the veterans of previous administrations; and the others, who are new to the top echelons of government. Sparring and maneuvering for position are bound to continue until the ultimate pecking order is established.

Of the meeting: Hamilton Jordan says cabinet meetings are a waste of time, and it is easy to understand why. Communication is limited. Most of the discussion dwells on routine matters that could be covered in memos. Carter prods his advisers for suggestions, which is all to the good. But his attention is selective. He picks up on the items in their reports that coincide with his own personal interests. He does not so much talk to them as at them, and he does not draw them out well. The size of the meeting—sixteen people sitting around the table with the President—makes decision-making almost impossible. But Carter could do more to encourage debate on such important matters as farm policy, minimum wages, and shoe imports, all of which were passed over quickly. Jordan has suggested that the President change the format, which some aides compare to show-and-tell.

Under the present arrangement, as one staff member says, the meetings mainly serve the purpose of allowing the President and his advisers to size each other up. This is a step toward communication. But Carter has to go further. Otherwise he will have trouble controlling the government, and the bureaucracies will meander off in their own directions. Just as the President needs the support of the public, he must have his own ministers behind him.

8

Bold Ventures

The Spokes of the Wheel

Stuart Eizenstat, the President's chief staff adviser on domestic policy, was worried about money. He quickly offered his senior staff colleagues rough long-range estimates of the cost of some of President Carter's major promises—$10 billion for tax reform, $15 billion or so for welfare, maybe another $10 billion for national health insurance. All this, he pointed out, had to be reconciled with one of the most fundamental of all Carter's campaign pledges, to balance the budget by 1980. "That," Eizenstat said, "is going to be absolutely hard to do."

Slouched down in his chair, coatless and tieless, Hamilton Jordan suggested ingenuously: "Why don't you just talk him out of that, Stu?"

Eizenstat winced, and most of the others laughed.

"Talking the President out of balancing the budget is not one of the things I'd like to try to do," Jody Powell said.

This was the morning of March 29, and a dozen or so White House aides had gathered for their daily 8:00 A.M. meeting in the Roosevelt Room, across the hall in the West Wing from the Oval Office and the Cabinet Room. Less formal than the Cabinet Room, the Roosevelt Room is still handsomely appointed—red carpeting, a gleaming conference table, Queen Anne and Chippendale furniture. In FDR's day, it contained an aquarium and was called the Fish Room. Nixon renamed it, in honor of Theodore Roosevelt, who had the West or Executive Wing added to the White House. A portrait of TR on horseback, in his Rough Rider regalia, still hangs on one wall. But next to it Carter has added a picture of the Democratic Roosevelt.

The staff meeting, which Jordan invited me to attend, had begun with a discussion of strategy for pushing the President's forthcoming energy program through Congress. But it soon turned into a rambling survey of the entire legislative landscape. Difficulties of one sort or another seemed to loom on almost every front. More immediate than Eizenstat's budget worries—"Yesterday I told the President that I wasn't an economist but I was beginning to get nervous about our ability to do all these things," he said—was the status of the President's $50 tax rebate proposal. This part of his economic stimulus package was in trouble in the Senate, and midway through the meeting Hamilton Jordan and Frank Moore, the President's chief legislative aide, left the room to discuss that problem directly with Carter.

The meeting broke up at 9:00. But two hours later the discussion resumed along similar lines when many of the same people gathered in Vice President Mondale's office, overlooking West Executive Avenue. This meeting had been called to begin laying out a revised Presidential agenda for the next few months, a second edition of the schedule that Mondale had submitted during the transition. Mondale, who presided over the session in his shirtsleeves, was relaxed and good-humored, munching licorice from a large bowl on his desk and occasionally lobbing pieces across the room to other members of the group. But again the conversation had a tone of anxiety and uneasiness.

Jack Watson thought that the President seemed to be moving too hurriedly in setting legislative goals. "We have to avoid arbitrary deadlines," he said. "We need to do what we can to slow the President down."

Jordan chuckled. "I think we ought to divvy it up," he said. "Jack, you slow him down, and Stu will get him to forget about balancing the budget."

Jordan's wisecracks did not alter the underlying mood of the meeting. The fact was that after ten weeks in power, many of Carter's own staff, Jordan included, were worried about the pace and direction of the Carter Presidency. In a sense, the President's aides were borrowing trouble. At the moment, to all outward appearances, the Chief Executive was in excellent political condition. His soaring ratings in public and private polls signaled that he was succeeding in accomplishing what he had set out to do right after the election—broadening and strengthening the base of personal support which had carried him to his narrow victory in November. His brief three-state excursion outside the White House in mid-March had demonstrated that his skills as a campaigner had been sharpened and enhanced by his tenure in the White House. Top-heavy Democratic majorities controlled both houses of Congress, and, they had an obvious stake in the success of the new Democratic President. The President's characteristic self-confidence seemed to be at a peak. In meetings with his cabinet he sounded as optimistic about the prospects for his program as he did on more public occasions, dismissing reports of discord between him and the legislators as exaggerations by the press.

His enthusiasm and energy were, to an extent, typical of the behavior of new Presidents. "I think there is a basic fundamental tendency for every guy when he arrives in the Oval Office, and sits down behind that desk, to try to do too much personally," Richard Cheney, who had headed Gerald Ford's White House staff, told me. "And I think they all find, I know that President Ford did, that sooner or later there are some things they cannot do."

But Carter had as yet given no indication he was prepared to accept any significant limitations. To keep up with the mountain of paperwork that piled on his desk he had taken a speed-reading course, and dragooned his staff and family into joining the class. At the start his schedulers had blocked out a fifty-five-hour work week. But after the first six weeks his appointments secretary, Tim Kraft, had reported to the senior staff that the President was actually putting in an average of seventy-one hours a week. "It's the kind of breakneck schedule I don't think he should try to put himself through for the next four years," Kraft said. At times the President did look weary. Yet he continued to rise each morning at 6:30, eager for new challenges to meet and surmount.

This headlong pace was a good part of the reason for the consternation among his staff. Many felt that the boss was moving too fast, in too many directions, spreading himself and the resources of his Presidency too thin. In the Congress, they feared he was creating potential bottlenecks, as well as potential enemies. "We're talking about ten or so major things," complained Frank Moore, "and eight of them have to go through Ways and Means." His attempt to cut off federal spending for a flock of dams had stirred congressional hostility which threatened to spread into other areas. His reorganization plan to lump together all existing federal agencies dealing with energy into one new Department of Energy had stalled on the Hill, because, Jordan argued, the President had committed himself to unveiling a massive program to meet the energy crisis by April 20. "If we hadn't put an arbitrary deadline on the energy policy proposals, Congress would have moved on the reorganization plan by June," Jordan told his colleagues in the Roosevelt Room. "Now they're going to hold it hostage until they get through with the policy legislation."

Jody Powell disagreed. "If we'd waited until late June on energy policy, we'd never had gotten it through this session."

Meanwhile, the President was forging ahead, setting new deadlines for himself and his administration. D day for tax reform was the end of September, a pledge he had publicly underlined during his visit to Clinton. "I give you my promise," he had told the crowd in Town Hall, "that next September 30, after long, detailed, and laborious analysis of the horribly complicated income tax laws, we will come out with a simpler system, so that 75 or 80 or 85 percent of all of you in this country can fill out your own income tax returns without anybody helping you, so that you will feel that you are not getting cheated and you will feel that everybody is paying their fair share."

Then there was the matter of reforming the welfare system, which was just as "horribly complicated" as the tax code. "On May 1," Carter had assured the people of Clinton and the rest of the country, "Joe Califano, a tough, knowledgeable administrator, who is trying to bring order out of chaos in the Department of Health, Education and Welfare, will come forward . . . and propose to the Congress a comprehensive revision of the entire welfare system."

"It's not Califano or anyone in the cabinet who is generating these ideas," Jack Watson remarked during the March 29 staff discussions. "Every one of these ideas comes in the form of a directive from the President."

"He just pulls these deadlines out of the air," someone else grumbled.

Jody Powell contended that the explanation was not always that simple.

"It's also a process of these cabinet people learning to watch what they say in front of the boss." Powell reconstructed the sequence of events which began during the transition conference on St. Simons. "Jimmy says, 'Joe, when can you have me a welfare reform, early on?' And everybody is in the first flush of pride and determination so Joe says: 'Well, the first of May.'

"Joe hasn't really looked at it that much, and besides, he's thinking that in a month or two he'll sit down and take another look at this thing. Before he knows it, the President has stood up in front of God and everybody and said: 'We're going to have this welfare thing on May 1.' "

But some deadlines did seem to be entirely the President's own making. Asked at his March 24 press conference about what his administration was doing to develop a comprehensive program to deal with inflation, the President announced: "We are now preparing a very strong anti-inflation package which will be delivered to the Congress and to the American people within the next couple of weeks." Caught off-guard, his staff was now scrambling to keep the President's promise. A proposal was in the works, but the consensus among the group in Mondale's office was that it would take longer than "a couple of weeks" to complete.

Jordan joked about the flap over the inflation plan. "I thought it was a well-planned move and I just hadn't been informed," he said. But he was troubled, too. "If we delay too long, *The Wall Street Journal* will say that the President can't get his economic program together."

Powell thought that press reaction would not be a serious problem. The inflation proposals would be ready only a week later than Carter had indicated, he said. "And I can handle that."

In the Roosevelt Room meeting, Jordan tried to ease the concern of his colleagues about the President's hyperactivity. "You're all talking about the down side, but there's an up side, too. It's like running in all those primaries. You get enough stuff up there and you'll slip some controversial stuff by them, simply because we've got so much stuff on the Hill."

But Jordan himself was not satisfied to rely on such a hit-and-miss approach. Something more had to be done. The conversation in Mondale's office had turned hopefully to a new type of schedule, which would better organize the President's time and efforts. But that begged the question of whether the President would really follow his schedule. Both meetings boiled down to the delicate problem of belling the cat, and this was something that Jordan had already tried to do on his own.

The week prior the March 29 staff meetings, Jordan had cleared his calendar of appointments, cut off his phone calls, and closed himself in his office for two days, mulling over the early weeks of the Carter administration. The result was a critique of

Carter's decision-making that ran on for nearly twenty pages, stamped "personal and confidential," and addressed to the President. Jordan began by reminding Carter that the Presidency is a "powerful and awesome" institution. This attitude had its advantages; it discouraged those around the President from burdening him with trivial matters. But it also created problems. The President's advisers tended to put more stress "on anticipating what you want," than on providing the frank and sometimes critical analysis which, Jordan presumed, the President really sought from his advisers.

Jordan's central point was that the President was making too many decisions in "a political vacuum," and at the last moment. The net result was to antagonize groups that had been important to Carter's candidacy and at the same time to make it more difficult to carry out his own program. Jordan cited as evidence the President's recent decisions on farm price supports and the minimum wage, both made, Jordan contended, with little opportunity for debate among his advisers. Agriculture Secretary Bergland had recommended to Carter the lowest increase in price supports he thought would be politically acceptable on the Hill. Then Carter submitted lower recommendations, which were far below what congressmen from the farm belt were demanding. On the minimum wage, the President had asked for an increase of only 20 cents, from $2.30 to $2.50, compared to the $3 standard the AFL-CIO wanted. George Meany called the Carter proposal "shameful" and "a bitter disappointment to everyone who looked to this administration for economic justice for the poor."

Jordan did not dispute the technical merits of the President's proposals on either issue. His point was that both were unrealistic politically and would be ignored in the subsequent bargaining on Capitol Hill. Carter's economic goals would not be furthered, he contended, if his economic proposals were "not even a factor" in the legislative process. The President, Jordan urged, needed to spend more of his own time weighing the political implications of his domestic decisions instead of relying mainly on written memorandums and the recommendations of the Economic Policy Group.

By contrast, in weighing foreign policy decisions, Jordan pointed out, Carter consulted personally and frequently with Vance and Brzezinski. Foreign policy was taking up more of Carter's time than domestic matters, Jordan complained, and he tactfully urged the President not to spend less time on international affairs but to devote more to issues at home. Jordan also made a case for tighter coordination of cabinet members, whose uncontrolled pursuit of their own goals could lead, he warned, to formation of opposition coalitions in Congress. "We have to pace ourselves," bearing in mind the problems and makeup of Congress and the need to build public support, he said.

Carter reacted to this critique "the way I knew he would," Jordan told me. "He was pissed off" and quarreled with many of its points. But he swallowed enough of his pride to praise it as "a good memo" and to urge Jordan to produce more of the same.

One element which the memo did not mention, but which seemed to contribute to the problems it outlined, was the way the President had decided that his staff should be organized. Soon after the election Jody Powell announced that the President-elect felt "it was not in his interest to have a single chief of staff" in the White House. Instead, Carter's White House senior staff would operate on what Powell called "the spokes of the wheel" approach, similar to the pattern Carter had used as governor. Each staffer would have relatively easy access to the President, Powell explained. "It also increases competition and helps to keep us on our toes."

Neither the phrase nor the idea was original. A similar scheme had been tried by Ford's top aide, Donald Rumsfeld, after Watergate blackened the image of a White House staff hierarchy. The result was reflected in a plaque presented to Rumsfeld's replacement and former deputy, Richard Cheney, by some of his colleagues shortly before Cheney left the White House. Mounted on the plaque was an old bicycle wheel, with most of its spokes broken and twisted. Underneath was this inscription: "A piece of rare artistry, conceived and developed by Donald Rumsfeld and modified by Richard Cheney."

"The basic message in that is that the spokes of the wheel concept is a nice concept, but it won't work," Cheney told me. "Sooner or later somebody has got to get everybody together and say: 'Goddamit, this is screwed up.' Somebody has to make certain that before the President signs off on a decision that he has all the relevant information and that he has taken into consideration economic, political, domestic, foreign, and all the other factors involved. Somebody has to police the process."

On occasion Ford's decision-making did not follow the established procedures, and the results, Cheney contended, pointed up the need for a staff chief. He recalled Ford's ill-fated promise to sign the controversial Common Situs Picketing bill, a pledge extracted from him by his Labor Secretary, John Dunlop, while he was meeting with the President on another matter. "Nobody else was aware of it," Cheney said. "Nobody else had a chance to say maybe we shouldn't do common situs picketing. The result was that ultimately we ended up in a situation where we had to back off our earlier position."

When Cheney moved out of the White House, he left behind him the busted bike wheel as a welcoming gift to Hamilton Jordan, who took over his office but not his job. Actually, Cheney's job no longer existed on the Carter White House's table of organization. His varied responsibilities had been divided up among four or five people. The critical job of monitoring the flow of paper in and out of the Oval Office had been turned over to Rick Hutcheson, a twenty-five-year-old assistant to Jordan during the campaign, who was named staff secretary. Jordan's major responsibilities are politics and appointments. Though he is the most influential of Carter's aides, with the possible exception of Powell, he has no authority to coordinate the rest of the staff or to assure that the President is fully informed before he acts and speaks. Moreover, during the first ten weeks of Carter's Presidency, Jordan's deep involvement in overseeing Presidential appointments distracted him and diminished his influence on other matters.

With no effective monitor of sufficient influence built into the system, Carter relied on his own instincts and judgments and the opinions of those he personally respected. In this environment, the controlling majority of the Economic Policy Group gained what Jordan contended in his memo was a "disproportionate influence" on the President. The six-member EPG was dominated by what one Jordan aide called a "secretariat"—consisting of Lance, Blumenthal, and Schultze—who usually took a more conservative view of economic issues than the position of organized labor, represented by Ray Marshall. But, as Jordan pointed out, organized labor had done a great deal more to elect Carter than the business interests whose views were reflected by the dominant members of the EPG. He might have added that labor was in a position, through its considerable influence in Congress, to help or hurt Carter's legislative program.

Not only did Carter seem to be giving short shrift to labor's substantive positions, he was also overlooking the amenities and courtesies important to its leaders. At a senior staff meeting I attended early in March, Landon Butler, the White House liaison with the AFL-CIO, had urged his colleagues to keep labor leaders informed of administration decisions. "They're basically a political organization that serves a constituency," he said. "If they're taken by surprise on an issue, and it embarrasses them, it's just like embarrassing a congressmen. They're very good about agreeing to disagree, but they don't like to be taken by surprise."

Yet the AFL-CIO had been taken by surprise on the $2.50 minimum wage. "It's sort of like a slap in the face," Lane Kirkland, secretary-treasurer of the federation and heir apparent to George Meany, told me. "Before the President finally made up his mind, we would have appreciated the opportunity of a little warning, rather than to have to read about it in the paper."

I asked Kirkland if Carter's conduct had differed from the practice of previous administrations.

"It's not different from other unfriendly administrations," he said.

During the first ten weeks of his Presidency, as during the transition, Carter's image as a methodical and sensitive political planner had been overshadowed by other aspects of his personality. Restless and aggressive, he plunged ahead, sometimes heedless of the timetables established by his advisers and even of his own political interests. This style of governing, which was unsettling for his staff in the White House, was even more disturbing for the members of his own party on Capitol Hill.

Congress: Hanging Tough

"He'll get along well with Congress, better than anybody else you've seen lately," Charles Kirbo, Carter's friend and counselor predicted last fall, when we talked about the prospects for the Carter Presidency. Kirbo had made the rounds on Capitol Hill that summer when he served as chief talent scout during Carter's search for a Vice-Presidential running mate. "When I was dealing with Congress, I thought the harvest looked very fruitful. I think a lot of them are frustrated up there. They're looking forward to change. They know it couldn't be as bad as the situation they've got now."

To smooth the way for the new President's legislative program, Kirbo and other Carter advisers were counting heavily on the sense of relief the Democratic congressional majorities would feel, after eight long Republican years, on being able to deal at last with a President of their own party. Furthering the spirit of cooperation, the President's men anticipated, would be the realization by the congressional Democrats—291 in the House, 61 in the Senate—that to a considerable degree their political fortunes would be linked with the President. "Congress is determined to make the President look good," Frank Moore told his colleagues at the March 29 meeting. Carter's success, or lack of it, would reflect on the record of the leaders of the House and Senate, Moore reasoned. It would also greatly influence the reelection chances of all the Democratic members in the 1978 and 1980 elections.

The President's first White House breakfast with the Democratic congressional leaders had been marked by expressions of harmony on both sides. "The people of this country want us to work together," Carter said soberly. "We've got to work together."

"No man, Mr. President, will ever have a stronger backing than you will have," Tip O'Neill replied. "The word 'confrontation' will not be in our lexicon."

Despite these professions of goodwill on both sides, certain circumstances were bound to complicate the relations between the thirty-ninth President and the Ninety-fifth Congress. Under the last two Republican Presidents, the White House had blockaded most of the social and economic legislation offered by the Democratic Congresses. "It's impossible to exaggerate how much legislative backlog there is on the Hill because of the Ford vetoes," Eizenstat told the staff meeting in Mondale's office. Actually, as Eizenstat later told me, the problem began under the Nixon administration. "For eight years, for God's sake, you've had essentially negative Presidents in the sense of not having strong legislative programs that a Democratic Congress could buy. And so they developed their own legislative packages. And now that they have a Democratic President they're gung-ho to go straight forward on it." The attitude on the Hill, as one Senate aide put it, was "By God, we'll get these things now." As a result, while Carter was still putting his own program together, he was being pressured to deal with congressional initiatives, such as farm price supports and the minimum wage, which threatened his priorities.

Institutional factors also created a potential for friction. "For eight years the Democratic party in Congress has been the Democratic party of the nation," Robert Healy, administrative assistant to Senator John Culver of Iowa said. "Its position has been one of reflex opposition. Most of us, on the staffs, have come up during the Nixon years when our style was to fire off a nasty letter to the President. Now suddenly the Democrats are forced to operate for the first time as the majority party of the government. And it takes a while to get used to."

"They've been running with the bit in their teeth over there for a long time," Frank Moore said of the Democrats on Capitol Hill. He pointed out to me that the total size of congressional staffs had climbed from about 5,000 when Lyndon Johnson was President to 15,000. "They're well-paid, dedicated professionals. A lot of initiatives come from there. A lot of these guys are good, they're smart, and they're tough. And they've got to have something to do."

Moreover, Carter entered the White House just as Congress was taking pride in its new self-assertiveness. The House had confronted Richard Nixon directly over Watergate, had rejected the doctrine of executive privilege, and was on the verge of impeaching him when he resigned. Reacting to the sweeping use of Presidential authority in Indochina by both Nixon and Johnson, Congress had brought an end to the nation's military adventure there. And it had passed legislation requiring congressional approval for any future long-term United States armed involvement overseas. It also established procedures to assure an unprecedented congressional authority and responsibility over the federal budget. In short, the past four years had raised Congress's consciousness and left it with a new attitude toward the Chief Executive, whatever party he happened to belong to. "There's a feeling here that things have changed," a veteran adviser to one member of the Democratic hierarchy said. "These guys realize what their role is, and can be, and they don't ever want to return to being a rubber stamp for the White House."

The message was delivered directly to the President by Tip O'Neill at one of the early leadership breakfasts in the White House. Over coffee and doughnuts, Carter mentioned that his newly appointed cabinet members were being forced to spend an inordinate amount of time away from their desks, appearing before congressional committees on various legislative proposals. The congressional demands on their time were making it difficult for them to deal with the President's own agenda. "Couldn't I just have them for, say, three days a week?" he asked good-naturedly.

But O'Neill, who not long before had pledged the President infinite cooperation, was adamant. Congress had its own requirements and they could not be altered. Looking the President straight in the eye, the Speaker of the House said firmly: "We are a coequal branch of government." Carter let the matter drop; a few minutes later he called the meeting to a halt and made an abrupt exit.

On an intellectual level Carter could understand the need to grant Congress recognition and respect. But his visceral feelings were conditioned by his own demanding and impatient temperament, and by his experience as governor when he had been embroiled in almost continuous combat with the legislature. One of Carter's public indictments of the Georgia legislature, for its failure to enact his proposals, had been so scathing that George Busbee, now governor of the state and then senate majority leader, took the floor on a point of personal privilege to respond. Frank Moore, then an aide to Carter, recalls: "I almost got thrown off the third floor of the capitol. God, there was hostility."

On Carter's part, at least, the hostility lingered on. During his Presidential campaign he toured a farm in Sioux Falls, S.D., and paused at a cattle pen to look over some heifers. As he stared balefully at the cattle, some impulse led me to ask if they reminded him of the Georgia legislature. "No," he said without smiling. "They're more intelligent."

Although Carter may hold the national legislature in higher regard, this has not always been apparent. The Congress and the new President got off to a rough start partly because of the general confusion in the Carter camp during the transition and for some time afterward. "We hadn't worked out our own internal staff and procedures," Frank Moore told me. "There was a great sense of frustration among the Democrats on the Hill. People wondered, how does it work, who do you need to know? Do we go through Kirbo or do we go through Moore? Does Jordan really have the President's ear, or maybe Mondale is the guy we ought to be talking to. They wanted the game plan."

There was none as yet. The major item of concern to Congress was the appointments the new administration was making. After eight years of GOP rule, the Democrats felt, as Moore said: "Let's get the Republicans out; let's get our own people in." But the new administration was sluggish in filling jobs. And its negligence in consulting congressmen and responding to congressional suggestions was the cause of persistent grumbling, private and public.

"The appointments seemed like big things because nothing else was happening," Moore said. "Also, they were testing us a little bit. You know, we were the new kids on the block. And you can't overlook the fact that both O'Neill and Byrd were new in their jobs and they had to represent their respective institutions."

As the man in charge of the White House's congressional relations, Moore naturally bore the brunt of the criticism, a situation he has learned to accept if not to like. "I'm on the front line. I take the heat. I'm the lightning rod," he said. "That's what I get paid for." A rumpled forty-one-year-old Georgian, Moore first linked up with Carter in the 1966 gubernatorial campaign, and has been a jack-of-all-political-trades for him since. He was handicapped at the start by a small staff, which was later expanded, and his own lack of experience, a flaw which at least in some respects he has overcome.

"Up on the Hill the most valuable commodity is information," he said. "If you get the information before somebody else, it makes you look more important than somebody else. For example, I just called Senator Byrd's people and offered them a chance to call the other senators and say: 'The President has just called me, and a treaty is on the way up.' Most of it is a matter of timing. If I made that call after it's been in the early edition of the *Washington Star,* it ain't no good to anybody."

While I visited Moore in his office in February, I heard him discuss arrangements over the phone for the next week's leadership breakfast in the cabinet room. "Mondale had breakfast with Byrd this morning," Moore reported to Tim Kraft, "and Byrd complained that we don't get a full breakfast at the leadership meeting. And O'Neill has complained about that, too. . . .

"I don't think the President is going to change on that, and I don't want to change. You can't serve a full breakfast in the cabinet room. And I don't want to have to go back over to the family quarters to eat.

"We're going to have Republicans this time. That will increase it by six. That means there won't be room in the cabinet room for everybody to sit at the table. That means we'll drop Dan Rostenkowski off at one end and Dan Inouye at the other end. I'll take care of that."

Moore's early weeks in the liaison slot convinced him that little things mean a lot on the Hill. "A lot of times you can get a guy's vote just by having done a lot of little things. And a lot of times they'll vote against you, just out of damn spite. Confrontations are going to come, and we're going to be in plenty of them. But I want them to come on big things, important, substantive matters. I don't want them to come on small, unnecessary, needless little things, like somebody's not returning a phone call."

Moore is seemingly tireless, eager to please, and shrewd. His backslapping manner serves him well with some congressmen. But he lacks the finesse and grasp of substantive issues that made Lawrence O'Brien and Bryce Harlow effective White House ambassadors to the Hill. His favorite tie, decorated with the White House phone number (202-456-1414), struck one ranking Senate staffer as "a bit tacky." In March he was invited to address a breakfast meeting of ranking staffers of the Senate standing committees, eager for details of the administration programs. But one member of the group complained that "he spent all his time saying that 'we're really good guys and we're shaping up and we're going to take care of things like U.S. Marshal's appointments, which is what your bosses are really interested in.' For us, it was almost demeaning. And for him, it was a lost opportunity."

Despite all his efforts, in the early weeks some congressmen found it easier to talk to the President himself than to his liaison. Representative Theodore Weiss, newly elected to fill Bella Abzug's old seat, tried to reach Moore to get his help in blocking an interstate highway project scheduled to run through his Manhattan district. After two days, he gave up and "in absolute frustration" asked his secretary to call Carter at the White House.

To his astonishment, a few minutes later, Carter was on the line. "I picked up the phone," Weiss recalled, "and I heard the female voice on the other end say, 'I think he's on now, sir,' and she was not talking to me. Obviously, the President had been holding on the damn telephone."

The President suggested that Weiss first meet with Transportation Secretary Adams and then invited him to the White House to discuss the problem. Carter heard Weiss out for about fifteen minutes, but told him that he was going to support Adams' decision to go ahead with the highway project.

"Mr. President, in all likelihood my constituents are going to be challenging this in the courts," Weiss said. "And in all likelihood I'm going to be part of that legal action."

"I know that's very likely," Carter replied. "I want you to do what is right for your district."

Weiss was of course disappointed in the decision. But he could not help being impressed by Carter's accessibility to a very junior member of the House.

"We've learned the members," the President proudly told a group of publishers and broadcasters who visited the White House in March, "their special interests and capabilities and sensitivities. And I think we've worked out now an increasingly good relationship with them."

But good congressional relations could not be sustained by an occasional personal contact in the face of significant disagreements. Apart from the institutional friction between the two branches of government, the President's own political inclinations inevitably brought him into confrontation with Capitol Hill. In Georgia, when legislators dragged their feet on his programs, Carter had appealed over their heads directly to their constituents. This tactic worked fairly well for him there, and his advisers saw no reason why it would not be just as effective on the federal level.

"You'll find him respectful of the traditions and protocol of Congress," Hamilton Jordan told me last fall. "And you'll find him, in a very personal way, trying to sell his programs to them. But the bottom line will be that the programs Jimmy will advocate will be programs supported by the American people." In a crunch, Jordan said, Carter would never fail to do what he often did in Georgia, "go directly to the people to force the legislative branch into line."

A few weeks after inauguration day, Charles Kirbo sounded the same theme in an interview with David Broder of the *Washington Post*. His friend the President, Kirbo said, is "a bold fellow and some of his ideas are controversial." Congressional opposition would be a "continuing problem" and Kirbo expected Carter to go directly to the people to overcome it. "He's going to have to do it that way in some instances. That's the only way he'll get his program passed."

This sort of talk, which had an ominous ring on Capitol Hill, was derived from Carter's conception of his Presidency and his constituency. The populist theme of his campaign—"I owe the special interests nothing, I owe the people everything"—was more than just rhetoric. Carter's rise to national power had been made possible by his ability to cut across traditional interest group lines and carve out his own constituency. As President, he clearly intended to strengthen that constituency, and this put him on a collision course with Congress. The members of Congress depended for votes, and for financial backing, on a whole range of interest groups—local, regional, and national—from the Manhattanites in Weiss's district, fighting highway construction to the AFL-CIO and the NAM, the NEA, and the AMA, B'nai Brith and the Holy Name Societies, and so on and so forth. Presidents had generally understood this principle and adjusted to it, trading concessions on one issue for votes on another.

But Carter was determined to be different. Nothing better illustrated this determination, and the divergence between him and Congress, than his decision to cut the water project funds from the federal budget. This action was not listed in the Mondale agenda for the first three months of Carter's Presidency. But its origins could readily be traced to the Carter campaign and to the transition. His pledges to curb construction of federal dams were listed in the environment section of his "promises" book. And even before he took office, his transition staff had earmarked for cancellation on either economic, environmental, or safety grounds sixty-one water projects previously approved by Congress. On February 18, three days before the deadline for making changes in Ford's 1978 budget, the President picked out eighteen of these projects and decided to cut off their federal funding, pending further review by a special Interior Department panel. That would save $268 million in fiscal 1978 alone, and about $5 billion in the long run. But the significance of his action went far beyond the dollar sums.

The federal water projects epitomize insider politics in Washington, the collaboration of Congress and the bureaucracy to their mutual benefit. The dams bring benefits for the congressmen's constituents, or some of them. And they help provide the federal dam building agencies, the Corps of Engineers and the Bureau of Reclamation, with a reason for existence and expansion. The governing principle has been, "you can have what you want in your district or your state if you go along with one of mine," said Stewart Udall, who learned to understand the system first as a congressman in the 1950s, then as Interior Secretary under Kennedy and Johnson. "And we're all getting a little piece of pork out of the national treasury."

The President's attack on the water projects, coming at the beginning of the second month of his Presidency, was his most tangible action yet to carry out the theme set forth in the Mondale agenda of "Carter as an outsider who intends to shake things up in Washington." During the first month in the White House, Carter had tried to make that point symbolically. Now he was dealing in $45 billion worth of substance.

"During the campaign I committed myself to a prudent and responsible use of the taxpayers' money and to protection of the environment," he declared in a letter to Congress on February 21. "Today I am announcing a major review of water resource projects which will further both commitments." To demonstrate his fairness and objectivity, the President next day added to the original eighteen projects on what came to be called the White House "hit list," the $248 million Richard Russell Dam back home in Georgia.

This did nothing to mollify the senators and congressmen who, in many cases, had labored for years, persuading and finagling to get their local projects approved and funded. None had been consulted in advance on the President's proposed cuts, and many had not even been notified before the public announcement was made. When they got the news, their indignation was nearly unanimous. "One of the most shocking things that has ever happened to North Dakota in my lifetime," said seventy-nine-year-old Republican Senator Milton Young. But Young was among the least of the White House concerns. Among other lawmakers wounded by the hit list were such influential Democrats as House majority leader Jim Wright, House Interior Committee chairman Morris Udall, Senate Armed Services Committee chairman John Stennis, and Senate Finance Committee chairman Russell Long.

The aggrieved senators were invited to the White House on March 11 for a private briefing, but this did nothing to heal the breach. Long rose and introduced himself with heavy sarcasm: "My name is Russell Long, and I am the chairman of the Senate Finance Committee." As one troubled White House aide later recalled, Long "shouted and screamed" his objections. Gary Hart of Colorado claimed that he had been misinformed by the ad-

ministration when he tried to learn the reasons for cancellation of
two projects in his state. "I was lied to," he said, "and I don't like
being lied to." But when the President appeared to speak to his
irate guests, he refused to give any ground. Whereupon the angry
senators returned to the Hill and handed him the first serious
legislative defeat of his new Presidency.

Led by Long's equally resentful colleague from Louisiana, J.
Bennett Johnston, the Senate tacked a water projects amendment
on to the public works job bill, part of Carter's economic stimulus
package and therefore presumably immune to veto. This stipu-
lated in effect that all the money originally set aside for the dams
should be spent despite the President's action. It was Johnston, an
ardent supporter of Carter's candidacy, who during the campaign
had coined the catch phrase that never failed to draw a roar of
approval from Southern audiences: "Wouldn't it be nice to have
a President without an accent again?" But in the rancor over the
dams, both regional and party loyalties were discarded. Johnston's
amendment swept through the Senate by a 65 to 24 vote; thirty-
five Democrats were among the ayes, while only twenty were
opposed.

Jody Powell summed up the White House attitude when
reporters asked him if the President regretted the Senate action.
"I would say that the greatest regret would be by the people who
have to pay for these projects." Two weeks later the President
agreed to reinstate three dams out of the original list of nineteen
in the budget. But at the same time he recommended that fourteen
additional dams be reviewed for safety, environmental impact,
and economic feasibility, bringing the total number in immediate
or future jeopardy to thirty. The word went out from Capitol Hill
that unless the President backed away from his opposition to the
water projects, injured congressmen might take their revenge on
his major legislative proposals. But the word went back from the
White House that the President, as he often liked to describe his
position on a range of controversies, was "hanging tough" on the
dams.

"The dams are nonnegotiable," Hamilton Jordan told me at the end of March.

Had the President anticipated the negative reaction from Congress? "Oh hell, yes," Jordan said. But he had made his move anyhow, "because he doesn't believe that most of them are economically or environmentally sound. It's just not negotiable."

Jordan likened the President's opposition to the dams at home, despite the reaction of Congress, to his commitment to human rights abroad, despite the reaction of the Soviet Union. "Just like the dams are not negotiable domestically, human rights are not negotiable either." But as events in Moscow would demonstrate, to the President's distress, the Russians had nonnegotiable issues of their own.

Retreat from Moscow

In January, during one of his brief preinaugural trips to Washington, the President-elect received in his office in Blair House a man with a cause. The advocate was Harold Willens, the liberal Los Angeles businessman who had given his blessing to Carter's candidacy at an early and critical stage. Willens had been an active opponent of the Vietnam War, organizing political and financial resources behind the protest movement. Now his zeal and energy were focused on a related goal, nuclear arms control. In his talk with Carter he lobbied for the nomination of the dovish Paul Warnke as Chief U.S. arms negotiator, a choice Carter indicated he was inclined to make. More fundamentally, Willens spoke to the President-elect of the threat of nuclear holocaust and the need for new curbs on the weapons of ultimate destruction.

"You know how deeply I share your feelings," Carter told Willens. "If I can get control, slow down, reverse the arms race, that would be the most important thing I could accomplish in four years."

Willens realized he was being told what he wanted to hear

and what he wanted to believe. But he was impressed by the force and tone of Carter's remarks. And the new President's public utterances seemed to bear out what he had told Willens privately. In his inaugural address, Carter pledged himself and his country "to move this year a step toward our ultimate goal—the elimination of all nuclear weapons from this earth." A few days later, in his first interview as President, Carter called for a new treaty, "eliminating the testing of all nuclear devices instantly and completely," and "a fairly rapid ratification" of the strategic arms accord reached by President Ford with the Soviets at Vladivostok in 1974.

Before his administration was even a week old, then, Carter had provided strong evidence of his eagerness to slow the arms race. But the way he chose to go about it was as unorthodox as his conduct of domestic affairs. Indeed, his efforts to break new ground and set new standards proved just as irritating to his Soviet antagonists as to his presumably friendlier adversaries in Congress.

Not that anyone thought there was a simple or easy way. The intertwined problems of Soviet-American relations and nuclear weaponry had dominated U.S. foreign policy and factionalized domestic politics for more than thirty years. The controversy over these issues had not only pitted Democrats against Republicans but also divided most of the Democratic party into opposing camps, which in simplest terms were known as hawks and doves. Intensified by the Vietnam War, the conflict between these groups had nearly torn the party apart and doomed its candidates for the White House in 1968 and 1972. When the fighting in Vietnam ended for Americans, the intraparty warfare also subsided. But each side remained deeply committed to its views and intensely suspicious of the other camp.

From the time Carter emerged as a serious candidate, hawks and doves scrutinized him carefully, trying to determine where his sympathies lay. In his second televised campaign debate with Ford, which focused on foreign affairs, Carter's hard line—"Our

country is not strong anymore; we're not respected anymore.
. . . We've become fearful to compete with the Soviet Union on
an equal basis"—drove Ford into making his foolish denial of
Russian dominance in Eastern Europe and gave the hawks reason
to believe that the Democratic nominee would turn out to be one
of their own.

Thus they were all the more pained and disappointed in
January when they surveyed the first twenty or so appointments
made by Vance and Carter to fill key posts in the State Department and on the National Security Council staff. George McGovern was quoted as telling friends that he considered most of those
selected to be "excellent, quite close to those I would have made
myself." Alan Baron, a former McGovern aide, cheerfully noted
in his newsletter, the *Baron Report,* that the appointments "reflect
the moderate/liberal wing of the Democratic foreign policy establishment."

On this point, the hawks unhappily agreed with the doves.
But the hardliners would not accept this state of affairs without
a battle. "In our party there are two sides to the foreign policy
debate, two sides that are both in the mainstream of the Democratic party," Ben Wattenberg, an ally and adviser to Senator
Jackson, the preeminent hawk, declared at a panel discussion of
administration policy sponsored by the Democratic Forum a few
days after Carter's inauguration. Carter's foreign policy appointees "are either professional neutralists or are to be found on one
side of the divide," Wattenberg contended. "The point of view
that is missing happens to be the dominant point of view in the
Congress and the country." Wattenberg noted that *The Wall
Street Journal* had complained that Carter "seemed to be giving
us George McGovern's State Department." Speaking for himself
and other "like-minded Democrats," Wattenberg said: "We are
absolutely determined that we do not want to stand by while our
party is wrongly and inaccurately described as a party of mush
and weakness."

Whether or not those who shared Wattenberg's views dominated Congress and the country, they certainly did exercise great influence and power. Among their leaders, besides Senator Jackson, whose personal prestige was reinforced by his chairmanship of the Senate Arms Control Subcommittee, were George Meany and Lane Kirkland of the AFL-CIO. Not to be overlooked was the Committee on the Present Danger, established right after the election to warn the country of the "Soviet drive for dominance based upon an unparalleled military buildup." Its influential membership included such former Johnson administration officials as Dean Rusk, Eugene Rostow, and Henry Fowler, and ex-chief of Naval Operations Elmo Zumwalt. These and other spokesmen were articulate, knowledgeable, and strong in their convictions. Most important of all, they could draw on a power base of widespread public suspicion of the Soviets, fostered by three decades of hot and cold war.

The hawks had demonstrated their strength in Congress even before Carter's inauguration when they helped lay the groundwork for the withdrawal of the Sorensen nomination for CIA director. Later on, in March, they mustered 40 votes in the Senate against the Warnke nomination, despite an intensive effort by the President's allies led by the Senate whip, Alan Cranston. Though Warnke was confirmed, the size of the opposition vote was an ominous sign for the doves—and for the President. Even before the final roll call, the intense debate served as a warning that the hawks and their allies had the potential power to prevent ratification of a new arms treaty with the Russians. And certainly they could make the President pay a heavy political price for any agreement they might regard as an excessive concession to the Soviets.

Understandably, then, the President concluded that before he could negotiate successfully with the Russians, he had to reckon with the hawks. It was this circumstance that made the issue of human rights all the more important and appealing to him. Not that the President necessarily planned beforehand to employ human rights as a tactical political weapon. In fact, the evidence suggests that though his personal interest in this cause was always strong, the emphasis he gave to it gained a momentum of its own during the early weeks of the Presidency.

The first salvo in the human rights offense had been fired before the Carter administration was a week old, not from the White House, but from the State Department. And evidently it took the President as much by surprise as it did the Russians. Commenting on reports of harassment of the leading Soviet dissenter Andri Sakharov, the State Department formally warned Moscow that any attempt to intimidate him would "conflict with accepted international standards of human rights." Soviet ambassador Dobrynin immediately called Secretary of State Vance to protest.

The President's initial reaction was cautious and discreet. The State Department spokesman had commented without his knowledge, and for that matter without the knowledge of his Secretary of State, Carter told reporters. "What he said was my attitude," and the President had no intention of reprimanding the anonymous spokesman. He thought it would be more advisable in the future if such comments came from him directly. The United States did not want to "aggravate" its differences with the Soviet Union. But, Carter said, "We are not going to back down."

Nothing in the public response to this episode discouraged the President from going further. Early in February he wrote his dramatic personal letter to Sakharov, made public later in the month, the first in a series of Presidential utterances on human rights, which provoked anger in Moscow and elsewhere stirred feelings ranging from enthusiastic approval to anxious uncertainty.

Human rights was clearly a cause Carter believed in. His advocacy was consistent with the moral tone of his candidacy and with the religious faith that influenced his personality. At the same time, it was well suited to his overall domestic political strategy for building a consensus behind his efforts to reach an arms agreement with the Russians. "He feels that human rights is something that can bind our people together," Hamilton Jordan told me. "And in terms of the SALT talks, it provides a good argument against those who later on might accuse him of being soft on the Commies, to be able to point back to an experience where he was really tough with the Soviet Union."

The timing of the human rights campaign, early in Carter's Presidency, added to its effectiveness, Jordan believed. "In politics, just as in personal relations, first impressions are very important. One of the first impressions that American people have of their new President is that he's been tough with the Soviets on human rights. So when he comes back to sell us a SALT treaty, and he says it's good and it's fair and it protects our country, there will be some evidence for believing him."

As he generally claimed about all his actions and utterances as President, Carter contended that his human rights drive was the result of a deliberative process. "It's been something that's been carefully considered, thought about at great length," he told columnists Jack Germond and Jules Witcover. But in the next breath, he acknowledged, "I think it's had unprecedented results, more than we had anticipated."

"It ended up being a larger opportunity than the President realized," Jordan said. "It might be the best example of how we had not fully appreciated the significance of public statements by the President on international affairs. Seeing the ramifications, he decided they were good, and his statements should be continued."

Not all the ramifications were favorable, however. Early on, the President realized that if his stand on human rights was to be convincing, it would have to be extended to other countries besides the Soviet Union. "Obviously there are deprivations of human rights even more brutal than the ones on which we've commented up till now," he told his second press conference on Wednesday, February 23. As an example, he singled out the recent murders in Uganda of political foes of that country's brutal ruler, Idi Amin. "The actions there have disgusted the entire civilized world," Carter declared.

Amin must have seemed a safe enough target to the President; certainly he had few defenders in this country. But the unpredictable dictator promptly gave the new President a lesson in the risks of rhetoric. Two days after Carter's comments, Amin abruptly summoned all the two hundred or so Americans remaining in the country to a meeting; meanwhile, none were to be allowed to leave the country. Then he cabled a diatribe to Carter, challenging him to put his own house in order before criticizing other nations on human rights. Caught in a potential crisis that it had unwittingly helped to create, the embarrassed Carter administration could do little but cautiously express concern and ask other African countries to send soothing messages to Amin. After twice postponing the ominous meeting, and draining all the notoriety he could from the episode, Amin relented and announced that the Americans were free to come and go as they pleased.

Another complication developed when the administration made its recommendations on military aid. Secretary Vance asked Congress to cut support to Argentina, Ethiopia, and Uruguay because of their violations of human rights, but urged continued aid to other countries, including South Korea, despite "great concern" about their human rights policies. "In each case we must balance a political concern for human rights against economic or security goals," Vance explained. That sort of pragmatism may have been considered necessary by the State Department and the Pentagon. But it undercut Carter's claim that his support of dissenters in the Soviet Union was based on unswerving principle.

The Russians had their own interests to protect. Carter's pronouncements served to aggravate their concern over agitation for human rights within their own borders and about a surge of dissent in Poland, Czechoslovakia, and East Germany. Brezhnev struck back in a major speech on March 21, only six days before Vance was due in Moscow to begin SALT negotiations. "Washington's claims to teach others how to live cannot be accepted by any sovereign state, not to mention the fact that neither the situation in the United States itself, nor U.S. actions and policies in the world gave justification to such claims. I will repeat again: We will not tolerate interference in our internal affairs by anyone and under any pretext." Brezhnev warned that "normal development of relations on such a basis is, of course, unthinkable." As for the Vance visit, Brezhnev's skepticism was evident. "We will see what he will bring with him."

Carter professed to be undismayed by Brezhnev's harsh language. In a press conference on the eve of Vance's departure, he declared: "We go in good faith with high hopes to Moscow." Brezhnev understood that human rights and arms control were separate issues, the President claimed. "I have nothing that I have heard directly or indirectly from Mr. Brezhnev that would indicate that he is not very eager to see substantial progress made in arms limitations."

Then the President outlined for the press, the Russians, and the rest of the world the offer Vance would make to the Russians. The main proposal would scrap the ceilings on strategic nuclear weapons, which had been agreed to at Vladivostok, and substitute instead what the President called "substantial" reductions in existing weapons. As an alternative, the United States would be willing to ratify the Vladivostok agreements, but postpone any limits on the Soviet backfire bomber and on the U.S. cruise missile, a low-flying, pilotless drone, more accurate and harder to detect than other missiles. This missile was regarded by the Soviets as having major potential to alter the weapons balance against them. And in effect the President was telling the Russians that the United States would agree to limits on the cruise only if the Russians were willing to make substantial cuts in their existing weapons stockpiles.

On its face, this position seemed designed to ward off criticism from the hawks. In fact, Senator Jackson later disclosed that Carter's proposals closely paralleled recommendations he had submitted to the White House. But the Soviet attitude was a different matter. Brezhnev had made clear weeks before the Vance mission that the Russians wanted to hold firm to the Vladivostok accord, and wanted the cruise missile covered by its limits. Now Carter was pushing negotiations into an area well beyond the Vladivostok understanding, amid great public fanfare and in an atmosphere embittered by the human rights issue.

The sessions opened in Moscow on March 28 with a stern warning from Brezhnev to Vance on human rights. Unless the United States accepted the principle of "noninterference in internal affairs," the Soviet leader said, efforts to improve relations between the two countries would be impossible. Brezhnev did not even appear at a later session that day, when Vance presented Carter's proposals for deep cuts in nuclear weaponry. Two days later the talks collapsed, with each side rejecting the other's proposals. In an angry epilogue, Soviet foreign minister Andrei Gromyko held an extraordinary press conference, calling the U.S. approach a "cheap and shady maneuver" and an attempt to renege on the Vladivostok agreement. Vance hurried back home, and on the way some of his aides confided to reporters their feeling that the United States had misplayed its hand on SALT by pushing the Soviets too hard and too publicly, and ignoring the signs of resentment from the Russians.

Back in Washington the President sought to put the best face on the situation. "I can't certify to you," he told the press, that the Soviet irritation over human rights had not contributed to the failure in Moscow. But, he said, "We have no evidence that this was the case." At any rate, the President said: "I will not modify my human rights statements." He was "not discouraged at all" by the breakdown of the talks. His own explanation was that his proposal was "so substantive and such a radical departure . . . that the Soviets needed more time to consider it."

Guesses on future Soviet intentions are hazardous to make. But it seems likely that any change in their position would require some alteration at least in the tactics of the Carter administration. In his first confrontation with the Soviets, the President appeared to have been more concerned with domestic politics than with the realities of nuclear bargaining. Mindful of the potential opposition to an arms agreement, he sought to defuse it by advocating vigorous adherence to human rights and drastic changes in weapons limits. The Russians, disturbed and threatened on both fronts, and uncomfortable in the spotlight of publicity to which Carter had exposed them, reacted accordingly. Even Senator Jackson, who supported Carter's basic position, questioned his methods. "Frankly, I don't think I would have gone public on this," he said.

A few days before Vance left for Moscow, I asked Hamilton Jordan about the impact of the President's handling of human rights and other foreign policy issues. "I think it's good politics," he said. "The people who are upset are people who would prefer international relations conducted in a traditional way. This is a break with tradition. His international style of doing business is as different as his domestic style."

Being different appealed to the public, even if it irritated Congress and the Kremlin. Carter's style, at home and abroad, earned him widespread popularity. But his determination to break with the past had yet to be matched by a consistent pattern for dealing with the future.

9

The Guns of April

———————— ⭐ ————————

"Since the beginning of Franklin Roosevelt's term, the first one hundred days of an administration have been closely watched as a sign of what can be expected over the course of the entire administration," Stuart Eizenstat wrote late in April as Jimmy Carter's own first hundred days in the White House were drawing to an end. In a memo addressed to the President, but intended also to be discreetly leaked to the press, Eizenstat listed the "major initiatives" and "significant achievements" of Carter's early Presidency. He included nearly everything the President had done, or tried to do, from his economic and energy proposals to his commutation of Watergate burglar G. Gordon Liddy's sentence to his cutback in the use of White House limousines.

"As you know," Eizenstat wrote, "we have consciously tried *not* to emphasize the administration's first one hundred days out of a desire to avoid seeking hurried changes when more deliberate ones are needed." No one had expected Carter to match what

Roosevelt had accomplished in 1933, when the nation seemed on the brink of economic collapse. But the image of Presidential deliberativeness Eizenstat sought to depict hardly conformed to reality. Carter's hectic pace, which had unsettled his aides in March, accelerated in April. The last month of his hundred days culminated in a jumble of programs and deadlines, forced marches and sudden retreats, which blurred the thrust of his Presidency.

More clearly than it foretold the future, Carter's record illuminated some of the contradictions that define his personality and his politics. His devotion to methodical planning clashed with his impatience for action, his liberal commitments with his inherent conservatism, his belief in the limitations of government with his eagerness to use the powers of his office. And all these conflicts helped to shape the turbulent events of April.

The first major battleground was the rugged and uncertain terrain of the economy. Reducing unemployment and warding off inflation would have been a difficult enough task for the President in any case. But Carter made it harder for himself by assaulting Congress's cherished water projects and forging ahead on energy proposals whose full impact on inflation and economic growth no one could precisely ascertain in advance.

In January he had submitted to Congress his program for economic recovery, amounting to $31 billion spread out equally over two years. The centerpiece for the first year was the $50 tax rebate proposal, which the President estimated would channel about $11 billion in purchasing power to consumers. The rebate was never widely popular. Liberals questioned whether it was substantial enough to make much difference, and conservatives would have preferred a permanent tax cut as a rein on government spending. The rebate's main attraction was speed. If Congress moved quickly, the President said, checks could be mailed to taxpayers in the spring. "It is simply impossible for public works and public service employment programs to get money into the economic stream that quickly," he contended. In 1975 President Ford had submitted an economic recovery program, including a rebate, to the Ninety-fourth Congress, which completed action before the end of March. Carter certainly had reason to hope that this Democratic Congress would move on his program as rapidly as the Ninety-fourth had dealt with the proposals of his Republican predecessor.

The House did act expeditiously, though not enthusiastically. It approved the rebate on March 8, by a vote of 219 to 194. But as the rebate wound its tortuous way through the Senate, the sluggish economy was showing signs of revival. Unemployment, which had stood at 8 percent in November, was on the decline, dropping to 7.3 percent in March. Meanwhile, the price index was going in the opposite direction, intensifying concern about inflation. Doubts about the need for the rebate increased, and so did fears that it might contribute to inflation.

In the midst of this economic debate the President created another obstacle for the rebate by moving against the dams. Five of the thirty water projects he sought to eliminate were located in the home state of Louisiana's Russell Long, Senate Finance Committee chairman. Long, whose vigorous support was vital to the passage of any tax measure, now publicly spoke of the rebate with studied detachment. In mid-March he remarked archly that delay in action on the plan would give the President time for "thoughtful reconsideration" of the targeted projects. Senator Byrd, the majority leader, was more direct in expressing the attitude of the Senate Democrats. Chatting with reporters on April 2, Byrd observed that Carter's crusade against the dams was hurting efforts to muster a majority behind the rebate. Both the House and the Senate seemed ready to override the President on most of the dams he sought to eliminate, anyhow, and Byrd remarked: "I would hope that as it becomes more clear that the water projects are going to be funded, the situation in regard to votes for the tax rebate will improve." The hint was broad enough to be understood in the White House: backing off the water projects would avoid a losing confrontation in the Congress and gain some political capital to help the rebates.

But the President was in no mood to bargain. "I'm not much of a trader," he declared on April 7. "That is one of my political defects for which I have been criticized a great deal. But I am not inclined at all to trade a water project that's not needed, or my approval of it, in return for a vote on the tax refund which I think is needed for every member of Congress and the people that look to that Congress member for leadership." Later that very day the President sent to every Democratic member of the Senate, and to Republicans not yet committed on the issue, an eight-point letter vigorously arguing the case for the rebate. He contended that the economy still needed stimulating, warned that without the rebate consumer spending might weaken, and maintained that the rebate would "not add significantly" to inflationary pressures.

The President gave every indication of a man determined to fight for a cause he believed in. He had persuaded the AFL-CIO to throw its considerable influence on Capitol Hill behind the $50 refund plan. Though the labor leaders considered the rebate to be a paltry measure, they felt the economy would be damaged if taxpayers, once having been led to expect the $50, were denied it. Cabinet officials chimed in. "Our economy needs stimulus now, as well as late this year and next year," Labor Secretary Marshall declared in a speech in Detroit on April 12. "I worry about the economic outlook for the next year if we don't prevail." Next day, speaking to the National Press Club in Washington, Treasury Secretary Blumenthal pointed out that in the first five months of the fiscal year the federal government had somehow spent about $10 billion less than it had expected to. "It is doubtful that all of the shortfall will be made up," he said. "Therefore, from that point of view, the rebate does assume added significance."

But Blumenthal chose his words carefully. For even as he appeared to give the rebate his support in public, he had joined in an intense attack on the proposal within the councils of the administration. In the forefront of the opposition was the formidable figure of Bert Lance, who had had misgivings about the rebate from the beginning. Now Lance pointed to a range of improving economic statistics to argue that the economy no longer needed such a boost. Moreover, he contended that by supporting the rebate Carter was hurting his chances of winning the confidence of the business and financial community which, correctly or not, believed the rebate to be inflationary. Lance had gotten an earful of Wall Street's suspicions about the Carter administration at a meeting in New York late in March with officials of many of the nation's most powerful lending institutions. According to Eliot Janeway, the economic consultant who hosted the meeting, the financiers were impressed with Lance, "both with his sense and his influence." But Janeway himself doubted that either Lance or Carter could do much to overcome Wall Street's instinctive mistrust of a Democratic administration.

Still, Lance was determined to try. Dropping the rebate, he believed, would at least be taken as a sign of good faith. By April 13 he had raised enough doubts about the proposal so that the President called him and his other top advisers together to hash the matter out. Lance and Blumenthal hammered away at the concern of the business community about inflation and at the evidence that the economy was gaining strength. Mondale spoke out forcefully for the rebate, which he contended the economy still needed. Besides, the Vice President argued, the nation had been governed for eight years by Republican Presidents who catered to the hopes and fears of the business community, and the end result had been the worst recession since the 1930s. The Carter administration had no reason to expect that its gestures in that direction would have any better effect.

But Mondale had little support. Charles Schultze, the originator of the rebate idea, recalled that in December he had felt 95 percent certain that the rebate was necessary. Now, in mid-April, he said his certitude on that point had declined to 65 percent, or less. Hamilton Jordan, the President's top political operative, believed the administration could get the rebate through the Senate. And, Jordan told the President, if he should drop the plan now, he would likely face "some short-term political problems." But the issues that Lance had drawn were economic, not political, and Jordan could not argue economics with Lance. In the long run, he said, the best economics would probably be the best politics.

When the session ended, and Blumenthal went off to address the Press Club, Carter pondered the issue in his own mind. The minuses seemed to greatly outweigh the pluses. Time was running against the rebate. It had been conceived as a "quick fix." But by mid-April that possibility had faded and more days of struggle in the Senate lay ahead. Chances of winning were risky at best, and success would require an all-out effort by the White House. The President would be under pressure to give up ground on the water projects. Moreover, the battle over the rebate would be a distraction at a time when Carter wanted all the resources of the White House and the attention of the public and Congress focused on his energy proposal. Businessmen were bound to be uneasy about the effect of the energy taxes; it might help ease their anxiety to dispense with the rebate first.

Carter made his decision that night and announced it the next day. Signs of improvement in the economy had persuaded him that the rebate was no longer needed, he said. Political considerations were involved, but "I did not back off because I feared a political defeat." His decision, he claimed, had the support of the Democratic congressional leadership.

But that attitude was not unanimous on the Hill. Among the prominent dissenters was Senator Edmund Muskie, chairman of the Senate Budget Committee, who called Carter's action "a breach of his promise to the people." Said Muskie: "He did not consult with us adequately, gave us no warning, and retreated from a program that was a month in the making." Also resentful was Representative Al Ullman, chairman of the House Ways and Means Committee, who had led the battle for the rebate in the House. "I and a lot of other members put our necks on the line," Ullman complained. Carter's decision "was a little less than fair to those of us who supported the rebate against our better judgment and worked hard to get it passed."

On the day he disclosed his abandonment of the rebate, the President looked ahead to the next week's announcements of his anti-inflation program and his energy proposals, both of which presumably would call for public sacrifice. "It's not an easy thing to do," Carter told reporters. "But I think that in general I can live through the next week. And I believe that when the period is over, I hope and I do believe that the American people will think it's not only fair and equitable but also necessary."

But the public's attitude toward his proposals would depend not just on their merits, which inevitably would be argued at length, but on his own credibility. By dropping the tax rebate plan he won some points for flexibility in the face of changing circumstances. But the abruptness of his 180-degree turn raised questions in Congress and the country about his sureness of purpose and sense of direction. These same questions were subsequently underlined by his presentation of his programs to combat inflation and conserve energy.

His March 24 announcement that a "very strong" anti-inflation package would be ready within two weeks had caught his own aides off-guard, as was clear at the March 29 senior staff meeting I attended. The problem was not only time, but how to assemble meaningful proposals in view of the fact that Carter, during the transition period, had vowed not to ask Congress even for standby authority to impose wage and price controls. But the President wanted something in hand, and he wanted it fast. On April 8, on the CBS "Evening News," Eric Sevareid commented: "There are no signs the government will take any direct action on inflation. Its anti-inflation program about to be announced apparently will call only for talk—and polite talk, not even government jawboning —between industry, labor, and government—and on a now-and-then basis."

Rosalynn Carter watched Sevareid that night and was disturbed enough to repeat his remarks to her husband. His patience shortened, the President prodded his advisers harder.

Finally on April 15, about one week after Carter's self-imposed deadline, the program was unveiled. But the basic cause for disappointment, to anyone who had taken the President's earlier words at face value, was not the delay but the failure to present concrete new proposals. By and large the program lived up to Sevareid's suspicions. The President renewed his promise to balance the budget and pledged meanwhile "to discipline the growth of government spending." He called for voluntary cooperation in the exercise of self-restraint by business and labor, and announced that George Meany and General Electric president Reginald E. Jones had agreed to coordinate this collaboration. The most specific request he made of Congress was to renew the Council on Wage and Price Stability for two more years. "There are no magic solutions in the battle against inflation," the President said. "It can be won only by hard, day-to-day, unglamorous, and often politically unpopular efforts."

Corporate executives surveyed by *The Wall Street Journal* heartily endorsed the President's goal of cutting the inflation rate from 6 to 4 percent. But many noted that he had failed to spell out how he would accomplish this. His approach, with its emphasis on voluntarism, was in fact reminiscent of President Ford's efforts along the same lines. And Ford himself uncharitably remarked that his successor's attack on inflation "came in like a lion and is going out like a mouse."

Not only did the President's reliance on voluntary effort to restrain inflation give cause for skepticism; so also did his pledge to maintain fiscal discipline. On April 19, four days after the announcement of the anti-inflation program, Agriculture secretary Bergland disclosed that the President had decided to double the size of his original proposal for federal support payments on major farm crops. The changes had been decided on, Bergland said, "to gain stronger support among farm groups and on Capitol Hill." This was of course the argument Bergland had made originally to the President when he submitted his own price recommendations, which Carter had cut back sharply. By waiting a month to accept Bergland's reasoning, the President diminished his influence on this issue among the lawmakers and gave the appearance of yielding to political pressure.

But at the moment the President's attention was concentrated elsewhere. The farm price reversal came in the midst of the most intensive week of Carter's first hundred days, a period devoted to the disclosure and promotion of his energy programs.

From the beginning, the biggest obstacle the President faced in dealing with the infinite complexities of energy was that most Americans simply did not take the problem seriously. Until they did, it was clear that it would be impossible to generate political support for proposals that would involve disruption and sacrifice. Franklin Roosevelt faced a more critical but similar challenge in trying to awaken the country to the threat of Axis aggression—until the Japanese struck at Pearl Harbor. But Carter certainly could not wait for some sudden disaster on the energy front. Alternatively, he might have launched an extensive educational program, but that would have meant a prolonged effort, and the President was in no mood for indefinite delay. He decided to act swiftly—as Schlesinger put it at the March 21 cabinet meeting, "Damn the torpedoes, full speed ahead"—relying on a climactic television barrage to pound home the message that action was needed.

The decision to develop and unveil a full-scale energy program three months after inauguration day—which became the dominant priority of Carter's early Presidency—was entirely of Carter's own making. The seriousness of the energy problem was beyond dispute among persons knowledgeable in the field. And the bitter cold wave that greeted Carter's arrival in office had, for a time, literally brought the problem home to millions of Americans. But there was no overriding objective reason why the new President needed to propose a complete solution within three months instead of, say, six or nine months, or whenever his planners were ready.

In the midst of the furious race to meet the deadline, Pat Caddell told a friend that he was reminded of a passage from Barbara Tuchman's *The Guns of August:* Just after Europe had plunged into World War I, "the German Chancellor turns to a cohort and asks, 'How did this happen?' And the answer, 'If only one knew.' "

Carter's own background and inclinations offered the best explanation. His navy training in nuclear engineering had given him a good grounding in energy technology. His energy adviser, James Schlesinger, whose hard-driving personality was not unlike that of the President's, had early on won Carter's confidence and respect. It is part of Carter's style to seize upon one major issue —in Georgia it had been government reorganization—to dramatize his leadership. Finally, he believes in the potency of deadlines. "He likes action," Mark Siegel, one of Hamilton Jordan's deputies, said. "He thinks people work better with a gun at their heads."

In his memorandum on political strategy, Caddell had warned that before the President could deal effectively with the energy problem "he must convince the country not only that there is a real crisis, but that the public can gain from supporting a real energy program. The President will have to propose an energy program that is both equitable and fits into a larger set of economic and social concerns." But the President's timetable provided little opportunity for preparing the public or for combining his energy goals with such related economic and social proposals as an urban mass-transit program. Instead, energy was handled on a crash basis—and in isolation.

Carter was worried that if the program came to light in advance, on a piecemeal basis, the various groups whose interests were threatened would tear it apart, bit by bit. Thus on the President's orders, details of the developing energy blueprint were tightly held within Schlesinger's own staff. Not only was the public kept in the dark but so also, for the most part, were the cabinet and the White House staff.

As the April 20 deadline neared, concern about Schlesinger's plans increased among other administration officials. That became evident at a March 22 meeting of the White House senior staff that I attended. Jack Watson, the cabinet secretary, brought the matter up, pointing out that the President's chief economic advisers had little idea of what Schlesinger was up to. "What is in effect happening," Watson said, "is that the substance of the energy plan is being put together independent of economic impact and analysis. And that can be devastating. Some of these people want to negotiate with Schlesinger before the plans go to the President, before anything is blocked in. There really ought to be some shirtsleeve sessions."

To break the ice, Robert Lipshutz, who chairs the meetings of the senior staff, asked Schlesinger to provide a briefing for the group. In response, Schlesinger sent his public affairs director, James Bishop, with firm instructions to "just listen." Bishop followed orders, parrying specific questions from the President's top aides for ninety minutes, while their irritation mounted. When he reported to his chief on the rigors of his mission, Schlesinger smiled wryly. "It's good character building," he said.

But as Watson had noted, pressure for energy information was building at the cabinet level, too, chiefly from Schultze and Blumenthal, who could not be fended off so easily. They appealed to Jordan, who went to the President. Finally, on April 6, only two weeks before E day, Carter called together Schlesinger, Blumenthal, Schultze, Lance, Jordan, Powell, and Frank Moore to discuss the energy program. For five discordant hours Blumenthal and Schultze challenged many of Schlesinger's proposals, contending they would damage the economy by either retarding growth or boosting inflation. They succeeded in killing outright a ban on the sale of private homes by 1981 that did not meet government standards for insulation and heating. And they managed to get some modification of other measures. But in the end, the President in effect gave Schlesinger's program an exemption from economic standards on the grounds of national interest.

Still, Schlesinger continued to do his best to keep the final details secret. Asked for information about the impact of the plan so that Jordan's aides could pass it on to governors and mayors to help prepare them for the public reaction to the proposals,

Schlesinger again dispatched Bishop, who was as tight-lipped as ever. Bishop was asked questions, and Mark Siegel said later, "he basically didn't answer. Not in a way that was rude, but just unsatisfactory. The impression he wanted us to get was that the plan was so complex he couldn't explain it to laymen. The impression we got was that he was trying to hold on to as much information as he possibly could."

For all their efforts, Schlesinger and his aides could not maintain total security. Of necessity, draft proposals were submitted for appraisal to officials in OMB and other agencies. The predictable result was a series of leaks to the press and the public disclosure of much of the program.

Nevertheless, plenty of drama was left when the President at last made his presentation to the country. This was orchestrated in three movements: a televised address on Monday night, April 18, to outline the energy crisis; another televised speech, this time before a joint session of Congress on the night of April 20, to disclose his specific proposals; and as a finale, a televised press conference on April 22 to answer questions and set aside doubts.

In his April 18 speech the President's tone and language were somber. He sought to shock the nation into an awareness of the problem and, as a corollary, to make the legislation he would later propose seem less painful. Much of his program would be "unpopular," the President warned. He called the energy problem "unprecedented in our history," and, except for preventing war, "the greatest challenge that our country will face during our lifetime." Borrowing a phrase from Henry James, at Schlesinger's suggestion, he characterized the effort as "the moral equivalent of war."

The next afternoon, the President and his staff assembled in the Roosevelt Room to work on his address to Congress. The session dragged on past midnight. Gerald Rafshoon, one of a dozen participants, left at about 10:30. "I could see at the rate they were going Jimmy was not going to be very satisfied when they got through," he later said, "and that there was going to be some rewriting the next day." Sure enough, the next morning Carter and his aides returned to their editing and rewriting, and not until midafternoon did the President consider the job completed.

On television that night Carter resumed his gloomy tone. "This cannot be an inspirational speech," he warned Congress at the outset. "I don't expect much applause." Action was needed "to cope with a crisis that otherwise could overwhelm us." To achieve conservation, the "cornerstone" of his program, he proposed increasing the price of crude oil, through higher taxes, and of newly discovered natural gas, though he skipped over his campaign promise to deregulate the price of all natural gas. He called for a graduated excise tax on new gas-guzzling cars and a standby gasoline tax of five cents a gallon, to be added on each year that consumption of gasoline exceeded certain levels.

But to ease the pain, he offered a package of incentives and rewards. Revenues from the gasoline and oil taxes would be refunded to consumers, and substantial rebates would go to buyers of gas-efficient autos. Other tax credits were to be offered for home insulation and business investment in conservation.

"It will not be easy," the President said. "It will demand the best of us—our vision, our dedication, our courage, and our sense of common purpose."

Yet the President himself was not prepared to rest the chances of his program's success on such altruistic motives. At his press conference on April 22, the last act in the week's drama, he sought to brighten the bleak picture he had painted earlier. The inflationary impact of the energy package would be less than "one half of one percent per year," he asserted. As for production and employment, Carter claimed: "The most conservative and unfavorable analysis shows that it will have no adverse impact." In fact, he argued, some studies showed that his proposals would "actually increase the number of jobs [by] several hundred thousand and have a beneficial effect on our economy." No sooner had the press conference concluded than the White House press office rushed out a statement claiming that under the President's program, low- and moderate-income families would actually get back more in tax rebates than they would spend on higher energy prices. "By increasing the costs of energy and returning the proceeds to all Americans we can save energy, save money, and continue to have a healthy economy."

Suddenly, between Monday and Friday, the call for sacrifice had turned into a boon for the economy. The turnabout may have reassured some citizens and businessmen, as it was intended to. Yet it left the President vulnerable to critics who had already noted that his specific proposals were far milder than his rhetoric. Ralph Nader derided Carter as a "sheep in wolf's clothing." Ben Wattenberg, recalling the most dramatic phrase of Monday night's speech, likened the actual program to "the moral equivalent of a skirmish." Although *Time* magazine called the energy speeches "the most intensive effort by a U.S. President, in or out of wartime, to rally the nation behind a common cause," it acknowledged that Carter's later hedging made it appear that the program's greatest impact would be on habit and life-style. And even these impositions could be overcome by anyone willing and able to pay the extra price for big cars and central air-conditioning.

Afterwards, Schlesinger's staff boasted about the "nonpolitical way" the program had been developed. "Carter approached this as a problem-solving challenge," Jim Bishop claimed. "When people came to him and said you can't do that because the environmentalists would get mad, or the coal producers would get mad, he ignored them. He went right over their heads to the people."

To the extent that this was true, Carter's energy program had no constituency, except the people. Washington was swarming with the agents of various interest groups, who were ready to attack one part or another of the package. The President had told the country: "This is a carefully balanced program, depending for its fairness on all its major component parts." The entire program could be passed only if the President could muster behind it a broad base of public support. His television blitz had raised the level of public concern, but the results were far from overwhelming. A Gallup poll taken after Carter's energy week indicated that the number of Americans who considered energy a serious problem had climbed from 43 to 54 percent. The President needed to expand that base, but he had made that task harder by "mixing up the message," as Caddell put it. Caddell and others had argued that a hard-line approach was required to build a sense of urgency and idealism. "You can't make it work unless you make it tough," Caddell had told the President. "Making it easy on people won't work. You have to make it hard. Let them discover it's not really killing them." But by softening his tone, the President had weakened his point.

After energy, the next major deadline proclaimed by the President was for welfare reform. In Georgia, he once recalled, he had achieved a measure of reform by setting up day-care centers for retarded children and putting welfare mothers in charge. "They're the best workers in the state government," he said proudly. But a significant improvement in the national system would of course require an effort several magnitudes greater. The President knew this, yet the task turned out to be even more difficult than he had realized. Probably more than any other issue in his first hundred days, welfare forced a collision between Carter's personal beliefs and the commitments of this campaign and the realities of government.

Welfare reform was one of the oft-repeated promises of his candidacy. He pledged to streamline the system, shift the financial burden from the cities to the states and Washington, and establish one uniform payment across the nation. Nearly everyone who had thought about the matter, liberals and conservatives alike, agreed that the existing ramshackle welfare structure badly needed overhaul. But most professionals in the field also believed that any comprehensive change, to make welfare more efficient and more equitable, would cost more money. And this was a proposition that the President did not want to accept.

Soon after inauguration day Carter established a welfare study group composed of Labor Department and HEW officials, and other specialists, with orders to submit legislation by May 1. The deadline, based on Califano's casual estimate made during the transition, had been publicly underlined by the President, most emphatically during his appearance in Clinton on March 16. Later that month, when the study group met with the President, Califano presented a brief critique of the present system and a rough outline of some alternatives.

The President was appalled by the existing inequities and inefficiencies. But he was also deeply committed, privately and publicly, to fiscal discipline and to balancing the budget. As Stuart Eizenstat later recalled for his senior staff colleagues, Carter told Califano and his reform team: "I want you to go back and come up with a comprehensive welfare reform program under the assumption that we won't spend any more money than is currently being spent on welfare." At the same time, he also asked for proposals that would involve additional spending.

"They were frankly in a state of shock," Eizenstat said, "because it's virtually impossible to talk about a new design without spending more money. You've got to talk about something like $15 billion, even if you don't spend it all the first year."

In mid-April the group met with the President again. Califano presented several options, Nick Kotz reported in the *New Republic,* but added his view that none of them would be adequate unless the present level of spending was raised. "In that case, to hell with it," Carter said. "We're wasting our time."

More deliberations followed, but the President's response had in effect put an end to the prospect of welfare reform by May 1. In fact, the deadline made little sense to begin with. By May 1, Congress would be deeply immersed in the energy proposals which the President had made the top priority for his administration, and looking forward to the President's promised tax reform proposals. No matter what the President did, the lawmakers would have little time for welfare reform. Said Senator Byrd:

"Welfare reform will simply have to wait. We can't do welfare reform in this session of Congress."

On April 26, the White House announced through a press release that the President would present "recommendations" on welfare reform early the next week. But the release added that "questions on the legislative scheduling of the large number of administration proposals now before the Congress, as well as those to come, are still being considered."

On May 2, just after the hundred-day milestone had been reached, the President announced that the present welfare system was "worse than we had anticipated." The problem, he said, had turned out to be so complex that its solution would require "detailed analysis through computer models and working with governors." He established a new deadline—the first week in August—for submitting legislation to Congress. Meanwhile, he set forth twelve guidelines for reform, the first of which was that "the new system will be at no higher initial cost than the present systems combined."

No one could complain about the President's welfare goals, the *Washington Post* commented editorially. "Work, equity, generosity, economy, efficiency, family stability—a social policy could hardly be based on a more desirable set of values." But the paper added: "Nobody should be under the impression that the President has indicated how he intends to fulfill these ambitious goals."

Just as important a question—which applied not only to welfare but to Carter's other legislative goals—was how he would get congressional approval. By the end of Carter's first hundred days, Congress had passed only one of Carter's major legislative proposals, the measure granting him authority to begin government reorganization. He could expect quick action on his economic stimulus proposal, now that it had been shorn of the tax rebate. But that would still leave the legislative calendar crammed. Besides the massive energy package, by the end of the hundred days he had proposed major revisions in the food stamp program and sweeping election reforms that included public financing of congressional elections, universal voter registration, and direct popular election of the President. A controversial proposal to revise Social Security funding was due soon. And promised for later on, in addition to welfare reform, was the long-heralded recommendation for overhaul of the tax code.

"I'll have to depend upon, of course, the congressional leaders to decide in which order they will address these major efforts," the President acknowledged. Whatever order was established, Congress would have trouble finding the time to deal with all of it. But the more basic problem facing the President's program was finding the political support for it. Carter evidently intended to lean heavily on his personal standing with the public. But as his one hundredth day passed, this remained a rather slender reed.

Public and private polls indicated that the country's opinion of Carter as a man and as a President had improved considerably during his tenure in office. Even after the announcement of his controversial energy program, a *New York Times*–CBS News survey put his approval rating at 64 percent. But this was no better than par for any President during his early honeymoon period in office. Moreover, the *Times* reported, Carter's support appeared to stem from "an appreciation of the open, informal style of the Carter White House rather than from firm devotion to substantive administration policies." For example, only 47 percent of those surveyed endorsed his handling of the economy, and only 42 percent approved of his conduct of foreign affairs.

In short, the *Times*–CBS figures suggested support that was broad but relatively shallow. And these findings tallied with the conclusions of Patrick Caddell, the President's own pollster, based on his surveys taken for the Democratic National Committee.

At a briefing for White House aides that I attended early in April, Caddell pointed out the potential difficulties for the President. He began with the good news. Carter had enjoyed a big jump in popularity since his inauguration. His base of support had broadened, and he had "enormous potential" for increasing his strength across the political spectrum. The public gave him high marks in the categories of trust, dedication, and warmth. "On any question having to do with his concern, or keeping in touch with people, he gets a rating of 80 to 85 percent, which is very high."

Then came the worrisome news. Although the intensity of support for the President had increased, as measured by a series of cross-checking questions, it was still not particularly strong. "His superficial popularity has deepened, but his constituency is not defined," Caddell said. "There's a lot of long-run potential, but right now there's no particular group to fall back on."

"What you're saying," Mark Siegel broke in, "is that we don't have a political base."

"That's what I'm getting at," Caddell acknowledged. "The problem is, there is no anchor to his political support, even in the South." Much of the President's backing in the polls, Caddell said, came from normally Republican sections of the country. "When the farm belt, the Rocky Mountains, and the Midwest are your strongest areas, you need to worry."

Carter's ratings contrasted sharply with Mondale's. A graph of the Vice President's support would show a curve, high among traditional Democratic voters, lower among independents, dropping farther down among Republicans. Carter's support, Caddell reported, is almost a flat line," distributed fairly evenly among Democrats, independents, and Republicans. This could mean growth in the long run, but trouble in the short run. "What the figures say is that if the President doesn't have partisan battles he'll do fine," Caddell said. "But if he runs into partisan situations, he can lose." The biggest gains the President has made have come from independents and Republicans—voters "you don't expect to hold on to."

To test the President's strength, voters were asked if they would support Carter in 1980, running against an unnamed opponent. Only 10 percent of those who backed Ford and 55 percent of those who voted for Carter said yes.

"What would impress them?" Siegel asked. "We're not going

to get liberal programs. Would bold leadership help?"

That depends on the issue, Caddell said. Energy, the issue the President had chosen for his most forceful leadership, was not likely to build his political support. "Energy is something the President has to do," Caddell said. "But the political payoff is not great." The economy was still the single strongest issue, but because of inflation it offered more potential for harm than good. "No issue hurts the President more in the long run than inflation. He has not been hurt yet, but it could have a very wearing impact."

Inflation, Caddell pointed out, reaches people's lives directly, in grocery stores and gas stations across the country. "If you have no strong issues on your side, and inflation continues unabated, you're likely to have a severe political crisis."

Caddell cited government reorganization as an example of an issue that could strengthen Carter's appeal. "That's how government relates to people."

So far, "people are generally feeling better about the country," Caddell said. "But there's no clear view or focus on the President."

Jerry Rafshoon shook his head. "I see the President getting into so many different things it's beginning to blur," he said. "I watched this happen in Georgia."

Someone asked whether the President could strengthen himself by acting more like a traditional Democrat, attacking big business and offering more urban programs. But Caddell said this would be difficult for Carter. "He's set aside the traditional partisan symbols."

"This reminds me of last August," Rafshoon said, glumly recalling the high point in the campaign when Carter had a thirty-point lead over Ford in the polls. "We were very popular. Then suddenly the shit hit the fan."

Caddell had the last word: "We have to concentrate on solidifying our constituency." The 1978 congressional elections were not that far down the road, "and there is no question they will be viewed as a test of the President's leadership."

The political realities that faced Carter in April had in large measure been foreseen by Caddell in his political strategy memorandum last December. "The time is ripe for a political realignment in America," he had written. Neither Carter nor any other Democratic President could depend any longer for support on a coalition built along economic lines, Caddell argued. The political balance was shifting against the have-nots in favor of the haves. Older voters were getting more conservative, younger voters more concerned with environment and growth, rather than traditional economic problems. "The old language of American politics doesn't really affect these voters," Caddell wrote. "We must devise a context that is neither traditionally liberal nor traditionally conservative. What we require is not a stew, composed of bits and pieces of old policies, but a fundamentally new ideology."

If the old Democratic coalition was to be broadened and strengthened, Caddell said, "there needs to be some thought given to a better political definition of the issues and concerns that exist. Since Governor Carter is neither a traditional liberal nor a conservative, he is uniquely positioned to do this."

Here was a splendid political opportunity, but Carter had yet to take advantage of it. His economic policies had put distance between him and the groups that made up the old New Deal coalitions. But he had done little to create a new alliance. He had concentrated on building a personal following rather than a political base. If in his own mind he had a clear design for uniting politics and government, he shared it only partially even with those closest to him.

10

The Presidency

———— ⭐ ————

The Inner Circle

When Mark Siegel addressed a Washington Press Club luncheon on the politics of energy in April, he was introduced, archly, as "a member of Carter's outer circle." The thirty-year-old Siegel, who had been executive director of the Democratic National Committee before he joined Hamilton Jordan's staff at the White House, responded in the same vein. "I am really trying hard to get from the outer circle to the inner circle," he said. "But a few adjustments in my behavior have been demanded." He claimed that he had been advised that "at least three times a week, in answer to questions that normally would get a yes or no response, I should say: 'I wouldn't bet the family farm on that.'

"I don't know what that means," said Siegel, a resourceful and aggressive political operator, "but I will try it."

He had also been advised, he said, that "on Sunday mornings, instead of lox and bagels, I am to experiment with lox and grits. That would be a small price to pay to be a member of the inner circle."

Siegel's remarks pointed up at least one way in which Carter's early Presidency conformed to expectations and to precedent. As in most previous administrations, having roots in the President's home territory was a prime, though not essential, qualification for status in the White House and access to the Chief Executive.

But as Carter passed his hundredth day in office, the most striking point about his circle of advisers, wherever they came from, was their limited influence on the decisions that issued from the Oval Office. By scrapping the hierarchical structure favored by his Republican predecessors, Carter has so far forestalled anyone from filling the dominant role played by Richard Cheney and Donald Rumsfeld under Ford, and by H. R. Haldeman and Alexander Haig under Nixon. "There never has been anybody in the position of being right alongside Carter, touching on all the issues after the staff work has been done," said one veteran of the campaign. "Almost everybody who advises him is involved in formulating options in isolated areas."

"His chief of staff is named Jimmy Carter," Walter Mondale told me. "He is a guy with tremendous interest and capacity for detail himself."

Certain specialists, notably Brzezinski in national security and Schlesinger in energy, carried considerable weight in their particular areas. Those with more generalized backgrounds chipped in their advice on varied issues. But as Richard Moe, Mondale's senior staffer, observed: "With this President, I think a lot less depends on who is advising him than on how the President sees the issue." Dealing with the broad range of policy questions that confronted him in the White House, Carter has ultimately played a lone hand.

Still, within these limitations, it is possible to make out the hazy lines of a White House inner circle of a half-dozen advisers. These include Vice President Mondale, budget director Bert

Lance, Hamilton Jordan, and Jody Powell from the President's personal staff, and two unpaid part-time consultants, Gerald Rafshoon, specialist in media, and Patrick Caddell, pollster, analyst, and propounder of large ideas.

Missing from this group, largely through his own choice, is Charles Kirbo, Carter's most trusted adviser in the past. Though Carter still trusts him as much as ever, Kirbo's soft voice has only rarely been heard in Carter's inner councils during the first one hundred days. He chose to remain in Atlanta because, he said, he wanted to tend to his law practice. And perhaps also because, as an associate suggested, "Kirbo was too smart to come up to Washington and try to advise Carter on foreign policy stuff and other matters he really doesn't know much about."

Kirbo had always kept some distance between himself and Carter. He seldom appeared in the governor's office in Atlanta and did not travel with the candidate during the Presidential campaign. By keeping aloof from the day-to-day travail, he has maintained for himself a special perspective and a special position. But with Carter in the White House and Kirbo still in Atlanta, the gap between them has become greater and harder to bridge.

During the first one hundred days Kirbo did take on a few special assignments—helping to formulate regulations for upgrading the discharge of Vietnam veterans and working on conflict-of-interest rules for federal officials. He was given a special code number to ensure that his letters would go directly and promptly to the President. And the two men chatted on the phone several times. But when I talked to Kirbo in the White House early in May, he said it was only his fourth visit there since inauguration day.

As he nears sixty, Kirbo's white hair is thinning and his lean frame is running to paunch. The words come out slowly, as if he had rolled each around in his mind and measured it beforehand. "I have not kept up with what's going on as much as I would like to," he said. He has passed along suggestions for appointments and offered some himself, through the mail. But he has been reluctant to get overly involved. "I've sort of purposefully stayed away from the staff, sort of let it reach its own setup. Since I wasn't going to be here permanently, I didn't want them to depend on me."

No one doubts that in the event of a shattering crisis, the President would not hesitate to call on his friend. "If he needed me, I'd be available," Kirbo said. But unless he changes his mind and decides to come to Washington, Kirbo's involvement in Carter's Presidency is not likely to grow. "I had said before that it would be a diminishing role, and I think that's what has happened."

Kirbo acknowledged that some of Carter's newer advisers might hesitate to be direct and frank with the President. "The office itself is intimidating. In addition to that, he has a strong personality that tends to intimidate some people. But if they have that feeling, there's not much you can do about it." In any case, Kirbo does not believe Carter suffers from a lack of counsel. "I think he gets plenty of advice, maybe too damn much sometimes," he said. "You have to watch it, you can get just covered up with advice."

The gap in the advisory ranks created by Kirbo's absence from the scene has been filled, at least partly, by Mondale and Lance, two men with contrasting personalities and viewpoints. Mondale, at forty-nine, is an urbane, witty leader of the Washington establishment, moderate in taste, restrained in manner. Lance, three years younger, is a hard-driving self-starter from small-town Georgia, blunt and hearty, given to rural aphorisms. "You can't hoot with the owls and soar with the eagles," he chided two of his young aides, who, on the day I talked with their boss, seemed still to be recovering from their previous evening's entertainment.

More fundamentally, Lance is a self-proclaimed fiscal conservative while Mondale's opinions still reflect his training in the Hubert Humphrey school of liberalism. "I respect the Vice President's view," Lance said. "He happens to feel strongly that in certain areas the way to deal with problems is through the expenditure of federal moneys. My view is that if you bring about consistency and predictability in government and hold a tight rein on the deficit problem, the private sector will supply the additional revenues to do the same things he wants to accomplish through government."

During the transition period Carter announced that Mondale would be his "chief staff person," a designation that suggested primacy among his advisers. But the administration was not very old before some of its members began to refer to Lance as "the Assistant President," a notion which he did nothing to dispel. "It's not appropriate for me to put myself in that position by saying it," he said to me. "But if other people say it, I have no reason to quarrel with it." Thus though Mondale and Lance each publicly professed his respect and admiration for the other, the potential for internal rivalry and conflict was there.

Mondale characteristically preferred to treat the subject of his influence with Carter lightly. When we talked in the library of the Vice-Presidential residence, he was watching a televised Presidential press conference while packing for a speaking trip. "I've already told him what to say," he remarked, nodding at the screen. "I just want to be sure that he says it."

More seriously, Mondale claimed that he and Carter had "broken historical ground" by freeing the Vice President from the institutional and ceremonial duties that have occupied his predecessors. This left him free, Mondale said, to advise on a wide range of issues and handle special assignments such as intelligence oversight and election reform. This Vice President, his aides said, had been given unprecedented access to information and practically unlimited opportunity to comment on decisions while they are in the making. If nothing else this should make Mondale better prepared than most Presidential understudies. "I want you to be ready," Carter told Mondale. "If you have to take over, I don't want you to spend half a year learning this job."

But Mondale was careful not to overstate his role in Carter's policy-making in such major areas as budget, tax reform, energy, and foreign policy. "When we get into the crunch questions," he said, "you can't disregard the extent to which it's Carter himself who makes these judgments."Though Carter early on told Mondale, "Fritz, I want you to be more aggressive with me," the Vice President was at first reluctant to heed that advice. During the first one hundred days, Jordan felt that Mondale preferred to use him as "a sounding board" rather than argue with Carter directly. But by early May Mondale claimed he was becoming more assertive with the President. "When I think he's making a serious mistake, I'll go in and tell him. I've come to have more confidence in his willingness to take that kind of criticism."

Still, Carter's liberal critics are skeptical that Mondale will ever be a forceful champion for their side. In May a group of liberals who called on Mondale to complain about Carter's policies got "a polite hearing," but no more. "You win some and you lose some," was the gist of Mondale's response. "Mondale has never been a fighter and never won anything by fighting for it," one member of the delegation said afterward. "He is by nature a very cautious guy."

By all accounts, including his own, Lance is far less reticent with the President, and with everyone else. On the occasion of one of his first speeches in Washington, Lance made a point of seeking out each of the dozen or so economic reporters in the audience, to shake their hands and greet them by their first names, thus displaying the keenness of both his memory and his sense of public relations.

Lance's position in the White House is buttressed by what he calls the "all-inclusive" jurisdiction of the agency he runs, the congruence of his economic views with the President, and their friendship, which began in 1966. "Since the first day we knew each other," Lance said, he and Carter had had a strong relationship, "one of ease and understanding." Nearly every day since the inauguration Lance has crossed over from his second-floor office in the Executive Office Building to the White House to see the President, either with a group or in private. The area in which he offers advice, solicited or otherwise, is "very great." Though, as he conceded, he is not particularly knowledgeable about foreign affairs or some aspects of international economics, this does not necessarily prevent him from voicing his opinion in these and other unfamiliar areas.

"I think I have good judgment," he said. "I think I know something about people. I've watched them succeed and I've watched them fail, and I've seen all the in-betweens. So I'd always put forth a caveat and say: 'This is an area I don't have much expertise in, but good judgment would say this might be a way to look at it.' You don't have to be a bridge designer to run a highway department."

Though Lance's view prevailed on the tax rebate controversy, some in the White House contended this was more because Carter already favored that position than because of the strength of Lance's arguments. "I think that Lance would like for his relationship with the President to be more than it is," a fellow Georgian observed. "It's more one-sided than it seems from outside. It's not that Carter draws on Lance a great deal. It's that Lance makes every effort to get in there and give his opinion."

However strong the personal relationship between Lance and Carter, it is certainly no firmer than the bond between the President and the two young leaders of his personal staff, Hamilton Jordan and Jody Powell. Jordan has worked for Carter since 1966, Powell since 1970, and these years represent a substantial portion of their adult lives. Their dominant roles in engineering the drive to the White House, and the absence of anyone else as directly and deeply involved, fostered a remarkable intimacy with Carter which has carried over to the White House.

Though Jordan and Powell are as close to the President as they were to the candidate, their almost exclusive hold on him had been loosened. "I think without trying to rate our influence, it is certainly less now than it was during the campaign," Powell told me. Carter's range of activities and responsibilities had, of course, greatly expanded, he pointed out, "and a lot more people are involved in much more fundamental ways." Another factor is that neither Jordan nor Powell is strongly committed to ideology or issues. Thus they have no great interest in arguing for or against any particular policy decision except as they feel it would help or hinder Carter's success.

Powell and Jordan maintain an amicable professional relationship; they are careful not to step on each other's toes. But they are not close personally and rarely spend time together away from their White House duties. If there is rivalry between them it is hard to discern, beyond an occasional humorous gibe. When I asked Powell his and Jordan's age, he said: "I'm thirty-three and Hamilton's thirty-two, and I think it shows."

Jordan (whose name, as Washington has come to learn, is pronounced Jurden) usually appears at the White House dressed much as he did during the campaign: work boots, old pants, no tie, and a windbreaker, and carrying a pair of tennis shorts and a toilet kit. This is part of the calculated irreverence with which he approaches a position which the Washington Post glowingly called "the second most powerful" in the government. He himself likens his duties to those of a short-order cook.

During the day I spent watching him on the job, he conferred for half an hour with Mary Schuman, an emissary from Eizenstat's staff, about appointments to the Civil Aeronautics Board. Jordan, who has been accused of tendencies toward male chauvinism, was looking for a woman candidate—preferably, he said, a Republican woman. "I think the Republicans should bear some of the burden of affirmative action."

Glancing at the list of prospects, he asked Schuman, "Which of these women do you recommend?"

"I don't know any of them," she said.

"How come?" Jordan asked. "I thought all you women knew each other."

Jordan at times has been just as flip with the President, whom he irritated by calling the meetings of the cabinet a waste of time.

"How would you know?" Carter shot back. "You never go to them."

The following Monday Jordan attended the regular cabinet

meeting, then sought out the President. "Well I went to one, and I was right," he said. "They're a waste of time."

But if Jordan feels free to needle the President, his criticism is usually confined to tactical matters. His memo complaining about the minimum wage and farm support decisions focused on the way the President had made them, and on their impact, rather than on the merits of the issues. Jordan sees himself as a political operator, rather than a policy adviser. Even so, this is a critical role, particularly in this Presidency, because in the process of running Carter's campaign, Jordan had gained a firsthand awareness of political forces which the President himself often seemed to overlook.

The contributions of Joseph Lester Powell, or Jody as everyone calls him, to the Carter Presidency are twofold. First, he is a shrewd judge of how the press would respond to the President's actions and utterances. "He is very good at reading in advance how an issue will get written and reflect on Carter," said a colleague. "He doesn't try much to influence policy. But he will go to the President and say: 'Jesus Christ, you can't do that. Here's what they'll do to us on that.'"

Perhaps just as important is his skill at dealing with reporters. For the most part the White House press corps has been willing to forgive his chronic disorganization—appointments slip from his memory, phone calls are seldom returned—because of his undisputed knowledge of the President's mind. When Powell, in his shirtsleeves, vest unbuttoned, hands gripping the podium, eyes squinting at his notes, conducts his daily briefing, the assembled journalists know that however biased he might be, he speaks with authority. A quick and clever tongue helps him to explain the President's positions, often more persuasively and cogently than the President himself. And an ample store of color and humor disarms hostile interrogators.

During the preinaugural transition, in the midst of a hot exchange with one aggressive reporter, Powell's sharp features relaxed in a friendly grin. "Look, we're both good folks, come from good families, and have a good education. The question is, where did we go wrong?" In the subsequent laughter the point in dispute was forgotten.

Prodded at a White House briefing to provide a sampling of letters and telegrams objecting to the President's pardon of draft evaders, Powell stalled for a moment, then said: "I might be willing to come dump all 4,800 of them right in the middle of the press room. We could all take off our clothes and jump up and down on them." That line of inquiry also was abandoned.

Powell said he enjoyed the "give-and-take" of the briefings. "It happens to appeal to my competitive instincts." He seemed far more relaxed at the White House than during the campaign, when the severe pressures sometimes transformed him into a sulking, angry figure. But even at the White House his sense of humor occasionally deserted him, particularly when he thought someone had departed from the unswerving loyalty to the administration which the press secretary himself exemplifies and demands from others. At a senior staff meeting I attended in March, Powell voiced his displeasure at some relatively minor criticism of the White House's congressional liaision staff, attributed to unnamed administration officials. "This has just got to stop," he said grimly. "It's not a serious problem yet, and I don't have any desire to figure out who's making an ass of himself. But it can be done. We can find out who's responsible. There's no goddam reason why we should be picking on each other. We have enough people on our ass from outside. And if you can't live without knocking your fellow staff person to the press, then maybe you should find somewhere else to work.

"Spread it around," he added, "because I'm dead serious about this."

A few weeks later, James Wooten, in a page-one story in *The New York Times* that was based mainly on interviews with unidentified White House aides, depicted a remote and cranky Chief Executive, intolerant of dissent, impatient with his staff and cabinet. Powell was furious. The story had touched a nerve. At the next press briefing he denounced Wooten's account as "a complete departure from the facts." And he disclosed that he had checked with about twenty members of the White House staff, all of whom assured him they had not been interviewed by Wooten. Powell's counterattack was motivated by his anxiety that because of the prestige of *The New York Times,* the article would start a wave of similar stories. But the intensity of his reaction served to call attention to the story and to lend credibility to its allegations of an intimidating atmosphere in the White House.

Powell's behavior reminded reporters of the siege mentality that prevailed at the White House under Richard Nixon and, to a lesser degree, under Lyndon Johnson. That attitude was in large part a reaction to the passionate opposition to the war in Vietnam. But no such inflammatory issue has confronted Carter's Presidency. Powell's tendency to us-against-them responses reflects his intense loyalty to Carter, his sense of opposition to the Washington establishment, and the normal adversary relationship between a press secretary and the press. Given Powell's temperament and his closeness to Carter, the danger is that the inevitable tensions with the media will be heightened to the point where they distort the outlook of both the press secretary and the President he serves.

Next to Powell and Jordan, probably the most important member of the senior staff is Stuart Eizenstat, the domestic policy chief. Eizenstat's experience in the Johnson White House, in the 1968 Humphrey campaign, and as issues coordinator of Carter's drive for the White House has given him a greater familiarity with policy issues than anyone else on the staff. "Stu is really coming into his own," Rafshoon told me. "During the campaign he was always the issues coordinator kind of person. You know what that means. But now he's into the substance of things, and he's just blossoming." In Jordan's view, Eizenstate is "indispensable" to the President. "He knows so much about everything."

But Eizenstat's traditional liberal viewpoint does not fit in with the basic thrust of Carter's drive to hold down federal spending. And his cautious schoolteacher manner does not match the bold and irreverent élan of his White House peers.

For all his solemnity, Eizenstat's colleagues contend that he has a mordant wit. Rafshoon recalls that during the campaign he, Jack Watson, and Eizenstat flew from Plains to Atlanta in a small chartered plane through a raging storm. "I can just see the headlines if we go down," Rafshoon told his companions: RAFSHOON, 2 OTHER CARTER AIDES DIE IN CRASH.

Watson quickly suggested an alternative: WATSON, 2 OTHER CARTER AIDES DIE IN CRASH.

But Eizenstat had a better idea: EIZENSTAT SURVIVES IN CRASH THAT KILLS 2 CARTER AIDES.

Rafshoon and Patrick Caddell both enjoy the benefits of being White House insiders and, at the same time, successful businessmen. They are not paid for their White House services, but their private endeavors certainly have not suffered from their well-publicized relationship with the President.

Actually, both were well established in their respective fields before Carter became an announced candidate for the Presidency. Rafshoon's advertising agency was the fourth or fifth largest in Atlanta. And Caddell had launched two successful enterprises: Cambridge Survey Research conducts polls for Democratic politicians; Cambridge Reports compiles extensive studies on public attitudes on political and economic issues for clients that have included a number of large corporations and at least one foreign government, Saudi Arabia. Caddell's most important client, so far as Carter is concerned, is the Democratic National Committee. The committee pays Caddell substantial sums to conduct periodic political surveys, including, of course, measurements of Carter's popularity and public reaction to his policies. In May Caddell and Rafshoon opened a Washington office on Pennsylvania Avenue two blocks from the White House, as a base for advising Carter and for joint consulting ventures in politics and private industry. "We'll be using the expertise we showed off in the Carter campaign," Rafshoon said.

Their dual roles have created the potential for conflict of

interest, or at least the appearance of conflict, though both men insisted they could avoid such problems. "I'm not an advocate for anybody, I'm not an attorney who's going to help you with some government agency," Rafshoon said. "And I know, so far as Jimmy is concerned, there's nothing I could do for anybody that he would help me on." Rafshoon told the President: "We're not going to go after any government contracts," adding facetiously: "For one thing, you couldn't deliver."

Caddell—whose contract with Saudi Arabia, which has since expired, stirred criticism during the campaign—contended that he sells a product, not a service. "I don't represent anybody, I sell research, like Jerry sells advertising." The conflict of interest question is "idle speculation to the detriment of my character without any reason behind it, and I'm getting really very defensive about it." But idle or not, the speculation is likely to continue, as long as Rafshoon and Caddell are involved in Carter's Presidency. They have the President's ear, and are privy to his private thoughts. It is hard to think of many large enterprises that are not ultimately affected by Presidential decisions. Carter has pledged to elevate the ethical standards for federal officials and his two key unofficial advisers will need to exercise restraint and vigilance to avoid embarrassing him or themselves.

At the White House, Rafshoon's major concern is Carter's image, particularly as it is conveyed over television. He has sent the President occasional memos—like Kirbo, he was given a special code number for his mail—and has seen him every two weeks or so. He has generally been on hand to advise on such major media events as the first fireside chat and the President's presentation of his energy program. "I don't get into the substance, except for the phrasing of it," he said. More generally he has offered advice on the political impact of the President's pronouncements. "I've been in politics and I know a lot about Jimmy Carter and what sells for Jimmy Carter and I have a pretty good gut feeling when he's good and when he's bad." Symbolism and style are part of his expertise. The guiding principle, he believes, is "Don't do anything in the way of style setting that doesn't feel natural." For example, he contended that Carter's early gestures toward austerity in the Presidency were effective because they were a natural reflection of his personality.

"Jimmy Carter is the tightest sonovabitch you'll ever meet," Rafshoon said. "He's tight with his own family, with his own money." During the campaign, Rafshoon bought Carter a blue pastel shirt for his second televised debate against Ford. Rafshoon and Carter wear the same size—14 ½ neck, 33 sleeve. So when the media adviser presented the shirt to the candidate he told him: "If you want to keep it after the debate, fine. If not, give it back and I'll wear it."

"How much did you pay for it?" Carter asked.

"Twenty dollars," Rafshoon said.

"Twenty dollars?" Carter said indignantly. "I've never had a shirt for more than eight dollars."

"He was really offended," said Rafshoon, who, when I talked to him, was still waiting for Carter to return either the shirt or the twenty dollars.

Just as Rafshoon specializes in images, Caddell deals in numbers and concepts. The numbers, of course, come from the polls. The concepts also are derived from the polls, in part. But they go beyond the statistics turned up by the surveys and are intended to reflect what Caddell believes are Carter's basic intentions and beliefs, along with Caddell's ideas for implementing them. His first major postelection effort at conceptualizing was the political strategy memorandum which set forth themes for the early days of the Carter Presidency. "I put it on paper," Caddell said. "But it was really his own thinking and it had come from a number of conversations we had." When I talked with him early in May, Caddell was thinking about establishing themes for the future—"Where you say, 'These are the goals, these are the programs, and this is how they fit together.' "

Caddell has conferred with the President "sometimes once a week, sometimes twice a week, sometimes once every three weeks.

It depends on his schedule." When they talked, usually at the end of the President's day, Carter was less interested in polling statistics "than in bouncing large concepts and ideas around. He wanted to know how he was doing with the people, what do they understand, and how does he break through to them."

The difficulty is, Caddell said, that the pace and the structure of the Presidency are not conducive to contemplation. "When I go to the White House I realize that I could not work in that place. I could not work somewhere where I would have no chance to think."

He recalled that Hamilton Jordan had called himself a short-order cook. "That's true," Caddell said. "Everybody there is a short-order cook, including the President."

Each of Carter's close advisers shares a piece of the Presidential action. But only Carter himself can assemble the pieces into a coherent whole. To accomplish this in the face of the varied and conflicting pressures that played upon him every hour of every day is one of the severest challenges of the Presidency.

POTUS at Work

May 3, 1977—Susan Clough takes Bach off the turntable and puts on Mozart. The classical concert, which will last all day, is intended for an audience of one, the President, who is busy next door in his study. Clough, who is slim, blonde, and thirty-two years old, worked for Carter when he was governor, stayed on in Atlanta to serve his successor, and rejoined Carter after he won the Presidential nomination. In addition to being the President's personal disc jockey, she is his personal secretary, and I am using her office as a sort of observation post for the day.

Weeks ago I asked Jody Powell for an opportunity to watch the President at work and to talk to him about his first hundred days in office, which ended Saturday, April 30, at noon. Last night Powell phoned to tell me the memo he had sent Carter about my request had finally been approved. "You're on with the President tomorrow." What this meant was not entirely clear. I had asked to sit in on some of the meetings on Carter's schedule, but Powell had doubts about this. "I've discovered that when somebody from outside sits in on meetings, the meetings don't happen," he said.

Carter came to office committed to running an open Presidency, and despite some inherent difficulties, he has managed to make himself relatively accessible to press and public. The President and his press secretary are mindful not only of the importance of keeping faith with his campaign promise but also of the political benefits of visibility.

Last month NBC was granted permission to film a documentary of the President at work, an event which Eizenstat, in his memo on Carter's first one hundred days, listed among the President's "key actions." John Chancellor and a camera crew followed Carter around for most of his day; the ground rules were that the President could turn off the mike he wore under his tie whenever he chose, and that the camera crew would leave the room whenever the President asked. Powell told the senior staff what he thought the TV program would achieve for the President: "I don't think there is a general public perception of how much time the President puts in working and studying and getting ready and preparing himself for these rather complicated things that he deals with. We're at least slightly vulnerable just because of the way the press works, being kind of overly fascinated with the glitter and less able to deal in depth with the substance." No one pointed out that Powell's criticism of the press echoed the press's criticism of the Carter White House—that it has placed too much stress on "glitter" and style, and too little on substance.

Carter had mixed feelings about the arrangement with the network. Near the close of the televised day, he was heard to complain over his open mike that he had spent time talking with Chancellor that he otherwise would have devoted to paperwork. "Maybe it'll pay off," he added skeptically. It certainly seemed to. Though NBC was not as substantive as Powell had implied it might be, it did offer Americans an hour-long glimpse of their Chief Executive hard at work, which was what Powell really wanted. John J. O'Connor, *The New York Times* television critic, said the program "verged on a glossy commercial for the Presidency and its occupants." But Carter still grumbled to Powell about the time he had lost.

As I have learned in the course of gathering information for this book, some officials in the White House feel anxious about the presence of an outsider, even one without a camera. One reaction is simply to avoid saying anything that might be controversial, the course Mondale took at the cabinet meeting I attended. On another occasion, Mondale entered Hamilton Jordan's office while I was there and, when I stayed put, said to Jordan: "I just came by to congratulate you on the great job you're doing and to tell you how well I think everything is going." I took the hint and left. Fortunately, most people here have been less inhibited.

Another limitation on the openness of government and particularly on the Presidency is security. The fact that the President is under armed guard, day and night, wherever he goes, is particularly evident here in the heart of the West Wing. A White House press pass, issued by the Secret Service, gets me as far as the White House press room, but no further. A uniformed member of the Executive Protective Service, which supplements the Secret Service at the White House, is posted outside Jody Powell's door. Passage beyond that point requires escort by a White House staff member. Everyone working at the White House, with the exception of the President and a few close aides, wears a staff identification card with a photograph on a neck chain.

The agents in the corridor outside the President's office are there to protect confidential documents and, of course, the President. They are courteous but vigilant. About 8:00 A.M. the President, whose first meeting of the day has been, as usual, his national security briefing with Brzezinski, leaves his office for a breakfast with the Democratic congressional leaders in the dining room. The study door is open. With Susan Clough at my side I look in, then enter the room, taking notes on the books and furnishings. Suddenly there is a stir in the corridor and one of the agents glares at me and says something to Clough, who ushers me out swiftly. The President has left his briefing papers on top of his desk and no one can be allowed in the room.

I apologize to Clough for this breach and walk down the hall, about fifty feet, to the men's room. When I return, an agent asks me to wait while he phones Clough, who comes out to the corridor and brings me back into her office, a procedure which is repeated several times during the day. "These men are charged with the President's life," Susan Clough reminds me.

This is, of course, a grave responsibility. In a cautionary memorandum to Carter during the transition, Stephen Hess noted that the British journalist Henry Fairlie had written that the protection given Presidents "has gone beyond the stage of mere farce and become a threat to Democracy." Nevertheless, Hess advised Carter that before he cut down on his guards he should read a random sample of the crank letters he was sure to receive. "In 1961–62 I had the opportunity to see the threats that were sent to General Eisenhower, who was both in retirement and the most respected man in the nation," Hess wrote. "There are, unfortunately, unbalanced people whose capacity to injure a President must be taken seriously."

It is hard to argue that the President should be less secure. Still, as Hess advised Carter: "You should not become a captive of your protectors." It is difficult for a President not to be. The danger of isolation is just as real, if much less critical than that of physical violence. Jim Wooten's story in *The New York Times* about Carter's alleged isolation, which made Jody Powell so angry, reported that the President had instructed Secret Service agents to bar staffers from his office. Powell denied this, and several people I talked to at the White House refused to believe it. But Wooten later told me his information came from a Secret Service agent. At any rate, it seems clear that Carter guards his time and privacy jealously.

This morning he must be feeling extra pressure. The day after tomorrow he will leave on his first overseas trip as President, to attend the economic summit conference in London, and he is trying to prepare for the conference while keeping up with his regular routine. His breakfast with the congressional leadership, scheduled for an hour, turned into a fractious gathering and ran overtime. He does not get back to his study until 9:20, twenty minutes behind schedule. He works at shifting the balance between his in and out boxes until 9:45, when he appears in the doorway outside Clough's office to say hello.

The President is wearing a gray suit, a gray shirt, and a yellow striped tie. His face is ruddy, but the weary lines show through. He has been up and driving himself since 6:30, and he seems edgy and preoccupied. We shake hands and he says, "I don't know exactly when your article is running, so I don't know what would be the most efficient way for you to spend your time." I am struck both by his forgetting I am working on a book— Powell's memo had reminded him of this yesterday—and by his concern that time, his or mine, should be utilized efficiently. I explain about the book, and he says: "I'm going to a meeting on airplane engine noise in the Cabinet Room." This sounds like an implicit invitation. But when I mention that Powell had misgivings about my sitting in on meetings, he says: "You better work that out with Jody," and hurries to the Cabinet Room.

The meeting is an attempt to resolve a bureaucratic dispute which, like many other problems confronting the President, combines the complications of economics and technology. Last December, the Federal Aviation Administration established noise standards that would require the airlines to buy new engines or refit old ones on about 1,500 planes in the next eight years. Transportation Secretary Adams has proposed that funds from the federal tax on plane tickets be used to help the airlines meet the cost, and in this he has the support of the Council on Environmental Quality and the Environmental Protection Agency. But the Office of Management and Budget has protested that the subsidy for the airlines will be a cash drain on the budget. Adams is scheduled to testify on the issue Thursday before a congressional committee.

Officials of all the agencies involved make their case to the President. Carter is supposed to spend only fifteen minutes in the meeting, but he stays on for nearly three-quarters of an hour. Before returning to his study, he pauses to explain briefly, rapidly, and in more technical detail than I can absorb the agreement that has been reached, which Adams will present on the Hill. It is a compromise of sorts, basically favoring Transportation over OMB. The President was intensely involved and for the moment he seems as gratified by the outcome as if he had just concluded a SALT agreement with the Russians.

Promptly at 10:30 Jody Powell and his deputy, Rex Granum, arrive for their daily meeting with the President, which precedes Powell's own briefing of the press. I mention to Powell that the President had indicated he might not object to my attending some meetings. Powell shakes his head and says: "That's what he tells you." He has been through other situations like this, and had his ears burned by the President afterward, an experience he prefers to avoid. But he relents enough to let me attend his session with Carter.

The study is a warm and pleasant room, with gold carpeting, long white curtains, a painting of Rosalynn and Amy over the fireplace, and a photograph of the President's mother on the wall. I sit on a beige couch, next to where the President's cardigan sweater is neatly folded, and Powell and Granum sit in two green easy chairs, which Susan Clough has mentioned she thinks badly need reupholstering. On the President's desk are a group of reference books—*Roget's Thesaurus,* the *American Heritage Dictionary,* two congressional directories, the *World Almanac,* a congressional pictorial directory, and the Bible. A globe, about two feet in diameter, is to the President's left. Behind him, mounted on the wall, is a working replica of an eighteenth-century flintlock rifle, a gift from some friends in Georgia.

Carter is in his shirtsleeves. Uppermost in his mind are the problems that came up earlier at his breakfast with the congressional leadership. This morning's friction was only to be expected, given the events of the last few days. Last week, Defense Secretary Harold Brown, with the help of some conservative Democrats, succeeded briefly in amending the congressional budget resolution to restore some cuts in the administration's Pentagon spending request. But Brown's abrupt move outraged the House leadership, which had spent weeks patching the resolution together from a series of compromises. Liberal Democrats, still angry about the President's withdrawal of the $50 tax rebate, retaliated by helping to defeat the amended version of the budget resolution, sending it back to committee. "This is the U.S. Congress, not the Georgia legislature," said Robert N. Giaimo, chairman of the House budget committee.

The House leadership had not fully recovered from their rancor when the President invited them to the White House yesterday to outline his spending proposals for the future, making clear that he intended to balance the budget by 1980, if necessary at the cost of social and economic programs. The leaders brooded about this overnight and got some of their resentment off their chests at breakfast this morning. As Hamilton Jordan later tells me: "They gave him a lot of stuff about acting more like a Democrat."

The legislators and the President also picked at the old water projects wound. Last month the President had trimmed the list of dams he wanted eliminated to eighteen. But yesterday, the House appropriations subcommittee voted to fund seventeen of the eighteen projects, a rebuff which the President does not choose to ignore.

"You'll probably get a question on the water projects," the President tells his press aides.

Powell suggests a response to the reporters. "When you sent your recommendations to the Congress, you said this was a waste of taxpayers' money. And you still think this a waste of taxpayers' money." The President's initial objections to the projects were also based on environmental and safety factors. But now the strategy seems to be to base his case mainly on cost, which fits in with his renewed emphasis on balancing the budget.

Carter nods in agreement. "I told the congressional leaders we are headed for a confrontation on the water projects." This is one of several fronts where he expects to battle Congress over spending. "This will probably be an inducement to them to tie the water projects to some bill that will be hard for me to veto."

"Sooner or later you're going to have to veto something," Powell says.

The President grins. "I'm sort of looking forward to it."

Granum points out that the press office may also be asked about congressional displeasure with the President's stress on fiscal restraint yesterday. Should that be combined with the water projects controversy or handled separately?

"Take the stronger of the two alternatives," Carter says quickly.

Powell mentions a meeting on the afternoon schedule with the ambassadors to five Latin American and Caribbean countries. One reason for the meeting is to announce that the First Lady will visit Latin America and the Caribbean in June. But its main purpose is to give the ambassadors advance notice of the President's decision on sugar imports, which will not be disclosed publicly until tomorrow.

"Is that going to make the sugar growers unhappy?" Powell asks.

The President strokes his chin, then briefly summarizes his plans for the troubled sugar industry. The administration is not going to ask Congress for a curb on imports. But it will recommend subsidies for sugar growers of up to two cents a pound, if the price falls below 13.5 cents a pound. Carter does not think the growers will be unhappy.

Powell wonders what it actually costs to raise sugar.

"If you mean what the sugar farmers claim it costs," Carter

says drily, "that's about 15 cents a pound."

Later in the day, Carter says, he will meet with energy adviser Schlesinger to "get this uranium enrichment thing settled." Last month the President announced he intended to "defer indefinitely" the use of plutonium fuel in nuclear power plants and proposed instead to increase production of enriched uranium. The power industry attacked him for being too restrictive, but some environmentalists complained he had not been restrictive enough.

The President says the administration's position on nuclear fuel needs to be better explained. Meanwhile he is looking forward to a forthcoming conference on new sources of energy. In India, he says, half of the energy supply comes from wood and dung.

Powell cannot resist. "The District of Columbia alone could provide half the dung we need," he says. "I can just see a pipeline leading out of the press briefing room."

Powell and Granum go down the hall to the press office, and I go the other way to talk to Tim Kraft, the President's appointments secretary. Kraft, who is thirty-six and sports a Pancho Villa moustache, managed Carter's drive for Democratic convention delegates in Iowa. On the January night last year when he received the Iowa results, which made him the front-runner for the nomination, Carter told Kraft over the phone: "I guess I won't send you to Alaska after all." Instead Kraft went to Pennsylvania and coordinated Carter's victory there, which paved the road to the White House for both of them.

In some past administrations, the holders of Kraft's job have wielded great power and caused considerable resentment by tightly controlling access to the President. But Kraft does not operate that way. The President's long-range schedule, which Kraft draws up every two weeks, is submitted to the senior staff for comment before it goes to the President. And he often defers to last-minute requests for additions to the schedule.

In theory, at least, any of the senior staffers is free to knock on the door of the President's study whenever he is there alone. But Kraft tells me: "They don't do it very often, and they don't do it with something that's not important."

Certain items are regular fixtures on Carter's schedule. He meets daily with Brzezinski, Powell, and Frank Moore, twice weekly with Lance and Schultze on the economy, and with Mondale, Turner, and Brzezinski on intelligence. Once a week, he lunches with the Vice President, meets with his senior staff, and of course, attends his cabinet meeting. Most of the rest of the schedule is made up of what Kraft calls "add-on items," last-minute requests for a few minutes for ceremonial occasions, handshakes with distinguished visitors or old friends, consultation with aides.

Then there is the paperwork. Though Carter complains of the volume, his own requests for information produce a flood of memos. And he finds it almost impossible to resist reading anything that reaches his desk. "That man is clogged up with paper," Pat Caddell told me. Caddell was shocked, after attending a dreary cabinet meeting, to get a copy of the minutes with "OK-JC" scrawled on it. "I thought to myself: 'I'll be a sonovabitch, I'll bet he sat down and read the cabinet minutes.' "

After studying the President's routine for the first six weeks, Kraft concluded he was scheduling him too tightly. So he began blocking out contingency time, to allow for some of the inevitable last-minute requests, and keeping a tighter rein on additions. He managed to cut the President's work week from seventy to sixty-seven hours, though this does not take into account the time Carter spends on paperwork in the residence during the evening and on weekends. "He's seeing fewer people now," Kraft says, "but there's still room for necessary access."

And the add-on requests still come in "hot and heavy." While we are chatting, Landon Butler, the White House liaison with organized labor, stops by to ask for "five minutes" with the President this afternoon for Leonard Woodcock. "It's most important and it has nothing to do with auto emissions." Kraft makes a note, and Woodcock goes on the schedule. The President gets a brief memo from Butler explaining the purpose of his visit; Woodcock

wants Carter to discuss his plans for national health insurance—
a cause close to Woodcock's heart—when the President addresses
the UAW convention later in the month.

The Woodcock meeting is one of three additions to the schedule since the morning. The others are a chat with Don Tucker, a
candidate for vice chairman of the Civil Aeronautics Board,
whom Hamilton Jordan wants the President to see, and the meeting on uranium with Schlesinger, which Carter had mentioned to
Powell and Granum.

At 11:20 the President leaves the study for the Oval Office
and his only ceremonial appointment of the day. He is presented
with a CBS record album of his preinaugural gala. Proceeds from
the sales of the record will go to the National Endowment for the
Arts. This is what is known in the lexicon of the White House
press office as a photo opportunity. Press cameras click while the
President accepts the album and thanks the record company officials. In five minutes the photographers leave and Mondale,
Turner, and Brzezinski arrive for an intelligence meeting.

Before leaving I take a long look at the Oval Office. It is a
museum room. The Presidential seal is in plaster relief on the
ceiling, the only known replica of Charles Willson Peale's (ca.
1776) portrait of Washington hangs above the mantel, and an
eighteenth-century painting of Benjamin Franklin is to the right
of the door. Also on display are busts of Franklin and Truman,
a statuette of Lincoln, on loan from the Metropolitan Museum of
Art, a pair of Chinese vases, nearly three hundred years old, and
a tall case clock made in Boston early in the nineteenth century.
The massive oak desk, made from the timbers of H.M.S. *Resolute*
and a gift from Queen Victoria to Rutherford B. Hayes, was last
used by John Kennedy. Carter had it brought back to the White
House from the Smithsonian. On it is a plaque bearing Truman's
old motto: "The buck stops here," a line that Carter appropriated
for his campaign against Ford.

Since the early days of his Presidency Carter has used the
Oval Office only for ceremonies and meetings, preferring to do

most of his work a short corridor away in the cozier quarters of the study. Ford spent more time in the Oval Office, using the study only as an occasional hideaway. In the Nixon Presidency the study was occupied by Alexander Butterfield, the Haldeman aide who first disclosed the existence of Nixon's taping system in the White House. When Nixon sought seclusion he walked next door, across West Executive Avenue, to a small office in the Executive Office Building, which offers even more privacy than the study. That office is available to Carter, too, of course, but he rarely uses it. "I think he's so conscientious about time that he doesn't like to spend the five to seven minutes it takes to get back and forth," says Susan Clough.

Clough's small office has a history of its own. It was originally designed to house the White House's first telephone, back in 1909, when President Taft expanded the West Wing. During Harding's Presidency, some say, it served as a trysting place for the President and his mistress, Nan Britton. Kennedy installed a private phone in the cubicle, to make calls outside the White House switchboard, and Nixon kept a couch there for napping.

At 12:10 the intelligence meeting breaks up, Carter returns to his study for paperwork, and at 12:30 he stops by Clough's office to let her know he is going to the residence for lunch. This is an indulgence the President grants himself only occasionally. Most days, when he does not have luncheon meetings, he has a light snack at his desk. A sign in the small pantry adjoining the study reminds the White House stewards what POTUS, the official acronym for President of the United States, prefers. "POTUS will have soup (cup) or sandwich for lunch, but not both." It is signed: "The management."

Carter is back from lunch a few minutes after 1:00 P.M., in plenty of time for the next item on his schedule, a five-minute visit with Jane Fortson, a young woman who served in the Peanut Brigade. This was the group of Georgians who traveled from primary state to primary state, ringing doorbells on Carter's behalf during his quest for the nomination. His visitor is the niece of Ben Fortson, Georgia's longtime secretary of state, who has achieved a measure of national renown by likening Carter to a south Georgia turtle, an animal so stubborn that instead of going around obstacles it pushes them out of its way.

At 2:15 President Carter leaves the study for the cabinet room and his meeting with the Latin American ambassadors. He is still chatting with Jordan, who had stopped by the study to discuss Republican candidates for a seat on the Federal Election Commission. Rosalynn Carter joins them at the door to the cabinet room and she and the President take seats at the head of the table. Also present are Brzezinski and Robert Strauss, the former Democratic party chairman who is now the President's chief trade negotiator.

The President tells the ambassadors that the purpose of the First Lady's trip in June will be "to express our deep friendship for our neighbors in the south and also to conduct substantive talks with the leaders of these countries." He refers to his wife as "a political partner of mine" and adds that "perhaps as much as any other President's wife, she participates in and is aware of what government is—in both domestic and foreign affairs."

Mrs. Carter is said by some people in a position to know to be an important influence on her husband. But her public role in his administration has so far been limited and vague, and her qualifications for conducting substantive talks on foreign policy are not immediately apparent. It is hard to see how her hosts to the south can regard her visit as anything more than a goodwill tour, in the patronizing pattern of past Yankee diplomacy.

A press pool which had been allowed to witness the announcement of the First Lady's trip leaves when that is concluded, and the President and the ambassadors get down to the business of trade and sugar. I am permitted to stay.

Victor McIntyre, the ambassador from Trinidad-Tobago, who is spokesman for the diplomats, says their countries feel they should have "unrestricted accessibility" to United States markets. They are looking forward to an international trade agreement that would guarantee sugar prices.

The United States also favors such an agreement, the President says. Meanwhile, he says, he has made a decision on United States policy on sugar imports. "Can I talk to you all confidentially? I would like to be very frank with you on my own thinking . . ."

Strauss is stirring uneasily in his seat. Carter interrupts himself and asks: "Is that all right, Bob?"

"Whatever you say, Mr. President, is all right."

But Carter presses him. "What's your concern?"

"I just wanted to be certain that there wouldn't be any adverse market effect or anything like that because of something you said that you might not be absolutely certain on until tomorrow," Strauss explains. "I know the decision is imminent in your mind. But we do have a serious market problem tomorrow."

Carter turns back to the ambassadors. "I would just like to speak to you frankly, but not have you quote me until tomorrow."

"Until four o'clock tomorrow," Strauss interjects.

"Until after four o'clock tomorrow," the President repeats, "because I've got to firm up our position. But I wanted to consult with you first."

The ambassadors seem nonplused. This exercise was arranged so the administration could demonstrate goodwill for its hemispheric neighbors by consulting, or at least informing, them in advance of its decision on sugar imports. But now this courtesy is being withheld, pending a pledge of confidentiality.

The President seems to be responding to Strauss's anxiety about the commodity market. Strauss has little background in international affairs. He was chosen for his job mainly because in four years of dealing with the various factions of the Democratic party he gained a reputation as a conciliator and negotiator. But his style seems more suited to political back rooms than diplomatic councils.

McIntyre wants to get on with business. "Mr. President, if you want an embargo, we will agree to it."

"An embargo on my word, not on the shipments," Carter says quickly. Everyone laughs and the situation eases.

The President wants to avoid reimposing sugar quotas "provided we can work that out." But he wants to keep the price of sugar at a reasonable level. He mentions that his Vice President is from Minnesota, the biggest producer of beet sugar, and Senator Long is from Louisiana, the leading cane sugar state. "My own inclination would be to establish a reasonable price support level for sugar that would approximate production costs and not put quotas on sugar. I'm going to try to make the decision before I leave for London tomorrow, and Mr. Strauss will stay in touch with you."

"Can you give them a few hours' notice before we make the public announcement?" Carter asks Strauss.

"I can give them an hour's notice," Strauss says. "We have yet to consult with the leadership on the Hill, so it's very important that the embargo on news of this be kept."

Rosalynn Carter, who has been a silent witness to these proceedings, now takes her leave.

After a brief general discussion of trade problems, the President tells the ambassadors that Strauss has his complete confidence. "Whatever he says, he's speaking for me. We're close friends, we understand each other. He probably has as good a relationship or better with the congressional leadership than I do. He understands them better."

The President thanks his guests for coming and once more asks for their discretion. "Before I leave Thursday, we will have had a chance to consult with the congressional leaders, and then make the announcement. Until then, we hope you'll honor the confidentiality."*

The afternoon is winding down. The President squeezes in some more paperwork before and after his twenty-minute meeting with Schlesinger on nuclear power. The only other item left on his

*In the next morning's *Washington Post,* Bill Curry reported that the administration had decided to forgo restrictions on imported sugar and instead pay a two cents a pound subsidy to the sugar farmers. The news was attributed to unidentified "sources."

schedule is a 5:00 P.M. phone call to the meeting of the American Society of Newspaper Editors in Honolulu. After that he will play tennis. Carter has played tennis since childhood; in fact, there was a tennis court on the family farm. He has taken to using the White House courts frequently, with Jordan, Clough, and other staffers. Clough says he lobs well and hits the ball hard down either sideline.

About 4:30 Brzezinski appears at the door to the study, looks into Clough's cubicle, and confesses: "I have a moral dilemma." He had agreed to be part of a tennis foursome with the President, but he has just remembered a conflicting date with Senator Byrd. After the National Security Adviser makes his excuses to the Chief Executive, I am invited into the study.

The President looks wearier for the day's tedium and tension. Charles Kirbo thinks Carter is pushing himself too hard. "He doesn't allow himself enough breaks," Kirbo told me. But the toughest part of today's schedule is behind Carter, and he now seems more relaxed than he did this morning. He may have taken the time to reflect that his conflict with Congress over spending, however irritating, probably helped him politically with the public by strengthening his image as a careful man with the taxpayer's dollar. At any rate, he seems cheerful and confident as he puts his feet on his desk and talks about his political identity.

Right after the election Carter had been worried because many people were uncertain about his beliefs and purposes. Now, having studied the polls, he thinks the perception of him is clearer and much improved. "There has been a general increase in the number of people who consider me to be competent, who consider me to be in charge of the government, who consider me to have proven a capability of working better with Congress, at least better than my predecessors," he says. "There's been a substantial shift in my placement on the political spectrum by the people of this country toward the conservative, and I think that's probably an accurate assessment, on economic affairs."

The last three words in that sentence are an example of a

familiar Carter rhetorical device, the dangling qualifier. He used these hedges often during the campaign, to the frustration of his rivals and the press, and he continues to use them as President. Having declared his conservative leanings, he nevertheless kept for himself a small opening to the left. Presumably this is intended to placate liberals in his party, though many of them feel that if a President is conservative "on economic affairs," it does not help much for him to be liberal about anything else.

Carter says the current assessment of him is the same view the country held before the Presidential conventions last summer. Following the conventions, the Republicans "made a massive and to some degree successful effort to paint me as being irresponsible in the management of fiscal affairs." This is true, though the opposition's attempts to depict him as a free spender were aided by Carter's own campaign rhetoric and promises.

At the moment Carter is less concerned about his domestic image than about the impression he has made abroad. "Foreign countries, I think, have some doubts about what I stand for and about the consistency of my foreign policy." Their uncertainty, he feels, stems from his introducing "new emphases" into U.S. foreign policy—his stress on human rights, his SALT proposals, his efforts to curb the proliferation of nuclear weapons.

But on balance Carter is satisfied with the impression he has created in his first hundred days. "Of course, I think I'm much better than folks think," he says with a smile. "But it's certainly an improvement."

During his campaign Carter talked often of the damage that had been done to the credibility of government by Watergate, Vietnam, and other public traumas. In an interview right after his nomination, Carter said that the American people were prepared to give their government only "one more chance." He added: "If there should be any more lying or scandal or betrayal of trust on my part or the part of other leaders, it would be a devastating blow."

Carter feels he has worked hard to rebuild trust. "That's one reason I've been so insistent on a new openness." He mentioned his twice-a-month press conferences, the telephone call-in radio show, his meetings with editors and broadcasters, his trips to Clinton and West Virginia. "I've tried to project into the public consciousness options, questions, and new ideas, on diplomatic affairs, for example, where formerly those ideas were discussed only in secret."

This effort "cuts both ways," Carter says. Delay in reaching solutions creates the appearance of failure. "But it also lets the American people know their government has confidence in them in a mature way to know the facts. If you reveal only the minor successes then it always looks like you've had successes. Of course I would rather have 100 percent successes. But I think the American people now feel that I might make mistakes, but I would let them know what's going on, at least more than my predecessors have."

Besides, Carter claims: "I think we're loosening up other people's ideas and thought processes." After the SALT talks collapsed, "Gromyko had his first press conference in his whole life, for instance." And he claims that the Arabs and the Israelis are now more willing to discuss their many deep-rooted differences.

Still, the President acknowledges that some of his "judgmental assessments" may have been mistaken. He mentions his public disclosure of his SALT proposals again, his criticism of West Germany's plan to sell a nuclear reprocessing plant to Brazil, and his attempt to eliminate funding for the federal water projects. "These kinds of things have caused, I think, legitimate criticism, that I've disturbed long-standing, amicable arrangements. That's a judgment I've had to make. It may be that some of these discussions could better have been carried out in secret or private. It's a matter of judgment."

Carter feels that he needs to repair relationships with West Germany, with Brazil, and perhaps with the Soviet Union. "But as they get to know me, to know that my intentions are honest and legitimate, I think that those original mistakes and the emphasis on public disclosure will be accepted."

Meanwhile, he points out that before he made his recent

statement on nonproliferation of nuclear weapons, he consulted with West German chancellor Schmidt. "And the same day I made my statement on it, he made a similar statement. That kind of thing is something I've learned from having more experience in office."

I ask him gingerly, in view of his remarks that morning to Powell and Granum, if that same principle applies to his dealings with Congress. "Yes, I think so. For instance I believe I know much more clearly now what the problems are with the House budget committee, where they've got an almost unanimous built-in vote by Republicans against whatever they propose, and their balance of a majority of Democrats is very tenuous. I don't think we were adequately sensitive about their problems because I didn't know the history of congressional action in the past. Now I've learned."

The President's mellow mood even extends to the bitter controversy over the water projects. "Had I called in or met with congressional leaders, the chairmen of committees, and told them what I had in mind, that it was a campaign commitment that I was going to pursue aggressively, I think it would have been better."

But it is still not clear to me, despite the President's confession of error, how much he feels he needs to adjust, and how much he intends to rely on the possibility of others adjusting to him. He believes that some of his goals are bound to cause conflict, no matter what his tactics are. "Some confrontations, when they're inevitable there's no nice way to do them, no pleasant way to have them, and I'm destined for a lot more."

We talk briefly about the changes in national politics that his election reflected, about the shrinking New Deal coalition and, ultimately, about his own support. He says this is difficult to identify. "First of all, I have a coalition of what might generically be called consumers, which is a natural constituency of a basically populist philosophy. When it comes down to a choice between what's best for customers compared to manufacturers, my natural inclination is to do what's good for customers."

In the next breath he adds, "I'm strongly committed to high competition and the free enterprise system. I grew up with it, I'm a small businessman, and I'm committed to that concept."

As the President surveys the political landscape, his support seems to be almost all-inclusive. He claims a "natural constituency" among environmentalists. "They trust me I think even when I make some difficult decisions." The South is a regional stronghold for its native son. "I think sectionalism will be deemphasized as the years go by but it still exists to some degree." Poor voters and black voters are on his side. "They feel that I'll treat them fairly." He has "a fairly good rating" with young people. His standing with women has greatly improved since the campaign. "I think my relationship with organized labor is still there—compared with some of the alternatives." And farmers are "another good constituency," though, the President notes, "they would prefer higher price supports than I would prefer."

But it is easier for Carter to describe his constituencies than it is for him to explain his overall approach to government. He mentions a soon-to-be-published collection of his speeches going back to his early utterances as governor of Georgia. "There's an amazing consistency in my speeches, in what I emphasized as being important. It's hard for me to describe because it's part of my consciousness. But I'd say basic morality is there. Not that I'm better than other people," he says. "But things like human rights and practical approaches to ultimate peace, these kinds of things are inherent in the speeches I made years ago. As far as describing an ideology or philosophy, I think it would be encompassed in what I said. I think it's fairly well laid out so far as basic principles are concerned. Of course the practical application of them will just have to grow as the days go by."

Jody Powell enters the study and interrupts, to remind the President of his phone call to the newspaper editors meeting in Honolulu. "I thought you might want to take a minute or two to get ready," Powell says. The President will make a brief statement on his first hundred days in office and then answer questions.

Powell suggests that Carter use this opportunity to answer the frequently heard criticism that he is trying to do too many things at once. "You have to decide what needs to be done, get it out on the table," Powell coaches him. "It may not be the easiest thing in the world to do, you may never get it all done, but at some point, if we just don't set it out, that this is the way things ought to be, we'll continue to do less than what we're capable of doing.

"This gets at the idea," Powell explains, "that the political approach never proposes anything that you're not sure you can do, so you look 100 percent successful."

Carter listens, then writes quickly on a yellow legal pad, outlining what he will say. The phone call comes in and he tells the panel: "I'd like to say that the basic thrust of my administration in its early life has been to try to carry out the campaign commitments that I've made for the last two years, without regard to the difficulty of the questions that we face and regardless of how they've either been deliberately ignored or aborted by officials in past administrations."

While Powell listens anxiously, leaning forward in his chair and chewing on his pen, Carter briefly summarizes what he has done so far, and what he intends to do in the future. "I am very determined to carry forward the proposals I've made to Congress." If someone has a better solution to present, he is willing to adjust. "But I am not naturally inclined to overcompromise, and I don't have any apology for what we have done so far." For a few minutes the President answers questions from the panel, then the phone call is concluded and he turns back to me.

I ask him whether by striking out in so many directions he is not running the risk, in Caddell's phrase, of overbuilding expectations. "Sometimes, when you just announce that there's a problem, people assume that you already know the solution to it," he says. "When you put forward proposals to Congress there's quite often a sense on that part of the public that Congress will automatically adopt it. And when Congress passes legislation, there's an automatic assumption quite often that the program can be immediately implemented. So I think there's an inherent, built-in overexpectation when a major problem is addressed."

But the President is not daunted. He mentions his campaign promises book, whose publication he describes as "unprecedented" in American politics. "An analysis shows that those promises are reasonable and that the time schedules give me enough flexibility to fulfill them. I would rather go ahead and be very aggressive in addressing many kinds of problems that are important to the well-being of the American people and take my chances with prospective failure."

Time for one more question. Is he concerned that, as Kirbo had suggested, some of his aides might be intimidated by his office and his personality?

Carter grins. "My own sense is that there is an inadequate degree of intimidation."

More seriously, he quickly sketches his decision-making process. "I generally have options presented to me. When there is a consensus, most of the time I go along with my advisers. If they disagree, then they ask for discussion with me like this morning on airplane noise control. We had a pretty good exchange. On sessions where we discuss energy questions, or SALT, I really believe there is absolute openness of expression."

The President is standing now, with his suit coat on, ready to leave for the tennis courts. He has been at his desk for ten hours and has more hours of paperwork facing him after dinner. I thank him for his time and walk down the corridor, past the guards, out of the White House.

Outside, it is very different from the unique cocoon that Carter and every other President inhabits. Carter wants to be thought of as the servant of the people, and may even think of himself that way. He is by nature uncomfortable with pomp and he has tried manfully to make the point that a President can behave naturally. He walked home from his inauguration, and he puts on blue jeans when he goes back to his study after dinner. However calculated some of this may be, his efforts to strip away the trappings of the Presidency are undoubtedly healthy for him and for the public.

But no matter how hard he tries, he cannot escape from a sense of his own importance. The office, as Hamilton Jordan reminded him, is "awesome," and some of that awe attaches to the man. He works in an environment entirely designed to meet his needs, suit his tastes, and ensure his safety. Within the White House his time is the most precious commodity, conserved mainly for his own use and occasionally doled out to the Leonard Wood-cocks and the Jane Fortsons. Even a sixty-seven-hour week does not have enough minutes to deal with every crisis, real or potential. Facts flow to him constantly from every corner of the country and the world. He has more information than anyone else—and more than anyone can really comprehend. Spending a few hours inside Carter's White House helps one to understand Johnson and Vietnam, Nixon and Watergate. It must be very easy for a President to rationalize his decisions and very hard for him to remember he is not above the law. For his own sake, and the country's, POTUS must be constantly scrutinized and challenged, by his advisers, the press, and the public.

My experience today tends to reinforce some impressions of Jimmy Carter formed over the past hundred days, and the past two years. His tough talk to his press aides about Congress typified his natural combativeness. His absorption in the controversy over airplane noise reflected his fascination with technology. His awkward treatment of the Latin American ambassadors was an example of his insensitivity to certain traditional amenities. In the campaign he sometimes did not bother to introduce other Democratic candidates who shared the platform with him.

During our conversation in his study, Carter pointed with satisfaction to the present public assessment of him as leaning toward economic conservatism. Many liberals in his own party complain that he is the most conservative Democratic President since Grover Cleveland. This is probably true, but it does not necessarily help define him.

Carter himself evidently would rather not be defined. Anyone who wants to know what he believes, he suggested, should read his speeches. The strongest hint he could offer was that they emphasized morality. It is not uncommon for politicians to resist being labeled. But Carter has been more adroit than most. When Carter's Presidency was only a few weeks old, Jerry Rafshoon predicted that the major issue of the 1980 Presidential campaign would be: "Just what does Jimmy Carter really stand for?" This ambiguity, for as long as it persists, is a mixed political blessing. It allows some to see Carter as they want him to be, but makes others uneasy.

Some of those searching for an explanation of the political man have been struck by Carter's apparent interest in structure and process. In a thoughtful essay in *The Wilson Quarterly,* Jack Knott and Aaron Wildavsky suggested that Carter is less concerned with policy than he is with procedures for making policy. It is true that the new President has been greatly attracted to such ideas as welfare reform, tax reform, and government reorganization. But a major reason is that he believes these reforms can be carried out without the additional massive funding that the sort of government programs traditionally favored by liberals would require. Once he was told that welfare could not be readily reformed without additional cost, he postponed welfare reform. Another limitation to the definition of Carter as a proceduralist is that it does not explain his enthusiasm for such issues as human rights, a highly abstract concept which was one of the dominant concerns of his first hundred days.

Much of the puzzlement over Carter results from the timing of his entry into politics, when he was nearly forty and had already achieved a fair measure of success in life. His values and beliefs had been shaped largely by his experiences in the navy and as a businessman. And these attitudes were combined with a set of standards reflecting his strong religious beliefs. Most of our recent Presidents, except Eisenhower, got into politics when their lives were still in a formative stage. And Eisenhower was a towering figure in the establishment by the time he first ran for office. Truman was thirty-eight when he became a county judge in Missouri. But he had few achievements to look back on, and he was sponsored by the Pendergast machine.

Carter plunged into the political arena in 1962 as an outsider, battling the courthouse clique for the state senate seat which he won only after a bitter recount. This stance, as the challenger of entrenched political power, is a posture he has tried to maintain ever since. He has found it both natural and advantageous to present himself as antipolitical, or at least apolitical. His attempt to remain free of the obligations and customs that bind other politicians is in part a virtue and a strength. But it also is a potential weakness. More than most major political figures, Carter tends to personalize his involvement in public affairs and to make judgments based largely on his own life experience and instincts rather than on any intellectual or political framework. He is a moralist, more so than any President since Woodrow Wilson, and his opinions are shaped by a strict code of rights and wrongs.

Carter's aides and advisers say he intends to do what is right for the people. But even assuming that he knows what is right, that is irrelevant unless he can explain his views clearly and persuasively. To lead, the President must be able to teach—his staff, his cabinet, the interest groups, and the public—and also to learn. The President, no matter how wise and powerful, cannot control events. He needs support, an alliance of some form or another. This requires the sort of accommodation and give-and-take which are part of the political tradition, but which seem distant to Carter's nature.

In a hundred days Carter made a vigorous but erratic start on his Presidency. He set a refreshing tone of openness, innovation, and action and demonstrated a capacity for moving the country. But he will not take it very far until he establishes where he is going and why. Referring to his promises book, the President said he was prepared to take his chances on failure to keep the pledges he made. This is a high-stakes gamble for all of us. As Carter himself has said, the nation may not be able to stand another failure in the Presidency.

Sources and
Acknowledgments

─────────── ★ ───────────

Most of the material in this book that is not part of the public record was based on my own reporting and interviewing, some of it going back to the campaign. I am grateful to the many people in the administration, including the President and the Vice President, for their time and their forbearance in allowing me to watch them at work. Special thanks are due to Jody Powell and the White House press staff for their assistance, and to Billie Shaddix, director of White House photographic services, and his staff who provided the pictures for this book.

For general background on the first hundred days I relied on the *Los Angeles Times,* the *Washington Post,* the *Washington Star, The New York Times, Time, Newsweek, The Wall Street Journal,* the *Baron Report,* and *New Republic.* I was fortunate in having the aid of the library staff of the Los Angeles *Times*'s Washington Bureau—Gloria Doyle, Diana Moore, and Leta Naugle Serafim. I have cited below persons who provided specific information, along with books and articles that were particularly useful. In addition, I want to thank for their general assistance and advice Bill Boyarsky, Robert Donovan, Paul Houston, Don Irwin, Norman Kempster, Grayson Mitchell, Ronald Ostrow, Kenneth Reich, Gaylord Shaw, and Paul Steiger of the *Los Angeles Times;* Frank Cormier and Richard Meyer of the Associated Press; Al Hunt of *The Wall Street Journal;* Martin Plissner of CBS; David Rush of NBC; John Stacks and Stanley Cloud of *Time;* Henry Hubbard, Tom DeFrank, and Thelma McMahon of *Newsweek;* Helen McMasters of Cox Newspapers; Stephen Hess of the Brookings Institution, Vic Gold, and Anita Mitchell.

Chapter 1. The Long Night

Stanley Cloud of *Time* shared his notes on events on the fifteenth floor of the Omni.

Helen Dewar of the *Washington Post* witnessed Carter's grumbling aboard *Peanut One.*

Chapter 2. Campaign

Off and Running

Martin Schram's *Running for President 1976* recounts the visit to the Doral and contains the text of the Jordan-Rafshoon memos.

Gordon Weil, in *The Long Shot,* describes Carter's role at the governors' conference and the McGovern Vice-Presidential strategy.

The Candidate

Neal R. Peirce's *The Deep South States of America* discusses Carter's qualified populism and his campaign against Sanders.

Why Not the Best? is the source for information on Carter's early life.

Chapter 3. "The Sweetest White People on Earth"

Jeff Prugh provided the first detailed account of the church conference in the *Los Angeles Times,* November 15, 1976.

James McCartney of Knight Newspapers reported additional information on the conference in the *Chicago Tribune,* November 22, 1976.

Chapter 4. The Best Laid Plans

The chronicle of Nixon's Presidency referred to is *Nixon in the White House* by Rowland Evans and Robert Novak.

John Stacks of *Time* reported on the rift between Jordan and Watson in *Time,* November 29, 1976.

Norman Kempster reported on the Sorensen nomination in the *Los Angeles Times,* January 28, 1977.

Chapter 5. The New Beginning

Strategy of Symbols

Richard Meyer of the Associated Press was the first to report on the Mondale agenda, January 19, 1977.

Paul Steiger analyzed Carter's tax statement in the *Los Angeles Times,* February 11, 1977.

Arthur Schlesinger's *Coming of the New Deal* describes Mrs. Roosevelt's visit to the bonus marchers.

Chapter 6. Road Show

Edward Walsh described the planning involved in the trip to Clinton in the *Washington Post,* March 16, 1977. See also "Carter on Show," by John Osborne, *New Republic,* April 2, 1977.

Chapter 7. The Cabinet: Morning Report

The account of the cabinet meeting is based on a tape recording supplemented by my notes and the notes of Rex Granum and Jane Frank.

Schlesinger reports Kennedy's attitude toward his cabinet in *A Thousand Days.*

Nixon in the White House describes Nixon's frustration with his cabinet.

Chapter 8. Bold Ventures

Congress: Hanging Tough

David Broder's interview with Kirbo was published, February 22, 1977, in the *Washington Post.*

Chapter 9. The Guns of April

Evans and Novak reported on Lance's meeting with the financiers in the *Washington Post* April 4, 1977.

Nick Kotz's article "The Politics of Welfare Reform" appeared in the *New Republic,* May 14, 1977.

Chapter 10. The Presidency

The Inner Circle

James Wooten's article ran in *The New York Times,* April 25, 1977.

Charles Mohr discussed Caddell's clients in *The New York Times,* August 2, 1976.

POTUS at Work

Stanley Cloud describes his day with Carter in *Time,* April 18, 1977.

Dom Bonafede discusses Presidential scheduling in "The Time Machine," the *National Journal,* April 9, 1977.

Carter's comment that the public would give government "one more chance" was reported in *The New York Times,* August 5, 1976.

Index

———— ⭐ ————

291